Emile Zola is a towering literary figure of the nineteenth century. His main literary achievement was his twenty-volume novel cycle, *Les Rougon-Macquart* (1870–93). In this series he combines a novelist's skills with those of the investigative journalist to examine the social, sexual and moral landscape of the late nineteenth century in a way that scandalised bourgeois society. In 1898 Zola crowned his literary career with a political act, his famous open letter ('J'accuse. . . !') to the President of the French Republic in defence of Alfred Dreyfus. These newly commissioned essays offer readings of individual novels as well as analyses of Zola's originality, his representation of society, sexuality and gender, his relations with the painters of his time, his narrative art, and his role in the Dreyfus Affair. The Companion also includes a chronology, detailed summaries of all of Zola's novels, suggestions for further reading, and information about specialist resources.

THE CAMBRIDGE
COMPANION TO
ZOLA

EDITED BY
BRIAN NELSON

CAMBRIDGE
UNIVERSITY PRESS

CAMBRIDGE UNIVERSITY PRESS
Cambridge, New York, Melbourne, Madrid, Cape Town,
Singapore, São Paulo, Delhi, Tokyo, Mexico City

Cambridge University Press
The Edinburgh Building, Cambridge CB2 8RU, UK

Published in the United States of America by
Cambridge University Press, New York

www.cambridge.org
Information on this title: www.cambridge.org/9780521543767

First published 2007

A catalogue record for this publication is available from the British Library

ISBN 978-0-521-83594-7 Hardback
ISBN 978-0-521-54376-7 Paperback

CONTENTS

CONTENTS

NOTES ON CONTRIBUTORS

DAVID BAGULEY is Emeritus Professor of French at the University of Western Ontario and Durham University. He is the author of several studies on Zola and literary naturalism, notably *Naturalist Fiction: The Entropic Vision* (Cambridge, 1990 and 2005) and *Le Naturalisme et ses genres* (1995), as well as a recent study of Napoleon III (*Napoleon III and His Regime: An Extravaganza*) (2000). He edited the volumes of the Cabeen bibliography for the nineteenth century (1994) and has published bibliographies of criticism on Zola and his works.

RAE BETH GORDON is Professor of French and Comparative Literatures and Cultures at the University of Connecticut and at the University of Paris-8. She is the author of *Ornament, Fantasy and Desire in Nineteenth-Century French Literature* (1992) and *Why the French Love Jerry Lewis: From Cabaret to Early Cinema* (2001); the latter was named 'Outstanding Academic Book' in the Performing Arts category by *Choice*. She has published numerous essays on correlations between medical science, art history, aesthetics, and literature. A book-length study of Darwinism in the Parisian music-hall, entitled *Dances with Darwin*, is forthcoming.

SUSAN HARROW is Professor in French at the University of Sheffield. She researches in the field of modern French poetry and narrative. Her study of poetry from Rimbaud to Réda, *The Material, the Real and the Fractured Self*, appeared in 2004. She is the author of a short study of Zola's *La Curée* (1998), and is currently completing a monograph, *Zola, The Body Modern: Pressures and Prospects of Representation*. She is joint editor of *Romance Studies*.

ROBERT LETHBRIDGE is Emeritus Professor of French Language and Literature in the University of London. He is currently Master of Fitzwilliam College, Cambridge. He has published widely on a number of nineteenth-century French authors, notably on Zola and Maupassant. His recent work has been devoted to the relationship between literature and the visual arts in the *fin de siècle*, developing some of the interdisciplinary perspectives opened up by essays in his (edited with Peter Collier) *Artistic Relations: Literature and the Visual Arts in Nineteenth-Century France* (1994).

VALERIE MINOGUE is Emeritus Professor of French at the University of Wales, Swansea. She is the co-founder (with Brian Nelson) of the journal *Romance Studies*, of which she was General Editor from 1995 to 2004. She is the author of *Proust: 'Du côté de chez Swann'* (1973); *Nathalie Sarraute: The War of the Words* (1981); *Zola: 'L'Assommoir'* (1991); and co-editor of *Nathalie Sarraute, Œuvres complètes* (with Notes and commentaries), under the general editorship of Jean-Yves Tadié (1996, 2001). She is currently President of the London Emile Zola Society.

OWEN MORGAN is Emeritus Professor of French at McMaster University, Hamilton, Ontario. He was associate general editor of vols. VI to X of the Franco-Canadian edition of Zola's letters (1987–95) and is the co-author, with Alain Pagès, of *Guide Emile Zola* (2002). He is currently completing, in collaboration with Dorothy Speirs, a second supplement to the *Correspondance*.

BRIAN NELSON is Professor of French Studies at Monash University, Melbourne, and editor of the *Australian Journal of French Studies*. His publications include *Zola and the Bourgeoisie* and *Emile Zola: A Selective Analytical Bibliography*. His recent editorial work includes *Practising Theory: Pierre Bourdieu and the Field of Cultural Production* (with Jeff Browitt) and *After Blanchot: Literature, Criticism, Philosophy* (with Leslie Hill and Dimitris Vardoulakis). He has translated and edited Zola's *Au Bonheur des Dames*, *Pot-Bouille*, *La Curée* and *Le Ventre de Paris*.

SANDY PETREY is Professor of French and Comparative Literature at SUNY-Stony Brook. His principal research interest is the intersection of the realist novel and contemporary critical theory, which he has addressed in *History in the Text* (1980), *Realism and Revolution* (1988), *Speech Acts and Literary Theory* (1990), and *In the Court of the Pear King* (2005).

CHANTAL PIERRE-GNASSOUNOU is *maître de conférences* at the University of Paris III – Sorbonne Nouvelle. She has a particular interest in genetic criticism and is a member of the Centre d'Etudes sur Zola et le Naturalisme at the Institut des Textes et Manuscrits Modernes in Paris. She is the author of *Zola. Les fortunes de la fiction* (1999).

JULIA PRZYBOS is Professor of French and Comparative Literature at Hunter College and the Graduate Center, City University of New York. Her *L'Entreprise mélodramatique* was published by José Corti and won the Gilbert Chinard Literary Prize in 1987. Her book *Zoom sur les Décadents* (2002) is a study of decadent fiction in the cultural context of *fin de siècle* France. She is currently writing a book on the role of physiology in realist and naturalist fiction.

HANNAH THOMPSON is Lecturer in French at Royal Holloway, University of London. Her research interests include nineteenth-century fictions of desire, sexuality and the body, gender theory and depictions of Paris. She has published several articles on Zola and is the author of *Naturalism Redressed: Identity and Clothing in the Novels of Emile Zola* (2004) and editor of *New Approaches to Zola* (2003).

NICHOLAS WHITE is a Fellow of Emmanuel College, Cambridge, where he is Director of Studies in Modern and Medieval Languages. He is the author of *The Family in Crisis in Late Nineteenth-Century French Fiction* (Cambridge, 1999). His editorial work includes Emile Zola, *L'Assommoir* (1996), *Scarlet Letters: Fictions of Adultery from Antiquity to the 1990s* (1997), J.-K. Huysmans, *A rebours* (1999), whose translator, Margaret Mauldon, won the Scott Moncrieff Prize, and *Currencies: Fiscal Fortunes and Cultural Capital in the French Nineteenth Century* (2005). He was co-founder of *Dix-Neuf*, the journal of the UK Society of Dix-Neuviémistes, and he reviews for the *TLS*. His current research concerns the debates about, and depictions of, divorce in nineteenth-century France.

ACKNOWLEDGMENTS

I would like to thank all my contributors for their patience and for their collaboration in bringing this project to fruition. My warm thanks are due to the following friends and colleagues for their help and advice: Philip Anderson, Marie-Rose Auguste, David Baguley, Valerie Minogue and Robert Savage. Finally, I am grateful to my editors at Cambridge University Press, Linda Bree, Maartje Scheltens, Jayne Aldhouse and Linda Woodward, for making the project such a pleasant and rewarding experience.

ZOLA'S NOVELS: A SUMMARY

The summaries below provide, without commentary, the basic plot lines of Zola's novels

Early works

La Confession de Claude (1865)

Claude, a young and impoverished poet, lives with a prostitute, Laurence, whom he attempts to save. Jacques, their neighbour, becomes Laurence's lover, and Jacques' mistress, Marie, dies. Claude is finally able to summon the strength to break with Laurence.

Le Voeu d'une morte (1866)

Daniel Raimbault, a generous young man, loves Jeanne, whose mother has provided him with financial support. He gives her up to his best friend, Georges.

Les Mystères de Marseille (1867)

Philippe Cayol loves Blanche de Cazalis, whose rich uncle is a prominent politician living in Marseilles. Philippe's brother, Marius, tries to protect the lovers from the uncle's wrath. Blanche gives birth to an illegitimate daughter before entering a convent.

Thérèse Raquin (1867)

Thérèse and her lover, Laurent, murder Camille, Thérèse's husband. Their remorse destroys their passion for each other, and they finally commit suicide under the gaze of Camille's mother, who has become completely paralysed.

Madeleine Férat (1868)

Guillaume, a shy dreamer, is the husband of Madeleine. They live happily together until Madeleine's former lover, Jacques, who is an old schoolfriend of Guillaume, reappears after an absence of many years. Madeleine, still under Jacques' spell, commits suicide under the vengeful eye of an old Protestant servant who imagines herself to be an agent of divine retribution.

Les Rougon-Macquart

La Fortune des Rougon (1871)

This is a political novel which also recounts the origins of the Rougon-Macquart family in Plassans. Dide, an orphan with a streak of insanity, marries a local peasant, Rougon, from which union springs the acquisitive Rougon branch, fathered by Pierre. From Dide's adulterous liaison with the drunken poacher Macquart are born Antoine, whose descendants are the proletarian Macquart line, and Ursule, from whose marriage to a Marseilles tradesman, Mouret, spring the bourgeois adventurers and the provincial bourgeoisie. The ambitious Pierre, a liberal Republican, and his wife Félicité, use the scare resulting from Louis-Napoleon's *coup d'état* to secure for Pierre a government post. His half-brother, Antoine Macquart, duplicitously uses Republican ideas to enrich himself. Silvère Mouret, who embodies the true spirit of the Republic, dies on the battlefield.

La Curée (1871)

Aristide Rougon, Pierre's son, adopts the name Saccard and makes his fortune in the frenzied property development that accompanied the Haussmannisation of Paris during the Second Empire. His wife, Renée, conducts an 'incestuous' relationship with her stepson, Maxime (Saccard's son by his first marriage) against the exotic background of a tropical hothouse. She dies, exploited by both men.

Le Ventre de Paris (1873)

Florent, having escaped from deportation to Cayenne after Louis-Napoleon's *coup d'état* of 1851, returns to Paris and is taken in by his brother, Quenu, and Quenu's wife, Lisa Macquart, daughter of Antoine, who own a *charcuterie* near Les Halles, the great new food markets built at the beginning of the Second Empire. Florent leads an amateurish conspiracy against the regime, is denounced by Lisa, and is once again deported. The 'Fat' are restored to their complacency by their expulsion of the 'Thin'.

La Conquête de Plassans (1874)

Faujas, a priest sent to Plassans to act as a secret agent for the imperial regime, lodges with François Mouret and his wife, Marthe, daughter of Pierre and Félicité Rougon. He effects a reconciliation of Bonapartists and monarchists through his hold over Marthe, who is infected with a religious hysteria that drives François mad. The theme of hereditary insanity is thus seen in duplicate, and all perish when François, crazed by jealousy, sets fire to the house.

La Faute de l'abbé Mouret (1875)

Serge Mouret, son of François Mouret and Marthe Rougon, is a priest whose cult of the Virgin results in a brain-fever involving amnesia. He is nursed by a young girl, Albine, and by his uncle, Pascal, in Le Paradou, a ruined château whose garden provides an idyllic background for the love that develops between Albine and Serge. They make love under the Tree of Life. But the Church, through the fearsome figure of the Friar Archangias, reasserts its hold over Serge, and Albine dies of grief. The only happy character is Serge's half-witted sister, Désirée, who symbolises animal enjoyment unmarred by human intelligence.

Son Excellence Eugène Rougon (1876)

Eugène Rougon, the elder son of Pierre and Félicité Rougon, Minister of State under Napoleon III, is the chief executant of the policies of the Emperor's regime. He loves power for its own sake. He is temporarily deposed by the scheming temptress, Clorinde Balbi, but returns to power by deliberately withholding information about an attempted assassination of the Emperor, so that the Ministry which has supplanted him might be overthrown. The brutal repression he organises is followed by a 'liberal' and opportunistic phase.

L'Assommoir (1877)

Gervaise Macquart, daughter of Antoine Macquart, is abandoned in Paris with her sons, Claude and Etienne, by their father, Lantier. She subsequently marries Coupeau, a zinc-worker. They have a daughter, Nana, and achieve comparative prosperity when Gervaise establishes a laundry in the working-class district of the Goutte d'Or. Coupeau, however, falls from a roof and sustains an injury that leads him into a life of idleness and alcoholism. Lantier's return to lodge with the Coupeau family marks the beginning of Gervaise's and Coupeau's decline into abject poverty (and Nana's into debauchery). Coupeau dies of alcoholism and Gervaise from hunger.

Une page d'amour (1878)

Hélène Grandjean (née Mouret; she is the daughter of François Mouret and Ursule Macquart) is a widow who lives with her daughter, Jeanne, in the bourgeois district of Passy in Paris. She meets, through Jeanne's illness,

Dr Henri Deberle. After wrestling with their scruples, they become lovers. Hélène experiences the passion her late husband could not arouse in her. But Jeanne, jealous of her mother's transfer of affection, dies, breaking the link between the lovers. Hélène marries an older admirer and goes to live in Marseilles.

Nana (1880)

Nana, the daughter of Gervaise and Coupeau, reappears as a sexually magnetic prostitute/actress, described in a newspaper article as 'The Golden Fly', the product of a diseased family and class. She avenges the ruling class's tyranny over the proletariat by infecting the aristocracy with her own disease. She leads a brilliant career, rapidly conquering Parisian society, ruining all men who fall under her spell – especially Count Muffat, Chamberlain to the Empress. Nana herself meets a terrible death, returning to Paris after a brief absence to die from smallpox on the day war with Prussia is declared.

Pot-Bouille (1882)

The ambitious Octave Mouret, elder son of François and Marthe Mouret, begins to make his fortune in Paris by using sex to advance his career. He lodges in a new apartment house and soon discovers that the lives of its 'respectable' bourgeois inhabitants are a continual series of adulterous liaisons. The building is a 'melting-pot' of deception, depravity and hypocrisy.

Au Bonheur des Dames (1883)

Octave Mouret's rise to fortune is continued in his transformation of the draper's shop left to him by his wife, Caroline Hédouin, into Paris' first great department store: The Ladies' Paradise. Once more, he is shown making his fortune from women, channelling the desires of his female customers into a fever of buying. He falls in love, however, with a working-class shop-girl, the virtuous Denise Baudu. He marries her, a co-operative organisation of the store being the price she puts on the marriage.

La Joie de vivre (1884)

Pauline Quenu, Lisa Macquart's daughter, lives with her uncle Chanteau in a small fishing village in Normandy. She falls in love with his neurotic son, Lazare, who is so conscious of the brevity of life that he abandons any task for fear of not being able to finish it. She sacrifices her inherited fortune to assist him in his chimerical projects. However, he marries Louise, a rich banker's daughter, and settles down to a life of idle boredom. Pauline, in an attempt to rid herself of the jealous possessiveness she has inherited from her family, spends her life in ungrudging charity. Her ultimate success is shown in her altruistic release of Lazare to marry Louise, and the joy she gets from living.

Germinal (1885)

Etienne Lantier, son of Gervaise Macquart and her lover, Lantier, arrives as a stranger in the coal-mining community of Montsou, in north-eastern France. He lodges with the Maheu family, with whose daughter Catherine he falls in love, and becomes a worker in the mines. He becomes the leader of a violent uprising of the miners against their bourgeois masters. The strike fails through lack of proper direction and the mass hysteria of the starving workers. The miners are forced to return to work, only to be trapped in a flooding caused by the anarchist Souvarine. Catherine and Etienne are imprisoned underground for twenty days and only Etienne survives. His unpopularity in Montsou makes him leave the community to take up a political career in Paris.

L'Œuvre (1886)

Claude Lantier, the younger son of Gervaise Macquart and Lantier, is an artist who fails to gain admission to the Salon, because he refuses to compromise an unattainable artistic ideal in the interests of popular taste. Nothing he produces satisfies him and he progresses from one half-finished canvas to another until his frustration drives him to suicide.

La Terre (1887)

Jean Macquart, the son of Antoine Macquart and the brother of Gervaise, is a former soldier who settles down in the farming community of the Beauce, where he marries Françoise Mouche, the daughter of Père Fouan and the sister of Lise. Buteau, Lise's husband, kills Françoise and Fouan in his greed for more land. Jean leaves the Beauce to enlist in the war against Prussia.

Le Rêve (1888)

Angélique, the illegitimate daughter of Sidonie Rougon (*La Fortune des Rougon, La Curée*), lives in the town of Beaumont with a family of chasuble-makers. She attempts to model her life on that of the saints, and her dream seems fulfilled when she falls in love with Félicien, the son of the archbishop, Monseigneur de Hautecoeur. Monseigneur's opposition to the match almost kills Angélique, but he relents and the marriage takes place. But Angélique dies at the first kiss of love to join the virgin saints of her dreams.

La Bête humaine (1890)

Jacques Lantier, the son of Gervaise Macquart, is a train driver on the Paris–Le Havre line. He is beset by a hereditary madness which manifests itself in a desire to murder as a substitute for sex. He glimpses the murder, on a train, of Grandmorin, President of the Railway Company, by Roubaud, an assistant station-master, and Roubaud's wife, Séverine, who had been seduced by Grandmorin. Jacques becomes Séverine's lover. His sexual relationship with her encourages him to hope that his insanity is cured, but her confession of guilt arouses his desire to kill. They plan to murder Roubaud, but at the last moment, in an access of homicidal mania, Jacques murders Séverine instead. He meets his own end in a fight with his stoker, Pecqueux, jealous of his mistress Philomène's interest in Jacques. The two fall to their deaths from a moving train.

L'Argent (1891)

Aristide Saccard, having abandoned the world of property speculation, creates a banking company, the Banque Universelle, and attempts to wrest control of the stock exchange from the Jewish financier Gundermann. After a period of fantastic but artificial expansion, created by Saccard's financial and advertising genius, the bank collapses, ruining hundreds of small investors. Eugène Rougon enables his brother to be released from prison, and the latter flees to Belgium.

La Débâcle (1892)

Following his flight from the Beauce, Jean Macquart has enlisted to fight in the Franco-Prussian war. Through Jean's friendship with the intellectual Maurice Levasseur and their experience of warfare, Zola recounts the disastrous military defeat of France at Sedan and the Emperor's fall from power, aggravated by civil strife. After imprisonment and escape, the two are separated, Maurice joining the insurrectionists of the Commune and Jean joining the government troops. By chance, during the 'Bloody Week' which saw the Commune crushed, Jean shoots and kills Maurice across a barricade.

Le Docteur Pascal (1893)

Pascal Rougon, a doctor who lives near Plassans, is the chronicler of the Rougon-Macquart family, cataloguing its hereditary patterns and ills, and attempting by medical science to discover a cure. Pascal's joyous sexual relationship with his niece Clotilde echoes Zola's happiness with Jeanne Rozerot. His life's work appears to be destroyed when his mother, Félicité, and his servant, Martine, jealous of Clotilde, burn his precious notes. But hope for the future and for the regeneration of the family lives on in the birth of Pascal's and Clotilde's son shortly after Pascal's death.

Les Trois Villes

Lourdes (1894)
Pierre Froment, a priest, joins a pilgrimage to Lourdes, and begins to doubt the authenticity of the supernatural cures that are allegedly performed there.

Rome (1896)
Pierre Froment has written a book, *La Rome nouvelle*, based on his experiences in the Paris slums, in which he calls on the Pope, Leo XIII, to put himself at the head of the new socialist movements in Europe. To defend his book against the threat of condemnation by the Congregation of the Index, Pierre travels to Rome. He is disappointed to find the Church both conservative and corrupt.

Paris (1898)
Pierre Froment's elder brother, Guillaume, is a brilliant chemist who has invented a powerful explosive. Pierre dissuades his brother from putting the explosive at the disposal of anarchists. However, he falls under the influence of Guillaume and his circle of scientists and revolutionary social thinkers and activists, and gradually his Catholicism is replaced by the Religion of Science.

Les Quatre Evangiles

Fécondité (1899)
Pierre Froment and his wife Marie have produced four children: Mathieu, Marc, Luc and Jean. The family of Mathieu and his wife Marianne grows enormously over several generations; all those characters in the novel who practice birth control meet sad ends.

Travail (1901)
Luc Froment, a reform-minded engineer, founds an ideal socialist community, La Crêcherie – the model of a new and better civilisation.

Vérité (1903)

Marc Froment, a schoolteacher passionately devoted to truth and justice, struggles heroically and ultimately successfully on behalf of a Jewish colleague, Simon, who has been wrongfully accused of having sexually abused and murdered his young nephew. The real culprit is a monk, Gorgias.

FAMILY TREE OF THE ROUGON-MACQUART

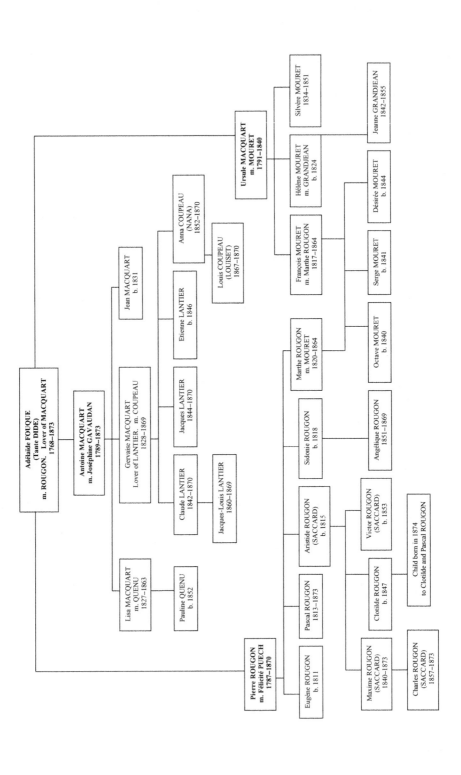

CHRONOLOGY

1840–1858: Childhood and adolescence in Provence

1840   Emile Zola born in Paris on 2 April, the only child of Francesco Zola (b. 1795), an engineer of Italian origin, and Emilie Aubert (b. 1819), the daughter of a glazier. The naturalist novelist was later proud that 'zolla' in Italian means 'clod of earth'.

1843   The Zola family moves to Aix-en-Provence, Francesco having been commissioned to build a dam and a canal necessary to provide the town with an adequate water supply. Aix will become the town of 'Plassans' in the Rougon-Macquart novels.

1847   Francesco Zola dies suddenly on 27 May, leaving the family nearly destitute.

1848   The rule of King Louis-Philippe (the so-called 'July Monarchy', which began in 1830) is overthrown and the Second Republic declared. Zola starts school at the Pension Notre-Dame.

1851   The Republic is dissolved after the *coup d'état* of Louis-Napoleon Bonaparte, who in the following year declares himself emperor as Napoleon III. Start of the Second Empire, the period that will provide the background for Zola's Rougon-Macquart cycle.

1852   Zola becomes a boarder at the Collège Bourbon in Aix (now the Lycée d'Aix), and forms friendships with Jean-Baptistin Baille and the future painter Paul Cézanne.

1858–1862: Paris and Bohemian life

1858   Moves to Paris with his mother in February. His father's friends secure for him a place and a scholarship at the Lycée Saint-Louis. In November he falls ill with 'brain fever' (typhoid) and convalescence is slow.

1859   Fails his *baccalauréat* twice.

1860 Finds employment as a copy clerk in the Excise Office of the Paris docks, but abandons it after two months, preferring to eke out an existence as an impecunious writer in the Latin Quarter of Paris. A period of severe hardship begins. These years see the height of the rebuilding programme undertaken by Baron Haussmann, Prefect of Paris from 1853 to 1869, which is reflected in several of Zola's novels.

1862–1865: The beginnings of a literary career

1862 Joins Hachette, the well-known publishing house, as a shipping clerk (February). Within a few months becomes the firm's head of publicity. This gives him special insight into the workings of the literary marketplace. He gets to know Michelet, Sainte-Beuve and Taine. Naturalised as a French citizen on 31 October.

1863 Makes his début as a journalist in January. On 1 May Manet's *Le Déjeuner sur l'herbe* exhibited at the Salon des Refusés, which Zola visits with Cézanne, who is now living in Paris.

1864 Zola's first literary work, *Contes à Ninon*, appears in October.

1865 Meets his future wife, Gabrielle-Alexandrine Meley (b. 1839); they marry in 1870. Publishes his first novel, *La Confession de Claude*, in November.

1866–1868: Literary journalism

1866 Leaves Hachette, determined to make a living by his writing. Becomes a literary critic on the recently launched daily *L'Evénement*. Writes a series of provocative articles attacking the art establishment, expressing reservations about Courbet, and praising Manet and Monet. Begins to frequent the Café Guerbois in the Batignolles district of Paris, the meeting-place of the future Impressionists. Antoine Guillemet takes Zola to meet Manet. *Mes Haines* (collected articles, mainly on literature and art) published in June. Summer months spent with Cézanne on the Seine at Bennecourt. *L'Evénement* suppressed by the authorities in November. *Le Voeu d'une morte* published in the same month.

1867 Article on Manet, 'Une nouvelle manière en peinture: Edouard Manet', published in *Revue du XIXe siècle* in January. *Les Mystères de Marseille* published in June. *Thérèse Raquin* published in December.

1868　Preface to second edition of *Thérèse Raquin*, in which Zola declares that he belongs to the literary school of 'naturalism', published in April. Manet's portrait of Zola exhibited at the Salon. 'Mon Salon' published in *L'Evénement illustré* in May. *Madeleine Férat* published in December.

1869–1871: Political journalism

1869　Writes for *La Tribune*, *Le Rappel* and *Le Gaulois*. Zola's proposal for a series of novels (later to be called *Les Rougon-Macquart*) accepted by the publisher Lacroix.

1870　Outbreak of the Franco-Prussian War leads in September to the fall of the Second Empire. The Zola family moves temporarily to Marseilles because of the war. The Third Republic is declared. Paris is besieged by Prussian forces. Spends several months in Bordeaux, reporting on the deliberations of the provisional Government of National Defence. *La Fortune des Rougon* begins to appear in serial form.

1871　Returns to Paris in March. Becomes a political reporter for *La Cloche*, *Le Sémaphore de Marseille* and *Le Corsaire*. Witnesses the civil war of the Commune and the carnage brought about by its fall. *La Fortune des Rougon*, the first novel in the Rougon-Macquart cycle, published in October.

1872–1877: Towards *L'Assommoir*

1872　*La Curée* published in February. Part of it had appeared in serial form from September to November 1871, but publication had been suspended by the censorship authorities.

1873　*Le Ventre de Paris* published in April by Georges Charpentier, Zola's new publisher. Forms friendships with the Goncourt brothers, Gustave Flaubert, Alphonse Daudet and Ivan Turgenev.

1874　*La Conquête de Plassans* published in May. First independent Impressionist exhibition. *Nouveaux Contes à Ninon* published in November.

1875　Employed as a foreign correspondent for the Russian newspaper *Vestnik Evropy* (*European Herald*), starting a monthly column in March (this will last until 1880). *La Faute de l'abbé Mouret* published in April.

1876　*Son Excellence Eugène Rougon* published in February. Second Impressionist exhibition. Becomes a drama critic for *Le Bien public* in April. *L'Assommoir* begins to appear in serial form and causes a sensation with its depiction of life in the Parisian slums. The Zolas move to a comfortable apartment at 23, rue de Boulogne (now rue Ballu).

1878–1885: From *L'Assommoir* to *Germinal*

1877 *L'Assommoir* published in book form and becomes a bestseller. Zola's fortune is made and he is recognised as the leading figure of the naturalist movement.

1878 Buys a house at Médan, on the Seine, forty kilometres west of Paris. *Une Page d'amour* published in June.

1879 *Nana* appears in serial form, before publication in book form in March of the following year. It attracts further scandal to Zola's name. A theatrical adaptation of *L'Assommoir* is successfully produced.

1880 Publication in May of *Les Soirées de Médan*, an anthology of short stories by Zola and some of his naturalist 'disciples', including Maupassant. In October, Zola loses his much-loved mother (her death following that of his literary mentor, Flaubert, earlier in the year). A period of depression follows and he suspends *Les Rougon-Macquart* for a year. *Le Roman expérimental*, which expounds the theory of naturalism, published in December (having appeared in *Vestnik Evropy* and *Le Voltaire* the previous year).

1881 More theoretical essays, *Le Naturalisme au théâtre* and *Les Romanciers naturalists*, are published.

1882 *Pot-Bouille* published in April. *Une Campagne*, a collection of articles written for *Le Figaro*, published.

1883 *Au Bonheur des Dames* published in March. Death of Manet on 30 April.

1884 *La Joie de vivre* published in March. Preface to catalogue of Manet exhibition.

1885 *Germinal* published in March. The play based on the novel is forbidden by the censorship authorities.

1886–1893: The end of *Les Rougon-Macquart*

1886 *L'Œuvre* published in April. Cézanne reacts badly to Zola's portrait of him in the novel, and ends their friendship.

1887 *La Terre* published in November. Five of Zola's 'disciples' sign a manifesto, published in *Le Figaro*, against the novel; they viciously denounce Zola as an onanistic pornographer.

1888   *Le Rêve* published in October. Zola begins a relationship with Jeanne Rozerot, a seamstress employed by Madame Zola.

1889   Birth of Denise, daughter of Zola and Jeanne, on 20 September. The Zolas move to 21*bis*, rue de Bruxelles. Zola's candidature for the Académie Française fails, as will his nineteen subsequent attempts to gain membership. He develops a keen interest in photography.

1890   *La Bête humaine* published in March.

1891   *L'Argent* published in March. Elected President of the Société des Gens de Lettres in April. Jacques, son of Zola and Jeanne, born 25 September.

1892   *La Débâcle* published in June.

1893   *Le Docteur Pascal*, the final novel in the Rougon-Macquart cycle, published in July.

1894–1898: *Les Trois Villes* and the Dreyfus Affair

1894   *Lourdes*, the first novel of the trilogy *Les Trois Villes*, published in August. On 22 December a Jewish army officer, Captain Alfred Dreyfus, is found guilty by court martial of spying for Germany and sentenced to life imprisonment in the penal colony on Devil's Island, off the coast of French Guiana.

1896   *Rome* published in May. Publishes a new series of articles in *Le Figaro*.

1897   New evidence suggests that Dreyfus' conviction was a miscarriage of justice. Zola publishes three articles in *Le Figaro* demanding a retrial.

1898   'J'accuse . . . !', Zola's open letter in support of Dreyfus, addressed to Félix Faure, President of the Republic, is published in *L'Aurore* on 13 January. Zola is tried for libel and sentenced to one year's imprisonment and a fine of 3,000 francs. *Paris* published in March. In July, while waiting for a retrial (granted on a technicality), Zola goes into voluntary exile in England.

1899–1902: *Les Quatre Evangiles* and the end of the Affair

1899   Returns to France in June after the Dreyfus case is reopened. *Fécondité*, the first of a series of four novels, *Les Quatre Evangiles*, published in October. Dreyfus is retried before a military tribunal in Rennes. He is again found guilty, but is granted a pardon (complete exoneration will not come until 1906).

1901   *Travail*, the second 'Gospel', published in May.

1902   On 29 September dies of carbon monoxide fumes from his bedroom stove, the chimney having been capped either by accident or by design. It is still widely believed that in effect Zola was assassinated by anti-Dreyfusards. Madame Zola survives. On 5 October Zola's funeral in Paris, at the Cimetière Montmartre, is witnessed by a crowd of 50,000.

1903   *Vérité*, the third 'Gospel', is published in March. *La Justice* was to have been the fourth novel in the series.

1908   Zola's remains are transferred to the Panthéon on 4 June.

The following abbreviations are used in this volume to refer to works by Zola:

RM   *Les Rougon-Macquart. Histoire naturelle et sociale d'une famille sous le Second Empire*, ed. Henri Mitterand, 5 vols. (Paris: Gallimard, 'Bibliothèque de la Pléiade', 1960–7)

OC   *Œuvres complètes*, ed. Henri Mitterand, 15 vols. (Paris: Tchou, 'Cercle du Livre Précieux', 1966–70)

Cor.   *Correspondance*, ed. Bard H. Bakker *et al.*, 10 vols. (Montreal/Paris: Presses de l'Université de Montréal/Editions du CNRS, 1978–95)

References to these works will be given in the form (RM ii 297) (except when an essay focuses on a single text, in which case only the page number will be given), (OC x 845), (Cor. xii 521), etc. The Cercle du Livre Précieux edition is in the process of being superseded by the Nouveau Monde Editions edition (see Further Reading), but is widely available in libraries worldwide. References to other items will be provided in full in a note on first mention, and in abbreviated form thereafter.

All quotations are accompanied by a translation into English, unless the meaning of the original is self-evident. The translation usually precedes the original, unless there is good reason – in the context of textual commentary, for example – to reverse the order. Translations are those of the individual contributors unless otherwise specified.

BNF, NAF, Ms   Bibliothèque nationale de France, Nouvelles acquisitions françaises, Manuscrit. . .

I

BRIAN NELSON

Zola and the nineteenth century

Unlike Flaubert, the 'hermit of Croisset', who turned away from his age in an attitude of ironic detachment, Emile Zola embraced his century in a way no French writer had done since Balzac. Zola's ambition was to emulate Balzac by writing a comprehensive history of contemporary society. Through the fortunes of his Rougon-Macquart family, he examined methodically the social, sexual and moral landscape of the late nineteenth century along with its political, financial and artistic contexts. Zola is the quintessential novelist of modernity, understood in terms of an overwhelming sense of tumultuous change. 'Why read Emile Zola?' asks Sandy Petrey in his chapter in this volume, answering himself thus: 'Because his representation of society's impact on the individuals within it memorably depicts what it means to be a human being in the modern world.'

The motor of change was the rapid expansion of capitalism, with all that that entailed in terms of the altered shapes of the city, new forms of social practice and economic organisation, and heightened political pressures. Zola was fascinated by change, and specifically by the emergence of a new, mass society. Henri Mitterand has argued that Zola was 'the first novelist . . . to make the crowd a character in itself' ['le premier romancier . . . à faire de la foule un personnage en soi'];[1] while Henry James noted Zola's ability to 'make his characters swarm',[2] arguing that it was both the 'fortune' and the 'doom' of the Rougon-Macquart cycle to 'deal with things almost always in gregarious forms, to be a picture of *numbers*, of classes, crowds, confusions, movements, industries'.[3] Industrialisation brought with it urban poverty and prostitution, class conflict, the rise of mass movements, the birth of a consumer culture, and the struggle between the forces of secularism and religion. As Erich Auerbach commented in *Mimesis*, his classic study of the representation of reality in Western literature, Zola 'is one of the very few authors of the century who created their work out of the great problems of the age'.[4]

Zola's epic type of realism is reflected not only in the vast sweep of his work, but also in its variety and complexity. In addition to his thirty-one novels, he wrote five collections of short stories, a large body of art, drama and literary criticism, several plays and libretti, and numerous articles on political and social issues published in the French press at various stages of his career as a journalist. He was actively engaged in his age. He was a major critic of literature and painting, and a significant political commentator long before the Dreyfus Affair. His main achievement, however, was his twenty-volume novel cycle, *Les Rougon-Macquart*, which was to rival Balzac's *Comédie humaine*, a collection of about ninety interlocking novels and stories portraying French society during the second quarter of the nineteenth century, and which showed how the novel could become a vehicle for mature commentary on modern society. In eight months, during 1868 and 1869, Zola outlined the twenty novels he intended to write on the theme of heredity: a family, the Rougon-Macquarts, tainted with alcoholism and mental instability, were to intermarry, to proliferate, and to pass on their inherited weaknesses to subsequent generations. Their fortunes would be followed over several decades. Zola began work on the series in 1870 and devoted himself to it for the next quarter of a century. The summary of Zola's novels provided at the beginning of this volume indicates the roles played by the various family members and its three branches, who spread through all levels of society. The Rougons represent the upper-class hunt for wealth and position, their members rising to occupy commanding positions in the worlds of government and finance; the Mourets are the bourgeois tradesmen and provincial bourgeosie; and the Macquarts, with the exception of Lisa Macquart (*Le Ventre de Paris*) are the submerged proletariat. Nicholas White, in his chapter on 'Family histories and family plots', analyses the role of the family in relation to the narrative structure and thematic configurations of Zola's vast project, seen in the context of the cultural values and intellectual discourses of the nineteenth century, and Zola's own planning notes for the Rougon-Macquart series.

Auerbach concludes his comments on two passages from *Germinal* with these remarks:

> Zola knows how these people thought and talked. He also knows every detail of the technical side of mining; he knows the psychology of the various classes of workers and of the administration, the functioning of the central management, the competition between the capitalist groups, the cooperation of the interests of capital with the government, the army. But he did not confine himself to writing novels about industrial workers. His purpose was to comprise – as Balzac had done, but much more methodically and painstakingly – the whole

life of the period (the Second Empire): the people of Paris, the rural population, the theater, the department stores, the stock exchange, and very much more besides. He made himself an expert in all fields; everywhere he penetrated into social structure and technology. An unimaginable amount of intelligence and labour went into the Rougon-Macquart.[5]

Materialism and imagination

As a writer, Zola was, in many respects, a typical product of his times. This is most evident in his enthusiasm for science and his acceptance of scientific determinism, which was the prevailing philosophy of the latter part of the nineteenth century. Converted from a youthful romantic idealism to realism in art and literature, Zola began promoting a scientific view of literature inspired by the aims and methods of experimental medicine. He called this new form of realism 'naturalism'. His fourth novel, *Thérèse Raquin* (1867), a compelling tale of adultery and murder, applied these ideas and attracted much critical attention. The subtitle of the Rougon-Macquart cycle, 'A Natural and Social History of a Family under the Second Empire', suggests Zola's two interconnected aims: to use fiction to demonstrate a number of 'scientific' notions about the ways in which human behaviour is determined by heredity and environment; and to use the symbolic possibilities of a family whose heredity is tainted to represent a diseased society – the immoral and corrupt, yet dynamic and vital, France of the Second Empire (1852–70). Zola set out, in the Rougon-Macquart cycle, to tear the mask from the Second Empire, and to expose the frantic pursuit of appetites of every kind that it unleashed. He was influenced by Balzac; by the views on heredity and environment of the positivist philosopher and cultural historian Hippolyte Taine, whose proclamation that 'virtue and vice are products like vitriol and sugar' he adopted as the epigraph of *Thérèse Raquin*; by Prosper Lucas, a largely forgotten nineteenth-century scientist, author of a treatise on natural heredity; and by the Darwinian view of man as essentially an animal (a translation of Darwin's *Origin of Species*, first published in 1859, appeared in French in 1865). Zola himself claimed to have based his method largely on the physiologist Claude Bernard's *Introduction à l'étude de la médecine expérimentale* (*Introduction to the Study of Experimental Medicine*), which he had read soon after its appearance in 1865. The 'truth' for which Zola aimed could only be attained, he argued, through meticulous documentation and research; the work of the novelist represented a form of practical sociology, complementing the work of the scientist, whose hope was to change the world not by judging it but by understanding it. When the laws determining the material conditions of human life were understood, man would have only to act on this understanding to improve society. Zola, in other words, was an early advocate of social engineering.

Zola was most truly a 'naturalist' (in the sense of being a writer who based his fiction on scientific theory, and in particular on methods developed by the natural sciences) in the early novels *Thérèse Raquin* and *Madeleine Férat* (1868). In his uncompromising preface to the second edition of *Thérèse Raquin*, he defended the 'scientific' purpose of the book: namely, a physiological rather than psychological analysis of the 'love' that brings two people of differing 'temperaments' together, and an attempt to present as an entirely physical, 'natural' process, the 'remorse' that follows their murder of an inconvenient husband. Theory and practice had diverged considerably by the time, over a decade later, he wrote his polemical essay 'Le Roman expérimental' ('The Experimental Novel', 1880). But in any case Zola's naturalism was not as naive and uncritical as is sometimes assumed. His formulation of the naturalist aesthetic, while it advocates a respect for truth that makes no concessions to self-indulgence, shows his clear awareness that 'observation' is not an unproblematic process. He recognises the importance of the observer in the act of observation, and this recognition is repeated in his celebrated formula, used in 'The Experimental Novel', in which he describes the work of art as 'a corner of nature seen through a temperament' ['un coin de la nature vue à travers un tempérament']. Zola fully acknowledges the importance, indeed the artistic necessity, of the selecting, structuring role of the individual artist and of the aesthetic he adopts. It is thus not surprising to find him, in a series of newspaper articles in 1866, leaping to the defence of Manet and the Impressionists – defending Manet as an artist with the courage to express his own temperament in defiance of current conventions. Zola's brilliant critical 'campaign' made Manet famous. Not only did he understand what modern painters like Manet were doing, but he was able to articulate it before they could. The rich (and often awkward) interchanges between Zola and the painters of his time are discussed by Robert Lethbridge in his wide-ranging chapter on Zola and contemporary painting.

Zola's representation of society is informed by a vast amount of dedicated first-hand observation, note-taking and research – in Les Halles, the Paris slums, the department stores, the theatre, the coal fields, the railways, the French countryside. Zola took his notebook down a mine to write *Germinal*; he travelled in a locomotive and studied the railway system and timetables to write *La Bête humaine*. He combines the vision of a painter with the approach of a sociologist and reporter in his observation of the modes of existence, the patterns, practices and distinctive languages that characterise particular communities and milieus. The texture of his novels is infused with an intense concern with concrete detail; and the detailed planning notes he assembled for each novel (published selectively in volume form by Henri Mitterand in 1987) represent a remarkable stock of documentary information about French society in the 1870s and 1880s.[6] Mitterand comments:

> What we find in this typical preparatory work for the successive novels in the Rougon-Macquart series are the three basic features of the ethnographic method: fieldwork, observation of the characteristics of particular groups (the railway workers on the Paris–Rouen line, the peasants of the Beauce, the shop workers of the Bon Marché), analysis and organisation of the phenomena observed in order to produce descriptive documents and syntheses.

> [On découvre bien dans cette activité caractéristique de la préparation des *Rougon-Macquart*, répété de roman en roman, les trois traits principaux de la méthode ethnographique: le travail sur le terrain, l'observation de phénomènes particuliers à des groupes restreints (les cheminots de la ligne Paris-Rouen, les paysans de Beauce, le personnel du Bon Marché), l'analyse et l'organisation des phénomènes observés pour élaborer des documents descriptifs et des synthèses.][7]

Zola's fiction acquires its power, however, not so much from its ethnographic richness as from its imaginative qualities. Zola is above all a narrative artist. Some of the chapters in this volume explore Zola's narrative art through detailed textual analysis. Susan Harrow argues that Zola's hybrid style in *Thérèse Raquin* subverts the reader's expectations (and the naturalist claim to transparency) in proto-modernist ways. Valerie Minogue brings out the narrative power and subtlety of Zola's representation of his alluring, terrifying and highly complex prostitute heroine in *Nana*. Chantal Pierre-Gnassounou, on the basis of a detailed examination of the voluminous planning notes Zola wrote for his novels, shows the extent to which, in his narrative practice, he went well beyond the procedures of the supposed naturalist method.

Zola's novels tend to be built in massively constructed blocks, huge chapters cemented together by recurring leitmotivs and a consummate gift for storytelling. In his narrative practice, he combines brilliantly the particular and the general, the individual and the mass, the everyday and the strange. His various narrative worlds, with their specific atmospheres, are always presented through the eyes of individuals, and are never separate from human experience. Often, the first chapter recounts the arrival of a stranger in a community – Gervaise Macquart in *L'Assommoir*, recently arrived in Paris, surveying the street from her hotel window, and later, walking round the neighbourhood before stopping to gaze up at the tenement house where her friend Coupeau lives; the abbé Faujas arriving in the small town of Plassans in *La Conquête de Plassans*; Florent in *Le Ventre de Paris*, suddenly appearing in the midst of the community of Les Halles; Etienne Lantier in *Germinal*, arriving in the mining community, being introduced to the communal life of the *coron*, and descending into the mine for the first time; Octave Mouret in *Pot-Bouille*, shown round the bourgeois apartment building in the rue de Choiseul before finding his own way; Denise Baudu in *Au Bonheur des Dames*, arriving in Paris and coming, open-mouthed, upon the new department store.

The interaction between people and their environment is evoked in Zola's famous physical descriptions, which are such a prominent feature of his novels. These descriptions are not, however, mechanical products of his aesthetic credo, objective 'copies' of the real; rather, they express the very meaning, and ideological tendencies, of his narratives. Consider, for example, the lengthy descriptions of the luxurious physical décor of bourgeois existence – houses, interiors, social gatherings – in *La Curée*. The main syntactic characteristic of these passages is (as Sandy Petrey points out in his chapter) the eclipse of human subjects by abstract nouns and things, suggesting the absence of any controlling human agency, and expressing a vision of a society which, organised under the aegis of the commodity, turns people into objects. Similarly, the descriptions of the sales in *Au Bonheur des Dames*, with their cascading images and rising pitch, suggest loss of control, the female shoppers' quasi-sexual abandonment to consumer dreams, at the same time mirroring the perpetual expansion that defines the economic principles of capitalism. Description of the physical realities of workers' lives reinforces the radicalism of novels like *L'Assommoir* and *Germinal* by pointing insistently to conditions of labour that are monstrously unjust.

Zola's descriptive style reveals a genius for dramatic pictorial representation. Did anyone before him see a tenement house as he did in the second chapter of *L'Assommoir*? Descriptions become highly metaphorical; the observed reality of the world is the foundation for a poetic vision. The originality of Zola's fiction lies in its movement, colour and intensity; and especially in its remarkable symbolising effects. Emblematic features of contemporary life – the market, the machine, the tenement building, the laundry, the mine, the apartment house, the department store, the stock exchange, the theatre, the city itself – are used as giant symbols of the society of his day. Zola sees allegories of contemporary life everywhere. In *La Curée*, the new city under construction at the hands of Haussmann's workmen becomes a vast symbol of the corruption, as well as the dynamism, of Second Empire society. In *Au Bonheur des Dames*, the department store is emblematic of the new dream world of consumer culture and of the changes in sexual attitudes and class relations taking place at the time. Zola's fictional naturalism becomes a kind of surnaturalism, as he infuses the material world with anthropomorphic life, magnifying reality and giving it a hyperbolic, hallucinatory quality.[8] The play of imagery and metaphor often assumes phantasmagoric dimensions. We think, for example, of Saccard in *La Curée*, swimming in a sea of gold coins – an image that aptly evokes his growing mastery as a speculator; the fantastic visions of food in *Le Ventre de Paris*; the still in *L'Assommoir*, oozing with poisonous alcohol like some malevolent beast, and Goujet's forge, where machines become giants and the noise of the overhead connecting belts becomes the flight of night birds; Nana's mansion, like a vast vagina, swallowing up men and their fortunes; the dream-like proliferation of clothing and lingerie in *Au Bonheur des Dames*; the devouring pithead in *Germinal*, lit by strange fires, rising spectrally out of the darkness.

Realist representation is imbued with mythic resonance. As Flaubert wrote: 'Nana turns into a myth, without ceasing to be real' ['Nana tourne au mythe, sans cesser d'être réelle'].[9] *Le Ventre de Paris* is simultaneously a description of Les Halles and the story of the eternal struggle between the Fat and the Thin. *Germinal* offers perhaps the most obvious examples of the fusion of reality and myth: the pithead, Le Voreux, is a modern figuration of the Minotaur, and is constantly compared to a monstrous beast which breathes, devours, digests and regurgitates. Reality is transfigured into a theatre of archetypal forces. Zola's fascination with these forces, and their central role in his creative project, are reflected in his repeated use in his preparatory sketches for his novels of the word 'poem': 'poème des désirs du mâle' (*Nana*), 'poème de l'activité moderne' (*Au Bonheur des Dames*), 'poème vivant de la terre' (*La Terre*).

Zola's use of myth is inseparable from his vision of history, and is essentially Darwinian. His conception of society is shaped by a biological model informed by a constant struggle between the life instinct and the death instinct, the forces of creation and destruction. His social vision is marked by an ambivalence characteristic of modernity itself – a pessimistic attitude towards the present, but optimism about the future. Progress, for Zola, cannot be imagined without a form of barely contained primitive regression, as witnessed by Jacques Lantier's feelings of both veneration and destructive hatred towards his locomotive in *La Bête humaine*. Despite his faith in science, Zola's vision is strongly marked by the anxiety that accompanied industrialisation and modernity. Scientific and technological progress bring alienation as well as liberation, and modern man feels trapped by forces he has created but cannot fully control. The demons of modernity are figured in images of destruction and catastrophe: the sinister still in *L'Assommoir*, the labyrinthine Le Voreux in *Germinal*, the runaway train in

La Bête humaine, the city in flames in *La Débâcle*. Zola's naturalist world is an entropic world, in which nature inevitably reverts to a state of chaos, despite all human effort to create order and to dominate its course.[10] But there is also emphasis on regeneration, on collapse being part of a larger cycle of integration and disintegration. Catastrophe has a cathartic function leading to regeneration. Zola's work always turns towards hope, as the very title of *Germinal* implies.

It is the mythopoeic quality of Zola's work that makes him one of the great figures of the French novel. Heredity serves as a structuring device, analogous to Balzac's use of recurring characters; and it has great dramatic force, allowing Zola to give a mythical dimension to his representation of the human condition. For Balzac, money and ambition were the mainsprings of human conduct; for Zola, human conduct was determined by heredity and environment, and they pursue his characters as relentlessly as the forces of fate in an ancient tragedy. As well as looking back to Balzac, Zola points forward to Proust – in the huge sweep of society he presents, in his inclusion of political and sexual themes, in his close attention to the particular idiom of individuals or groups, even in his representation (as in *La Curée* and *Nana*) of transvestism and homosexuality, but especially in his intense awareness of the disruptive effect of sex in breaking up formerly solid class barriers.

Class and sex

In 1876 Zola published in serial form his first novel of working-class life, *L'Assommoir*, which describes the social and moral degradation of that class in contemporary Paris. The novel focuses on the life and death of a washerwoman, Gervaise Macquart. It was hugely successful (the first bestseller in the history of the French novel), and it was also scandalous: the serialisation of the novel was interrupted by the government, and several bourgeois critics noisily accused Zola of pornography. These violently hostile reactions to *L'Assommoir*, together with the novel's immense commercial success (ironically, it made Zola rich), indicated that something significantly new had happened to the novel. In 1877, when the novel appeared in book form, Zola added a preface in response to the storm of controversy it had provoked. He characterised *L'Assommoir* as 'a work of truth, the first novel about the common people which does not tell lies but has the authentic smell of the people' ['une œuvre de vérité, le premier roman sur le peuple, qui ne mente pas et qui ait l'odeur du peuple' (RM ii 373–4)].

To understand the reasons for the scandal that surrounded the publication of *L'Assommoir*, and its success, we need to consider how the novel undermined the expectations of its contemporary readership. The novel in France was essentially a bourgeois genre, having developed in tandem with the bourgeoisie's political and material rise. It depended on a largely bourgeois readership, and was shaped by a bourgeois ideology of literary propriety. Conservative critics clearly considered that Zola had transgressed the limits of what could be written about. To focus entirely on urban workers was itself new and disturbing, and to make a working-class washerwoman a tragic heroine even more so. If the workers could take over the novel, perhaps they could also take over the government; the trauma of the Commune of 1871, when the people of Paris had repudiated their national government and set up their own, was still fresh in people's minds.

What also greatly disturbed bourgeois critics was Zola's unflinching realism, the sheer force and candour of his representation of the squalor of slum life, and especially his graphic portrayal, unprecedented in French fiction, of the workers' physical being, their bodies. Bourgeois thought generally concealed both the bourgeoisie's physical nature and the workers' humanity; this meant that Zola's emphasis on the body, by forcing the reader to recognise that the human condition is a universal, had a powerful subversive effect on the ideological justification for the capitalist hierarchy. As Jean Borie has argued, the bourgeoisie devised a complex mental system in which the body and the proletariat were alien and subservient.[11] In the artistic myths communicating that system, the body was either pornographic or subsumed by the soul, while workers, when not invisible, were either vicious drunkards or inspiringly resigned labourers on their way to becoming bourgeois.

What disoriented contemporary readers most, however, was not the subject matter of *L'Assommoir*, but its style: its use of working-class language and urban slang. The workers are intrusively present – they can be 'smelt' – in the very language of *L'Assommoir*. Language itself is – aggressively and provocatively – socialised. During the course of the narrative, popular speech is not simply sprinkled throughout the text but becomes, increasingly, the medium of narration. It is as if the characters themselves take on a narrative function, telling their own story. The language of the characters is absorbed by the (traditionally 'bourgeois') narrator without quotation marks, as if the novel were spoken via the collective voice of the Goutte-d'Or district, using the lexicon and syntax of the street.

Zola achieved this effect by use of a special form of the technique known as free indirect speech (*style indirect libre*). His brilliant ability to capture popular speech patterns, even when writing indirectly, reflects his powers of psychological empathy, a capacity for evoking the workers' own vision of the world; and it also has significant ideological implications. Not only are the expectations associated with conventional bourgeois narrative disrupted, but the reader is also brought into more direct and authentic contact with the characters and their culture, with their attitudes and values, than would have been the case had these been relayed exclusively by means of direct speech and conventional dialogue. It was his bold experiment with style that, according to Zola, explained why his bourgeois readers had been so upset. As he wrote in his preface:

> They have taken exception to the words. My crime is that I have had the literary curiosity to collect the language of the people and pour it into a carefully wrought mould. The form! The form is the great crime.
>
> [On s'est fâché contre les mots. Mon crime est d'avoir eu la curiosité littéraire de ramasser et de couler dans un moule très travaillé la langue du people. Ah! la forme, là est le grand crime! (RM ii 373)]

His 'great crime' was to have shown that the novel is not an intrinsically bourgeois genre, tied to bourgeois discourse.

The novel's central chapter (Chapter 7) describes Gervaise's celebration of her saint's day with a Rabelaisian feast where food, drink and companionship are the focus. The doors and windows are opened and the whole neighbourhood is invited to join in the merrymaking. The feast is a pivotal episode, marking the high point of Gervaise's professional success, but also a turning-point in her fortunes. The sheer extravagance of the feast suggests the lurking dangers of dissipation, and the occasion also marks the fateful return of Lantier, Gervaise's malevolent former lover. Gervaise decides to spend all of her hard-won savings on the meal, and even pawns her wedding ring in order to buy superior wine. Above all, the extravagance of the feast expresses defiance, through recklessness and prodigality, of the constrictions – the prudence and thrift – of a life always on the edge of starvation. The workers' plight is expressed through the very description of their pleasure: 'The whole shop was dying for a binge. They needed an absolute blow-out' ['Toute la boutique avait une sacrée envie de nocer. Il fallait une rigolade à la mort' (RM ii 558)]. The meal becomes an orgy, and the mounting excitement of the characters is matched by that of the narrative voice, which appears to blend joyously with the voices of the assembled company:

> Christ, yes, they really stuffed themselves! If you're going to do it, you might as well do it properly, eh? And if you only have a real blow-out once in a blue moon, you'd be bloody mad not to fill yourself up to the eyeballs. You could actually see their bellies getting bigger by the minute! The women looked pregnant. Every one of them was fit to burst, the greedy pigs! Their mouths wide open, grease all over their chins, their faces looked just like arses, and so red you'd swear they were rich people's arses, with money pouring out of them.

And the wine, my friends! The wine flowed round the table like the water in the Seine.

[Ah! nom de Dieu! oui, on s'en flanqua une bosse! Quand on y est, on y est, n'est-ce pas? et si l'on ne se paie qu'un gueuleton par-ci par là, on serait joliment godiche de ne pas s'en fourrer jusqu'aux oreilles. Vrai, on voyait les bedons se gonfler à mesure. Les dames étaient grosses. Ils pétaient dans leur peau, les sacrés goinfres! La bouche ouverte, le menton barbouillé de graisse, ils avaient des faces pareilles à des derrières, et si rouges, qu'on aurait dit des derrières de gens riches, crevant de prospérité.

Et le vin, donc, mes enfants! ça coulait autour de la table comme l'eau coule à la Seine.   (RM ii 579)]

The past definite tense used in the first sentence ('on s'en flanqua une bosse!') clearly identifies the passage as a part of the narrative, but the register and syntax – direct, simple, robustly colloquial – reflect the language of the characters. The characters' colloquial language is woven into the fabric of the narrative, absorbing the written discourse of the narrator. The use of *on* in the original is ambiguous (they? we?), blurring further the distinction between narrator and characters. A single voice dominates. The jovial apostrophe 'mes enfants!', its author and addressees uncertain, draws the reader into sharing in the general euphoria. The narrator sits at table with his characters, participating stylistically in the revelry and implicitly inviting the reader-spectator to join in too, thus subverting the moralistic perspectives on the workers' intemperance that so strongly marked contemporary discourse on social issues and contemporary reactions to the novel. Is it because Gervaise is self-indulgent and given to excess that she undergoes the tragedy of working people? Or is it because she undergoes the tragedy of working people that she becomes self-indulgent and given to excess? Is the feast an act of reprehensible folly, or an understandable symptom of the circumstances in which Gervaise lives?

The question of the narrator's sympathy, and its textual expression, is very important; the novel's style has clear ideological implications. Zola showed his readers things they would prefer not to see in a style making it impossible to look the other way. The ventriloquised storyteller is almost too close for comfort, right in our face. It is not only impossible to look the other way, but difficult to keep one's distance. The critical debate surrounding *L'Assommoir*, both at the time of the novel's appearance and since, involved what might be called a politics of representation. The fact that the urban proletariat were considered by the bourgeoisie to be beyond the limits of narrative, beneath the level of narrative representation, was held implicitly to justify their exclusion from political representation. The strident attacks on *L'Assommoir* for pornography were motivated as much by reactionary fear as by prudishness. The attacks Zola sustained thoughout his career for vulgarity, tastelessness, stylistic crudity and a purported obsession with the filthy underside of society were largely political in nature – attempts by the literary critical establishment to discredit and marginalise him.

Eight years after *L'Assommoir*, Zola published *Germinal*. Through his description of a miners' strike, he evokes the awakening of the workers' political consciousness. Paradoxically, it is in his portrayal of the miners' material and mental condition before their consciousness is aroused by their would-be leader, Etienne Lantier, that Zola is most subversive. The miners have a sense of social authority as a force in its own right, inscribed into the natural order of things. Their vision of the world is, in the Marxist sense, alienated. One of the strengths of *Germinal* is its demonstration of the ways in which bourgeois mystification and working-class alienation complement each other in the reinforcement of the dominant ideology. Like Marx, Zola saw that the true significance of social processes goes on 'behind the backs' of individual agents.

In *L'Assommoir* Zola had used narrative technique, and narrative voice in particular, to make articulate the inarticulate – to make us see and hear the world through the workers' eyes and voices. In *Germinal*, he does something similar; but in the later novel he also depicts a moment in history when the workers find a political voice. Irving Howe has commented: '*Germinal* releases one of the central myths of the modern era: the story of how the dumb acquire speech. All those at the bottom of history, for centuries objects of manipulation and control, begin to transform themselves into active subjects, determined to create their own history.'[12] The theme of the miners' learning to speak becomes a motif of the novel. Auerbach analyses the evening conversation between Etienne Lantier and the Maheu family in the third chapter of Part Three of *Germinal* – intended as one example of many such conversations – to show the stirrings of the miners' consciousness of their situation in response to Etienne's political eloquence.[13] The narration in the second chapter of Part Four of the visit of the miners' delegation, led by Maheu, to the mine-manager's house shows how the miners, though at first intimidated by the imposing surroundings (manifestations of the bourgeois world) and by their unaccustomed role (making demands rather than following orders), begin to speak and slowly gain in confidence as they articulate their grievances. And Maheu, their chosen spokesman, most of all: at first tongue-tied, reproached by the manager Hennebeau for heading a party of malcontents, he finds a tongue he did not even know he had. When Hennebeau tries to interrupt, Maheu cuts him short.

His voice was growing stronger. He raised his eyes and went on, looking straight at the manager . . . Moreover Maheu cut the manager short. Now he had taken off, the words were coming by themselves. Several times he listened to himself in amazement, as if a stranger had spoken inside him. These were things stored up in his chest, things he hadn't even known were there, and they were gushing out from his heart. He was saying their common poverty, the hard work, the life of a beast, the wife and kids in the house crying out from hunger.

[Sa voix se raffermissait. Il leva les yeux, il continua, en regardant le directeur . . . Du reste, Maheu coupa la parole au directeur. Maintenant, il était lancé, les mots venaient tout seuls. Par moments, il s'écoutait avec surprise, comme si un étranger avait parlé en lui. C'étaient des choses amassées au fond de sa poitrine, des choses qu'il ne savait même pas là, et qui sortaient, dans un gonflement de son coeur. Il disait leur misère à tous, le travail dur, la vie de brute, la femme et les petits criant la faim à la maison.   (RM iii 1320)]

Maheu discovers, in every sense, the power of speech. David Baguley, in his chapter on *Germinal*, offers a detailed reading of the novel with reference to its political message and its ambiguities, its narrative techniques, and its literary and mythical resonance.

Zola's social and sexual themes intersect at many points. In his sexual themes he ironically subverts the notion that bourgeois supremacy over the workers is a natural rather than a cultural phenomenon. His description of the secret adultery of Mme Hennebeau with her nephew, the engineer Négrel, exposes as myth the reactionary bourgeois supposition that they, unlike the workers, are above nature – that they are able to control their natural instincts and that their social supremacy is therefore justified. Hennebeau is at first enraged when he discovers that his wife is sleeping with her nephew; but he quickly decides to turn a blind eye to her infidelity, reflecting that it is better to be cuckolded by his bourgeois nephew than by his proletarian coachman. Adultery among the bourgeoisie was much more significant than among the working class because, as transgressors of their own law, the bourgeoisie put at risk an order of civilisation structured precisely to sustain their own privileged position. The more searchingly and explicitly Zola investigated the theme of adultery, the more he risked uncovering the arbitrariness and fragility of the whole bourgeois social order.

In *Pot-Bouille*, Zola lifted the lid on the realities of bourgeois mores, exposing the hypocrisy of the dominant class, who are no more able to control their natural instincts than the workers but are simply more dissimulating. The bourgeois go to extreme lengths to maintain the segregation between themselves and the lower classes, whom they insistently portray as dirty, immoral, promiscuous, stupid – at best a lesser type of human, at worst some kind of wild beast. But class difference is shown to be merely a matter of money and power, tenuously holding down the raging forces of sexuality and corruption beneath the surface. What we are left with is a melting-pot, a stew, an undifferentiated world where no clear boundaries remain.

Zola's naturalism, with its emphasis on integrity of representation, entailed a new explicitness in the depiction of sexuality. To say less than all would be to abdicate, as Zola saw it, from the novelist's intellectual and social function. He broke with academic convention to a degree hitherto unseen in literature. *Nana*, for example, represented a drastic advance towards erotic verisimilitude. The novel's opening scene dramatises this stripping away of cultural shields as Nana appears with progressively less clothing on the stage of a theatre that its director insists is a brothel.

Controversy and commitment

The subversive qualities of Zola's writings are clear. He broke taboos. His work was deemed scandalous in both form and content. At every stage of his life he was involved in controversy: as a journalist, he championed Manet and the Impressionists against the upholders of academic art; he was an outspoken critic of the Second Empire regime, and he attacked the stuffy moral conservatism of the early years of the Third Republic. As a novelist, he founded the naturalist school in opposition to 'polite' literature: there was the scandal of *L'Assommoir*, the provocation of *Nana*, the warning of *Germinal* ('Hasten to be just, or the earth will open up beneath our feet' ['Hâtez-vous d'être justes, sinon la terre s'ouvrira'](Cor. v 347)), the brutal candour of *La Terre*, and the sustained critique of organised religion in *Les Trois Villes* (1894–8). His whole career, in his fiction as well as in his essays and pamphlets, was punctuated by attacks on the bourgeoisie. The last line of *Le Ventre de Paris* is: 'What bastards decent people really are!' ['Quels gredins que les honnêtes gens!' (RM i 895)]. Zola never stopped being a danger to the established order. In 1898 he crowned his literary career with a political act, the famous open letter ('J'accuse . . . !') to the President of the Republic in defence of Alfred Dreyfus – a frontal attack on state power.[14]

The Dreyfus Affair provided a logical conclusion to Zola's career. His humanitarian vision and his compassion for the disinherited naturally allied him with all those who fought for truth and justice. He was consciously, and increasingly, a public writer. Squarely in the tradition of Voltaire and Victor Hugo, and anticipating the work of writers like Jean-Paul Sartre and Albert Camus in the twentieth century, his courageous stand in the Dreyfus Affair showed the public writer at his best. In 1893 a Jewish army officer,

Alfred Dreyfus, had been accused of spying for Germany. He had been court-martialled, found guilty of treason, and sentenced to life imprisonment on Devil's Island, off the coast of French Guiana. Despite clear evidence that emerged in 1897 showing that Dreyfus had been the victim of a conspiracy, the original verdict was upheld, to the outrage of Zola and his fellow Dreyfusards. By the time of 'J'accuse', French public opinion was polarised, not simply on the particular question of Dreyfus' innocence or guilt but on the future of the Republic itself. The Affair magnified and brought into question the fault-lines and divisions of the Third Republic and its major institutions. The clash of republicanism and anti-republicanism, clericalism and anti-clericalism, reaction and social reform, blind patriotism and rational criticism, was whipped up further by xenophobia and anti-Semitism.

The role Zola played in the Dreyfus Affair (described in chronological detail by Owen Morgan in his chapter) invites reflection on what it meant to be a public intellectual in late nineteenth-century France. The word 'intellectual' itself was a pejorative term first used by the anti-revisionist press: the Dreyfusards were the first official 'intellectuals'. To be an 'intellectual' meant speaking out in the name of justice; and for Zola to speak of justice was to speak in the name of the Republic. Zola's key strategy in his address to the jury at the time of his own trial for libel in connection with the publication of 'J'accuse' was to present the unjust condemnation of Dreyfus as an aberration from the true Republic of 1789 and its principles of liberty and justice.

> By now, gentlemen, the Dreyfus Affair is a very minor matter, very remote and very blurred, compared to the terrifying questions it has raised. There is no Dreyfus Affair any longer. There is only one issue: is France still the France of the Revolution and the Declaration of the Rights of Man, the France which gave the world liberty, and was supposed to give it justice?
>
> [L'affaire Dreyfus, ah! Messieurs, elle est devenue bien petite à l'heure actuelle, elle est bien perdue et bien lointaine, devant les terrifiantes questions qu'elle a soulevées. Il n'y a plus d'affaire Dreyfus, il s'agit désormais de savoir si la France est encore la France des droits de l'homme, celle qui a donné la liberté au monde et qui devait lui donner la justice.]
>
> (*La Vérité en marche*, OC xiv 937)

Zola, condemned to imprisonment for one year, went into exile in England. The day after his sentence the League of the Rights of Man was founded, identifying the case of Dreyfus (and that of Zola) with the French Revolution, civic education and the republican spirit. The Dreyfus Affair was of seminal importance in relation to the unique role French intellectuals were destined to play on the world stage in the twentieth century as a result of their historical legacy of revolution. As Tony Judt has written:

By the time of the emergence of the modern intellectual community, France, thanks to the Revolution, had become a universal model, her experience part of the collective European memory. Being French gave Parisian writers a uniquely dual identity and thus authorized them to bear a special burden. Henceforth, their marginality, their opposition, their elective condition of revolt and protestation within France itself was what elevated and integrated them into a superior, trans-national community and defined their cultural significance (in France and abroad); from Dreyfus on, this special confidence of French intellectuals would distinguish them from their peers in other cultures.[15]

* * *

So many currents of nineteenth-century thought and feeling circulate in Zola's writing (including contemporary psychology, as Rae Beth Gordon shows in her chapter on *La Bête humaine*). His work contains many contradictory strains; indeed, part of his abiding significance is to be found in the ways in which he exemplified and articulated the contradictions of his time.

In the early days, Zola was attacked almost as much by the humanitarian left as by the conservative right, on the grounds that he painted too black a picture of the lower classes. The critical controversies surrounding the ideological impact of his working-class texts reflect ambiguities in the texts themselves. For Zola, the power of mass working-class movements was a radically new element in human history, and it aroused in him an equivocal mixture of pity and dread. *L'Assommoir* and *Germinal* create a sense of humanitarian warmth and tragic pathos in their portrayal of the downtrodden, but Zola shows no solidarity with those who propound radical social and economic solutions. As a strike leader in *Germinal*, Etienne Lantier becomes a demagogue, an apostle of destruction unable to contain or control the repressed energies of the strikers once they are unleashed. The Commune, in *La Débâcle*, is seen not as the legitimate manifestation of an urge towards equality and autonomy, but as an aberration, a further symptom of the incurable malady which infected the body politic of the recently deceased Second Empire.

In his treatment of sex and marriage, Zola broke the mould of Victorian moral cant. Hannah Thompson suggests that it is Zola's interest in those sexualities and genders that deviate from the patriarchal norm that explains the continuing appeal of his novels. On the other hand, Zola admired what he saw as the bourgeois family ideal. The *bête noire* of the bourgeoisie, he was also a moralist who believed deeply in the traditional bourgeois virtues of self-discipline, hard work and moderation. Although the champion of the oppressed, he was an advocate of responsible bourgeois leadership. His biting attacks on callous greed and exploitation do not lead him to revolutionary socialism but to trust in an evolution towards a more moral, less class-ridden order, to be built, precisely, on the creative energy of the bourgeoisie. A vision of bourgeois paternalism is explicit in the last, highly didactic novels, particularly in *Travail* (*Work*, 1903), where a bourgeois Messiah creates a sentimental Utopia in which all problems have been dissolved and all classes live in harmony. Julia Przybos, in her chapter on Zola's utopias, analyses Zola's late fiction in the context of the idealistic tendencies of his work as a whole and the intellectual climate of the closing decades of the nineteenth century.

In September 1902 Zola was working on *Vérité* (*Truth*), a fictionalised account of the Dreyfus Affair, when he died, poisoned by carbon monoxide fumes from a blocked chimney. It was discovered that the chimney had been capped during repair work. Rumours of foul play, based on the many death threats the writer had received, seem to have been borne out by revelations made in the French press in 1953. Zola, it has been suggested, was murdered by an ill-wisher who blocked up his chimney flue one day and unblocked it the following morning. Did Zola pay with his life for his belief in the truth? We cannot know. We do know, however, that on 5 October 1902 50,000 people turned out for his funeral, including a delegation of miners from Anzin, who came all the way to Paris and chanted 'Germinal! Germinal! Germinal!' as they followed his hearse through the streets of the city.

NOTES

1 Henri Mitterand, *Zola: l'histoire et la fiction* (Paris: Presses Universitaires de France, 1990), p. 8.

2 'Emile Zola' (1903), in Henry James, *The House of Fiction*, ed. Leon Edel (London: Hart-Davis, 1957), pp. 220–49 (p. 233). Also in George J. Becker (ed.), *Documents of Modern Literary Realism* (Princeton: Princeton University Press, 1963), p. 518.

3 *The House of Fiction*, p. 227 (and *Documents*, p. 513).

4 Erich Auerbach, *Mimesis: The Representation of Reality in Western Literature*, trans. Willard R. Trask (Princeton: Princeton University Press, 1953 [1946]), p. 512.

5 *Mimesis*, p. 515.

6 Henri Mitterand (ed.), *Emile Zola: Carnets d'enquêtes. Une ethnographie inédite de la France* (Paris: Plon, 1987).

7 Henri Mitterand, *Le Regard et le signe. Poétique du roman réaliste et naturaliste* (Paris: Presses Universitaires de France, 1987), p. 80.

8 See Henri Mitterand, 'Zola, "ce rêveur définitif"', trans. Fiona Neilson, in Harold Bloom, ed., *Emile Zola* (New York and Philadelphia: Chelsea House, 2004), pp. 243–58 (first published in the *Australian Journal of French Studies*, 38, 3 (2001), 321–35).

9 Flaubert, *Correspondance* (15 February 1880).

10 See David Baguley, *Naturalist Fiction: The Entropic Vision* (Cambridge: Cambridge University Press, 1990) and Michel Serres, *Feux et signaux de brume: Zola* (Paris: Grasset, 1975).

11 Jean Borie, *Zola et les mythes, ou de la nausée au salut* (Paris: Seuil, 1971), p. 26.

12 Irving Howe, 'Zola: The Genius of *Germinal*', *Encounter*, 34 (April 1970), 53–61.

13 *Mimesis*, pp. 512–15.

14 Zola in fact made many journalistic interventions in the Dreyfus Affair. They are gathered together in English translation in Emile Zola, *The Dreyfus Affair: 'J'accuse' and Other Writings*, ed. Alain Pagès, trans. Eleanor Levieux (New Haven and London: Yale University Press, 1996).

15 Tony Judt, *Past Imperfect: French Intellectuals, 1944–1956* (Berkeley: University of California Press, 1992), p. 252.

RECOMMENDED READING

Auerbach, Erich, *Mimesis: The Representation of Reality in Western Literature*, trans. Willard R. Trask (Princeton: Princeton University Press, 1953 [1946]), pp. 506–15

Baguley, David, *Naturalist Fiction: The Entropic Vision* (Cambridge: Cambridge University Press, 1990)

Borie, Jean, *Zola et les mythes, ou de la nausée au salut* (Paris: Seuil, 1970)

Hemmings, F. W. J., *Emile Zola*, second edition (Oxford: Clarendon Press, 1964)

Mitterand, Henri, *Zola et le naturalisme* (Paris: Presses Universitaires de France, 'Que sais-je?', 1986)

Zola, 3 vols. (Paris: Fayard, 1999–2002)

Nelson, Brian, *Zola and the Bourgeoisie* (London: Macmillan; Totowa, New Jersey: Barnes & Noble, 1983)

Wilson, Angus, *Emile Zola: An Introductory Study of his Novels* (London: Secker & Warburg, 1964 [1953])

2

NICHOLAS WHITE

Family histories and family plots

Sexual and textual desire

It is a cliché to think of literary history in terms of family roles. The relationship of authors, particularly male ones, to previous generations of writers has often been understood in terms of Harold Bloom's famous notion of 'the anxiety of influence' and its explicitly Freudian model of Oedipal displacement. Indeed, it is hard to resist this model as one reads the private definition of Zola's Rougon-Macquart project, which he records under the title: 'Différences entre Balzac et moi' (RM v 1736–7). Ironically, this 'family romance' of literary identity depends on the primacy of Zola's fictional family: 'The scope [of my work] will be more restricted. I do not want to paint contemporary society, but a single family, by showing the play of race modified by milieu' ['Le cadre [de mon œuvre] sera plus restreint. Je ne veux pas peindre la société contemporaine, mais une seule famille, en montrant le jeu de la race modifiée par les milieux']. Novelists and dramatists have often enjoyed a paternal relationship to the characters they have created, and Zola is by no means alone in his reference in correspondence to his novels as 'my children', though such paternal mastery itself risks displacement, or disfigurement, in the hands of deconstructive readings born in the wake of Roland Barthes' notion of the Death of the Author, which questions the pre-eminent status attributed to authorial intention in traditional literary criticism. But whereas Marcel Proust's insights, for instance, can be brought into historical focus by the contemporaneous achievements of psychoanalysis and modernism, Zola seems to belong to a more naive world in which personal identity and literary form appeared coherent.

As Zola planned the Rougon-Macquart series in 1868–9, he wrote down lists of possible names for his characters, like the parents of children yet to be born, all too aware of the ways in which names generate connotations (RM v 1670, fols. 135–40, 144–51, 153–4, 157–63). (Conversely, Zola's notes from the geneticist Prosper Lucas [*Traité de l'hérédité naturelle*, 1847–50] refer to biological parents as 'two authors' ['deux auteurs' (RM v 1710)].) However, in Zola's begetting, which depends on and yet transcends biology, the author has the power to give his fictional progeny particular surnames as well as first names. In Zola's vast project, it is the family, and not individual characters, which has the authority of the eponym. Indeed, the novels tend themselves not to be named after individuals. To give a child a double-barrelled name at the start of the twenty-first century might be a feminist choice, or simply a bourgeois gesture; by contrast, Zola's use of the Rougon-Macquart name displays his willingness to embrace both the legitimate and illegitimate sides of the family he depicts.

The modern critical fix on the general category of desire is subject to stricter definition by one of Zola's scientific sources, Charles Letourneau's *Physiologie des passions*, which divides 'will' ['la volonté'] into '*desire*, when it is unreasoned and unavoidable, and *passion*, when desire is stubborn and lasting' ['*désir*, quand elle est irraisonnée, inéluctable, et *passion*, quand le désir est tenace et durable' (RM v 1681)]. Literature is particularly adept at exposing the contrary relationship to sexual desire which families exhibit: on the one hand, needing desire for self-perpetuation; on the other, fearing its corrosive and transgressive force. Quite simply, families may be both created and destroyed by desire. In the warning from Letourneau copied out by Zola, 'the sense of the voluptuous is dominant in the need to procreate' ['le sens voluptueux domine dans le besoin générateur' (RM v 1680)]. The power of Michel Foucault's famous assertion that even the Victorians (and certainly their risqué continental counterparts) were hooked on the discourses of sex (medical, sociological, criminological and psychological), and of Freud's thorough-going sexualisation of family relations at the end of the nineteenth century, needs to be understood against the fanciful desire on the part of 'Victorian' domesticity to define itself as a safe space to be preserved at all costs from sexual provocation.

Famously, in his preface to *La Fortune des Rougon*, Zola defines his fictional family precisely in terms of such procreative and excessive desire, and he identifies in this novelistic pattern an emblem of the historical moment: 'The great characteristic of the Rougon-Macquarts, the group or family which I propose to study, is their ravenous appetite, the great upsurge of our age, which pounces on pleasure' ['Les Rougon-Macquart, le groupe, la famille que je me propose d'étudier, a pour caractéristique le débordement des appétits, le large soulèvement de notre âge, qui se rue aux jouissances' (RM i 3)]. Only in the private 'Résumé des notes' ['Synopsis of notes'] which Zola jots down from his reading of Lucas do we see the trans-historical comparison between the 'thirsts' which define families: 'Just as the Medicis have a thirst for power and the Viscontis a thirst for cruelty, my family will have a thirst to satisfy its appetites, the abuse of physical and intellectual pleasure, a family released into the satisfactions of modern life' ['De même que les Médicis ont soif de pouvoir, les Visconti soif de cruauté, ma famille, aura soif de contenter ses appétits, abus de la jouissance physique et intellectuelle, famille lâchée dans l'assouvissement moderne' (RM v 1725)].

The distinction between a secure private domain and the dangers of *la vie publique* (not least the city-space of the street) was solidified by the nineteenth-century theory of separate spheres, which saw the home as a feminine space and public life as a male domain of politics, art, journalism and work. Nineteenth-century literature performed before its audience their fear that such a spatial separation of the genders might not hold good, and as such literature served as a particular reminder of the potential instability of family life. Narratologists might well see marriage as the pretext or the culmination of family plots, in other words as a fulfilment of the dream of affective stasis (or emotional security). We often find it at the fixed poles of storytelling, at (or towards) the beginning or the end of plots, whereas the process of narrative itself registers the displacements of the human heart. Novels, of course, may begin with a marriage, such as Emma Bovary's, or end with one, as is the case with Octave Mouret, twice. These possibilities of generic nuance within the very genre of the novel are illuminated by Northrop Frye's classic observation that 'comedy is much concerned with integrating the family and adjusting the family to society as a whole; tragedy is much concerned with breaking up the family and opposing it to the rest of society'.[1]

The narrative erosion of solid family structures is particularly visible in the much glossed novel of adultery. Even before the Rougon-Macquart series, Zola had in *Thérèse Raquin* already tried his hand at the tale of wifely transgression which is punished by death (and even before the tragic ending of the novel, by the ghostly return of the murdered husband, Camille). In a persistent fictional pattern, the autonomy of the newly wedded couple is interrupted by a male third party (Laurent), but the stability of the *ménage à trois* will not hold. The illusions of desire are deromanticised by the analytical force of physiology (in Zola's account of the 'temperaments' of the 'nervous' wife; the 'lymphatic' husband – as his name suggests, as sedate as camomile tea; and the 'sanguine' lover, as though the blood of a bull coursed through his veins).

Zola's notes from Prosper Lucas suggest that rather than viewing the family as a given, radical Utopian movements in nineteenth-century France such as Saint-Simonism and Fourierism were keen to revolutionise the family (or even destroy it): 'Saint-Simonism and communism overturn heredity and abolish the family. Fourierism transforms it' ['Le Saint-Simonisme et le

Communisme renversent l'hérédité et abolissent la famille. Le Fouriérisme la transforme' (RM v 1693)]. Unsurprised that radical social and political movements such as these should wrestle with the very idea of the family rather than simply accept it, Lucas himself is all too aware of the political issue posed in post-revolutionary France by the logic of heredity: 'heredity poses an immense problem – : for the *principle* and *succession* of property within the social order; and for the *principle* and *succession* of sovereignty within the political order' ['l'hérédité se pose en un problème immense – : dans l'ordre social, *principe* et *succession* de la propriété; politique, *principe* et *succession* de la souveraineté' (RM v 1693)]. Seen in this light, Zola's method appears so powerful because biological and sociopolitical orders are held in place by a common model of power.

Zola's family planning

Particular to Zola's great novelistic project is the reader's awareness that the family is not only the thematic focus of his writing, but also its grand structuring principle. The demands of the university syllabus often mean that students do not get to read *La Fortune des Rougon*, even though this novel explains the origins of the family tree, and in particular the way in which the sexual life of Adélaïde Fouque (known as Tante Dide) generates the rival narrative paths of the legitimate and illegitimate sides of the family. This gap in student knowledge does, however, replicate the experience of many of Zola's contemporary readers, who would have joined the novel series (often referred to as a *roman-fleuve*) only in 1876–7 via *L'Assommoir* and who may have found it hard to read all subsequent novels as they appeared. It is for this practical reason that Zola reproduced two versions of the family tree (one in 1878 with *Une page d'amour* to recap for his newly seduced readership; the other in 1893 to coincide with the conclusion of the entire series, *Le Docteur Pascal* – to be found in volumes II and V of *Les Rougon-Macquart* respectively). Whereas Proust's vast enterprise revolves around the psyche of a dominant narrator-character, Zola's characters come and go. Balzac is famed for introducing the device of the recurring character, but in Zola it is not so much character but rather characteristics which persist (as we shall see, only Octave Mouret truly dominates more than one novel). In the terms of Zola's 'Différences entre Balzac et moi', 'my characters do not need to return in different novels' ['mes personnages n'ont pas besoin de revenir dans les romans particuliers' (RM v 1737)]. Zola's reliance on a family tree allows him to explore a stock of cultural norms and connotations (or should one say 'ramifications'?): not least the tree of life (echoed in those diagrams of the human body where arteries resemble branches) and the tree of knowledge. As well as providing Zola with a shape for his project, the tree also encourages certain ways of thinking: organic development from a point of origin, beyond the mechanistic plotting of cause and effect.

The history of the tree as a traditional model of thought could be traced via the work of Frank Kermode, and of Gilles Deleuze and Felix Guattari. In his analysis of nineteenth-century thought, Kermode cites the gloss on *Hamlet* in Goethe's *Wilhelm Meister*: 'It is a tree with boughs, leaves, buds, blossoms and fruit. Are they not all one, and there by means of each other?'[2] Indeed, our understanding of literature itself may depend on the tree-like structure of rhetoric. In the words of Michel Charles, 'The tree is the emblem of rhetoric, which classifies and divides, and describes and orders a living architecture where everything is connected and has a function: branch, leaf and fruit' ['L'arbre est l'emblème de la rhétorique, qui classe et divise, décrit et ordonne une vivante architecture où tout se tient et où tout a une fonction: la branche, la feuille et le fruit'].[3] Deleuze and Guattari propose another botanical metaphor, the purposeful chaos of the rhizome as a counter-model of avant-garde practice at odds with the mainstream tradition of cultural production. The latter follows the vertical hierarchy of the 'livre-racine' ['book-root'], in which 'the tree is already the image of the world, or indeed the root is the image of the tree-world. It is the classic book, in the form of an organic, signifying interior of beauty' ['l'arbre est déjà l'image du monde, ou bien la racine est l'image de l'arbre-monde. C'est le livre classique, comme belle intériorité organique, signifiante'].[4] In Zola's 'livre-racine', the tree doubles as both theme and structure, or both object and model of analysis.

Zola criticism has been haunted by the aesthetic monuments of Flaubert and Proust, which stand either side of *Les Rougon-Macquart*, and the recent critical onus on the 'poetics' and symbolism of Zola's writing is intended to overshadow the wilful schematism of his authorial project. It would certainly be an error to imagine that the myriad effects of Zola's history of the Second Empire could be reduced to what we might call the arboreal logic of the family. Equally, though, it is hard to grasp the patterns of unfolding which shape the series without being aware of the family tree. In his notes, Zola writes down Letourneau's distinction between moral and intellectual 'impressions' made on the human organism: 'The first [impressions] relate to the exterior world, to society and family; the second ones are detached from the world, and relate to the play of cerebral faculties' ['Les premières tiennent au monde extérieur, société, famille; les secondes sont détachées du monde, et tiennent au jeu des facultés cérébrales']. By going to press, Zola offers us, in Letourneau's terms, an intellectual 'impression' of our moral 'impressions'.

An analysis of what might be termed Zola's family planning will account for each of these twenty novels. The bodily origin of this tree of novels, Tante Dide, is born in 1768, married to the gardener Rougon in 1786, by whom the very next year she has a son, Pierre Rougon. Glossed in the family tree of 1893 as 'heavy and placid' ['lourd et placide'], the gardener (whose job it is to impose green-fingered order and pattern, or law, on the chaos of nature) fathers the legitimate line of the family. Tante Dide's husband dies in 1788, and in 1789 (the very year of the French Revolution) the widow takes a lover, Macquart, 'unbalanced and a drunkard' ['déséquilibré et ivrogne']. By this smuggler (for whom, one might therefore flippantly remark, property is theft), she has a son in 1789, Antoine Macquart, and a daughter in 1791, Ursule Macquart. The illegitimate lines (for there are in fact two) are in this sense children of the Revolution. In this way the life and loves of Tante Dide form a maternal prehistory to this account of the Second Empire. As we read in Zola's 'Résumé des notes' distilled from Lucas, 'the constitutions of families begin with one individual' ['Les constitutions de famille commencent par un individu' (RM v 1723)].

La Fortune des Rougon examines not only the biological and social origins of the family but also the political origins of the Second Empire via the effect of Louis-Napoleon's *coup d'état* on provincial life in the southern town of Plassans. It is thus telling that 1789 should mark such a key rupture in Tante Dide's own sexual history, not least as the very vocabulary of legitimacy and illegitimacy comes to flavour the language of politics in the nineteenth century, with republics and empires claiming in turn to have the right of law on their side. This is worth comparing with Peter Brooks' analysis of Stendhal's *Le Rouge et le Noir* (1830), which, he notes, 'connects political issues of legitimacy and authority with paternity, itself inextricably bound up in the problem of legitimacy and authority'.[5] As Lynn Hunt has shown, the original Revolution of 1789 had already found in the family a potent method for thinking about politics.[6] To think of 1789 as an Oedipal moment in which sons displace fathers is not merely a subsequent critical imposition but a way of understanding the cultural symbolism of the Revolution which could be described as either childish or imaginative (with the king removed from playing cards and chessboards as well as the throne itself).

In his private 'Notes générales sur la marche de l'oeuvre' ['General notes on the progression of the work'], Zola is keen to historicise desire in such terms: 'The characteristic of the modern movement is the jostling of all ambitions, the fervour of democracy, and the accession of every class (from the familiarity of fathers and sons, the mixing and mingling of all individuals). My novel would have been impossible before '89' ['La caractéristique du mouvement moderne est la bousculade de toutes les ambitions, l'élan démocratique, l'avènement de toutes les classes (de la familiarité des pères et des fils, le mélange et le côtoiement de tous les individus). Mon roman eût été impossible avant 89' (RM v 1738)].

In addition to such figurative and symbolic force, the family became a conspicuous object of reform after 1789. The libertarian impulse of the Revolution led to a radical divorce law in 1792. It was not only the royal family which could be deposed. Subsequently, Napoleon himself used the divorce law to dispose of Josephine and it was not until the Restoration that divorce was finally quashed in 1816, but the Napoleonic Code of 1804 had already reasserted the principle of paternal authority. This was particularly important for the bourgeoisie, whose rise to prominence was of course accelerated by the events of 1789. During the *Ancien Régime* monarchs and aristocrats had depended upon the myth of God-given authority. The bourgeois father needed the myth-making of the Napoleonic Code as his power was otherwise grounded in the material value of his property, and recent history showed that such possessions could quickly be won and lost. If the bourgeois father was to rival the aristocracy, he required the secure transmission of his possessions by inheritance from father to son. The Napoleonic Code and bourgeois ideology highlight a metonymic relationship between the family and the state as microcosmic and macrocosmic structures of order.

Les Rougon-Macquart uses this very logic in inverted form to shape its own interpretative coherence: the disorder of the family provides the reader with a vision of the disequilibrium of Second Empire society, of which it is seen to be both emblem and performance, both cause and effect. In one sense, though, the thread which draws the series together is the family rather than the epoch. As Zola explains in the preface to *La Fortune des Rougon*, history had only intervened subsequently (with the collapse of the Second Empire and the onset of the Franco-Prussian War) to impose an aesthetically satisfying if politically turbulent closure on the hitherto open-ended context of his project, originally referred to as 'A Natural and Social History of a Family in the Nineteenth Century' ['Histoire naturelle et sociale d'une famille au XIXe siècle' (RM v 1671, 1746)].

Rougon or Macquart?

It is the rights of legitimacy that Pierre defends in amassing the 'fortune' advertised in the opening title of the series. The novels that follow can be placed on either side of this morally charged division of blood. Born between 1811 and 1820 (under Napoleon and then the Restoration), the five children Pierre fathers after his marriage in 1810 to Félicité Puech generate a range of novels: the political rise of their first son is marked in the sixth novel,

Son Excellence Eugène Rougon; the second son, Pascal, does not find his own textual space until the twentieth and concluding novel of the series; the second novel, *La Curée*, takes Pierre's son Aristide (known as Saccard) to the Paris of Baron Haussmann, to which we will return in the eighteenth novel, *L'Argent*; then the daughters follow, Sidonie also appearing in *La Curée*, and finally Marthe in the fourth novel, *La Conquête de Plassans*. Sidonie's daughter, Angélique, born in 1851, will emerge in that least naturalist of novels, *Le Rêve* (the sixteenth). Between 1827 and 1831 Antoine Macquart has three children by Joséphine Gavaudan ('vigorous, industrious, but intemperate' ['vigoureuse, travailleuse, mais intempérante']): in the final years of the Restoration, Lisa, of the third novel, *Le Ventre de Paris*, and Gervaise, of the seventh, *L'Assommoir*; and in the early days of the July Monarchy (Antoine having now married Joséphine), Jean is born, and he will farm in the fifteenth novel, *La Terre*, and fight in the nineteenth, *La Débâcle*.

The other illegitimate Macquart, Ursule, loses this shameful name in 1810 by marrying Mouret, by whom she will have three children between 1817 and 1834: François of *La Conquête de Plassans*; Hélène of the eighth novel, *Une page d'amour*; and Silvère, that heroic child of the *peuple*, whose naive love for Miette is traced in the opening chapter of the entire novel series. Resembling the icon of the Revolution, Marianne, consecrated in Delacroix's famous painting *Liberty Leading the People* (1830), Miette bears the flag of the anti-Napoleonic crowd in 1851, only to die in the final paragraphs of *La Fortune* from a gendarme's pistol shot. Although she is immortalised by such romantic politics, it seems that she and Silvère remain childless because they are themselves only children. Indeed, from this perspective, the plot of Silvère and Miette appears to be halted (or 'end-stopped') by this failure to have children.

On Antoine Macquart's side, Jean Macquart's progeny will not have their own novel, whilst the twelfth novel, *La Joie de vivre*, centres on Lisa Macquart's daughter, Pauline Quenu. Gervaise Macquart's achievement is not only to provide the focus for the first truly great (and notorious) novel of the series, *L'Assommoir*; she also gives birth between 1842 and 1852 to a string of canonical protagonists: first, Claude, the painter of *L'Œuvre* (the fourteenth novel); and second, Jacques, the mechanic of *La Bête humaine* (the seventeenth novel), who does not in fact appear in *L'Assommoir* but is added retroactively in order to fulfil the fictional demands of the project. Indeed, it would be wrong to imagine that the family tree represents a divine masterplan that governs novels which are merely written out once the author has conceived of the series. On the contrary, the initial plan for ten novels expands to the final twenty in order to accommodate the thematic variety of the historical fresco. The series not only recounts the organic development of the family; it is itself subject to that same organic logic, having its origins in *La Fortune des Rougon* without being dictated by its schema.

The third child, Etienne, the last Gervaise has by the slothful Lantier, leads the strike in *Germinal* (the thirteenth novel); and the fourth and final child, Anna, will be the courtesan of the ninth novel, *Nana*. Although she is the daughter of Gervaise's husband, Coupeau, Nana bears the genetic imprint of her mother's first lover, Lantier. Here it is as if polite society's cult of female virginity until marriage is brought to bear, strangely but scientifically, on working-class culture. The prim bourgeois stipulation of a woman's singular narrative path from virginal innocence to marital respectability seems in general, however, to have been less influential on proletarian culture of the time. (The reciprocal gaze of bourgeois and proletarian culture is writ large across the naturalist project as a whole, and finds its microcosm in the visit to the Louvre in Chapter 3 of *L'Assommoir*. Gervaise's abortive fantasies of economic security also have an unmistakably bourgeois ring to them.) All of this makes Lantier's rakish appreciation of Anna/Nana's precocious sexuality yet more perturbing.

It is worth recalling that this nineteenth-century writer and his twenty-first-century readers are separated (but also connected) by what many would be tempted to call the century of Crick and Watson (whose discovery of DNA has triggered the genetic revolution in recent science). As a result, the 'natural history' of *Les Rougon-Macquart* can strike us as outlandish as well as forward-looking. Zola was keen to borrow from the emerging human science of sociology and the new natural science of genetics so as to lend to his project the lustre of the new; preparatory note-taking from Letourneau and Lucas allowed Zola to write not only on the modern but as a modern. This 'natural history', which, as we are demonstrating here, accommodates all twenty novels, allows Zola to depict the 'social history' of class relations which his subtitle promises the reader as well.

It may be argued that many of the most dramatic and, indeed, canonical of Zola's novels are to be found on the illegitimate side of the tree, and this association of sexual transgression with the procreation of deviance and delinquency reflects a conservative ideology of the body. Moreover, this symbolic connection between transgression and imperfection is rationalised by the science of genetics. In Zola's notes from Lucas, we read: 'there are families where crime is passed on' ['il existe des familles dans lesquelles le crime se transmet' (RM v 1702)]. In Lucas' analogy: 'Interbreeding produces bad effects – *Interbreeding could be shown in adultery*' ['Le métissage produit de mauvais effets – *On pourrait montrer dans l'adultère le métissage*'], to which Henri Mitterand adds the footnote: 'Hence the history of the Macquart line, born of aunt Dide and the smuggler Macquart' ['De là, l'histoire de la branche

Macquart, issue de tante Dide et du contrebandier Macquart' (RM v 1700)].
In fact, Lucas also notes how illegitimacy can draw infantile qualities from
parental pleasures: 'The intellect and beauty of bastards – When the parents do not love each other, the children are ugly' ['L'esprit et la beauté des
bâtards – Quand les parents ne s'aiment pas, les enfants sont laids' (RM
v 1714)]. In his 'Résumé des notes' drawn from Lucas, Zola dreams of '*A
novel where* INTERBREEDING *would be shown in adultery*' ['*Un roman où
l'on montrerait le* MÉTISSAGE *dans l'adultère*' (RM v 1724)]. Tante Dide
establishes the initial 'crack' ['fêlure'] at the heart of the family structure,
like a quasi-geological as well as moral fault, and in the novels that follow
guilty sex seems to produce faulty behaviour in subsequent generations.

The fusion of legitimacy and illegitimacy

This focus on the family structure of the series allows us to appreciate the
nodal significance of novels which readers otherwise overlook. Vital in this
regard is the fourth novel, *La Conquête de Plassans*, which returns us to
Plassans in the wake of the *coup d'état*. For this novel is the only point at
which a pair of the three strands of Tante Dide's progeny reconnect sexually. In other words, the legitimate Rougon branch and the illegitimate
Mouret (née Macquart) branch grow back into one another and fuse in the
cousin marriage of Marthe Rougon (Pierre's daughter) and François Mouret
(Ursule's son). Between 1840 and 1844 they have three children: Serge and
Désirée, who share the very next novel, *La Faute de l'abbé Mouret*, and
Octave, who chooses a very different path in life – secular, urban and commercial. Given the significance of the tension between legitimacy and illegitimacy which we have glossed above, it is hard to resist the notion that
these children enjoy a key symbolic position in the family tree, at the point
where legitimacy and illegitimacy meet. In particular, it seems fitting that one
of these products of the licit and the illicit, Octave, should occasion Zola's
most extensive foray into the archetypal literature of illegitimacy, i.e., the
novel of adultery.

By contrast with Serge and Désirée, the life of the sexually and financially
rapacious Octave grows to fill two novels rather than one, unique in *Les
Rougon-Macquart* but appropriate for this most Balzacian of characters.
Arriving in Paris from the south at the start of the tenth novel, *Pot-Bouille*,
Octave seems to be following the well-worn path of the *roman d'éducation*
(or *Bildungsroman* as it is often called in honour of its founding text, Goethe's
Wilhelm Meisters Lehrjahre). Instead of simply giving us the tale of the
young man making his way on the stage of Parisian public life, *Pot-Bouille*
lures Octave into a house of bourgeois apartments on the rue de Choiseul,

where virtually the entire novel unfolds. The authority of the bourgeois patriarch, underpinned by the Napoleonic Code as we have seen above, is often said to be threatened by the uncertainty of paternity. Before blood tests and knowledge of DNA, it seemed that fatherhood was always uncertain (critics often refer to the Latin saying used by Freud: *pater semper incertus est*). Indeed, many critics have argued that the novel of adultery is the most conspicuous form of classic European fiction in the nineteenth century. As Tony Tanner explains, the particular focus on wifely adultery in classic novels such as Flaubert's *Madame Bovary* and Tolstoy's *Anna Karenina* reflects how uncertain paternity undermined bourgeois certainty about the transmission of property from father to son.[7] In the case of paternity, knowledge and power seem to be skew. Under the Napoleonic Code, the law of inheritance depended on its own fiction, at odds with the facts of nature.

Pot-Bouille exploits this patriarchal impotence. By the time Zola came to compose this homage to Flaubert (to which he refers privately as 'my *Sentimental Education*' ['mon *Education sentimentale*']), the sentimental novel had lost much of its pre-Flaubertian innocence and introspection. The ethos and tone of Zola's 'Flaubertian' novel are far removed from those of the *roman personnel* (Romantic prose fiction written by authors such as Constant, Chateaubriand, Fromentin and Nerval). With the tragedy of mismatched passions displaced by the comedy of revolving bedroom doors, Octave himself is subject to Zola's corrosive irony. His attempts to play the role of Don Juan are not only morally reprehensible but technically maladroit. Valérie Vabre laughs at the suggestion that she would have had an affair with the likes of Octave (though she is not above such behaviour and does have a mysterious lover). As a hysteric, Valérie is one of the three types of adulteress paraded on the conveyer belt of the bourgeois marriage market (which, by implication, Zola compares at the start of Chapter 2 with the paradoxically honest sale of sex on the street, as Mme Josserand marches her daughters home after yet one more failed bid to find a husband). Here the mimetic literature of types (with its attendant stereotypes, not least of gender) does not simply reflect commonly held and generally accepted opinions in a manner which would allow the author to make sense of the profusion of modernity for his readers. In fact, Zola the journalist had already written specific articles for *Le Figaro* between February and April 1881 on 'Divorce and literature', 'Adultery among the Bourgeoisie' and 'Decent Women', so as to define a set of female stereotypes which would make the fictional types in *Pot-Bouille* legible and recognisable to the readers of Zola the novelist (OC xiv 531–47).

The other women who fall victim to Octave's charms are Marie Pichon and Berthe Josserand. The first of these incarnates a naivety perhaps greater than

Emma Bovary's. Ironically named Marie (after the woman who falls pregnant whilst still sexually innocent), she enters marriage having barely read about love, let alone experienced it. Whereas Emma Bovary has grown up reading books, however sentimental, Marie Pichon has been denied access to literature. Indeed, the relationship between the novel as a genre and the constraints of family life have been subject to much critical gloss in recent times, and *Pot-Bouille* itself manipulates the intertextual echo-chamber of nineteenth-century fiction in order to question the moral function of Romantic literature. Marie's parents, the Vuillaumes, share the conservative fear that fiction provides a way for desire to invade the family. This issue is raised when Octave meets Marie's parents who have come over for tea. Octave displays surprise when the Vuillaumes explain that Marie (unlike Emma) was saved from the moral contamination of imaginative literature throughout her childhood. Indeed, it was only a few months before her marriage that her father allowed his blank canvas of a daughter access to George Sand's *André*, for Zola the epitome of naive Romantic sentiment against which, by implication, naturalist texts such as this offer a demystified vision of love.

The significance of novels in penetrating the supposedly safe space of the family which aims to keep young women pure is symbolised in the promiscuous passage of books which are borrowed, conveyed by a third party (Octave is virtually a pimp of literature), and even broken. The conveyance of books provides Octave with an alibi for entering the Pichon household. To feed Marie's sentimentality, Octave acquires from Campardon a copy of Sand's *André* for her to re-read. Its illusions about love are symbolically and physically broken when Octave returns to his prey, only to take her on the kitchen table. In such a scene of violation, the reader can hardly miss the significance of this particular novel falling to the ground from the table and damaging its spine. The decadence of the bourgeoisie of the Second Empire is registered in the concern Marie and Octave then show for the physical condition of the book. In a displacement of the Ideal by the Real, their concern is to deny all personal guilt – not for their moral Fall, however, but for the physical fall of the book from the table.

Berthe, the third type of adulteress, is characterised by her materialistic greed, and thus reflects the latter stages of Emma Bovary's descent into debt at the hands of Lheureux, in a fetishistic relationship to a reality which cannot match the Ideal. This 'wish for display' ['envie de paraître'], which Zola diagnoses in his journalism, underlines the fear that the bourgeois family cannot fence itself off from the public world beyond its walls, and in particular the idea that there is a morally provocative analogy between the process of marrying off young *bourgeoises* and the commercial sex of prostitution. This is Zola's way of reminding bourgeois readers that the other

Parisian world of the previous novel, *Nana*, is not so far away. The commercial aspect of marriage is institutionalised in the form of the dowry. To borrow the terms of a key sociological distinction, if prostitutes sell sex for pleasure, the bourgeoisie sell sex for reproduction. In this correspondence between the polite and the impolite, it is not just that the *bonne bourgeoise* may prostitute herself, but also that the prostitute may resemble the proud homemaker – hence the symbolic analogy between the interior of a middle-class drawing-room on the rue de Choiseul and the apparently respectable abode of Clarisse Bocquet, uncle Bachelard's low-life mistress.

Berthe's adultery is foreshadowed on her own wedding day in Chapter 8, as her brother-in-law-to-be falsely accuses his wife, Valérie, of an affair with Octave. The scene is one of painfully symmetrical and hypnotically metronomic counterpoint. In the very house of God, the reader is confronted by the connection between marriage and adultery as rival, yet dependent, discourses. Here both discourses are both spoken (the vow versus the accusation) and written (the printed Bible and mass-produced mass-books, versus the handwritten love-letter which is wrongly attributed and thus does not bear the stamp of unique individuality which romantic love seems to promise). The backstage drama of adultery displaces the nuptial performance before the altar, and even the bride's attention is drawn to the scene behind her at the back of the church. Like props in a farce, the congregation's mass-books and the bride's veil become alibi accoutrements to the backwards glance of middle-class morality. As the wedding vow is demoted to parenthesis, 'in an indifferent tone of voice'[8] ['au petit bonheur' (RM iii 147)], Berthe looks back at her own future, for she will indeed take Octave as her lover.

If *Pot-Bouille* charts the sexual seduction of women by Octave, *Au Bonheur des Dames* charts his commercial seduction of *la Parisienne* (and in its insistence on *bonheur*, continues to pose that key question in the rise of the modern cult of romantic and erotic love: namely, how happiness and pleasure can be connected). For all his seductive endeavours, both of Octave's novels end with his marriage, comically in *Pot-Bouille* and romantically in *Au Bonheur des Dames*. His marriage to Mme Hédouin at the end of *Pot-Bouille* allows Octave to transcend the *faux début* of his *Bildungsroman* and progress from the private (but porous) world of the bourgeois family to the public realm of capital. In her refusal to pander to Octave's 'way with women', Mme Hédouin offers him a vision of the 'ways of the world'. In other words, she socialises his childish desires (in a socio-economic as well as a psychoanalytical sense). She allows him to enter the adult world of commerce, towards which he seemed to be heading at the start of the novel. Although Octave does not simply triumph in an unambiguous way, and is subject to Zola's irony, the critique of the bourgeois family unit does depend on the kind of knowing cynicism that Octave embodies.

At odds with the official couple in the wedding at the end of the novel, a covert anti-couple emerges. For Octave and Valérie, seducer and hysteric, cannot resist a knowing but silent look as Octave leaves the church: 'as much as to say that they two alone were able to tell each other everything' ['Lui et elle auraient seuls pu tout se dire' (RM iii 375)]. In this literature which dreams of omniscience, the seducer and the hysteric seem to share a certain kind of intimate knowledge about sex, even if (or precisely because) they never share a bed. Though readers may feel exhilarated by the merry-go-round over which they seem to exercise the power of moral and critical judgment, the seducer and the hysteric stop them dead in their tracks. For in spite of everything, these transgressors of sexual norms, gendered male and female, represent a barely intuited ideal of what we might call the heterosocial couple (itself a perverse 'marriage' of the heterosexual and homosocial norms of patriarchy).

It is telling that the solidity which Mme Hédouin represents is immune to the process of narrative. When the reader starts the very next novel, *Au Bonheur des Dames*, it becomes clear that Mme Hédouin has disappeared in mysterious circumstances. She has shown Octave the way to commercial success, but cannot share it with him. The woman who finally tames him, Denise Baudu, offers another kind of resistance: the resistance of virginity. In a particular version of the Pygmalion plot, Denise works as a shop assistant for Octave, the orchestrator of the grand opera of the modern department store. She manages to halt the serial seductions of this Don Juan, as the only thing he cannot resist is resistance itself.

External and internal pressures

It may well be difficult to imagine plot-based literature which does not focus initially or ultimately on the nature of family life, although this is precisely the project of Des Esseintes, the anti-hero of *A rebours* (1884), written by Zola's contemporary Joris-Karl Huysmans. The plots of fiction and drama habitually turn on the making and breaking of family ties. This structure of intimacy may be endangered by external (and explosive) pressures with an outsider threatening the fulfilment of romance in a comedy by Molière such as *Tartuffe*, where the ultimate saving of young love promises the benign perpetuation of the family; or the de(con)struction of this unit of emotional and sexual coherence may come from within, from the internal (and implosive) disfiguring of such ties, infamously in the incest plot which is virtually as old as literature itself. The trajectory of Zola's own intimate relationship to relations of intimacy is trackable in his contrary treatments of the incest motif towards the beginning and at the end of *Les Rougon-Macquart*.

As the family tree grows, it also spreads, acquiring connections with ever more family trees in a process which anthropologists call exogamy. Though this brings with it hybrid vigour and the possibility of profiting from the property and capital of other families, it may also threaten the singular qualities of the family. The limited gene pool of rural communities had traditionally favoured the opposite process of endogamy – a good example would be *La Terre*. The endogamous impulse is also witnessed in the cousin marriage of *La Conquête de Plassans*. The most extreme form of endogamy is incest, of which *Les Rougon-Macquart* offers two conspicuous and contrary examples. In the second novel, *La Curée*, it enjoys the status of symptom in Zola's diagnosis of the moral decadence of the Second Empire. As the second half of the century unfolded, French society became ever more conscious of the feeling that its vitality was dissipating. In an echo of ancient Rome, this once vibrant Latin culture now seemed vulnerable to the barbarian hordes beyond its frontiers, not least from the Huns (in the form of Bismarck and the Prussians).

The relationship of reader to text was defined during the publication of *Les Rougon-Macquart* by a grand historical irony; whereas the characters are caught within the hubris of the Second Empire, the Third Republic readers of the 1870s and 1880s were only too aware of the nemesis of the Franco-Prussian War and the Commune which awaited the Empire. Nowhere is this cognitive gap between characters and readers greater than in the final words of *Nana* where Parisians merrily chant 'To Berlin! To Berlin! To Berlin!' ['A Berlin! à Berlin! à Berlin!' (RM ii 1485)] on the eve of the war. The parody of classical culture staged at the start of *Nana* dramatises this decadence as a frailty of the body in its military (Mars) and sexual (Venus) contexts. In *Nana* as in *La Curée*, incapacity in war is foreshadowed by perversion in love. Zola finally cashes in on the historical irony of this Third Republic retrospection on the Second Empire in the penultimate novel, *La Débâcle*, whose account of the crushing defeat at Sedan gives its readers what is in effect a version of the origins of their own Republic (just as Zola had thought of *La Fortune des Rougon* as the tale of *Les Origines*). This historical closure is followed in *Le Docteur Pascal* by the aesthetic and biological closure of the series. These final two novels provide a dual ending: *La Débâcle* closing the narrative of public history under the Second Empire; *Le Docteur Pascal* logically falling after this regime change. Like the series as a whole, therefore, it offers a Third Republic retrospection on the Second Empire. This retrospection takes the form of Pascal's attempt as a scientist to construct the genetic history of his own family.

Although Zola is not attracted to the ludic reflexivity of the proto-modernist novel, and though *Le Docteur Pascal* is in formal terms certainly not an early version of Gide or Proust, it is hard not to see in this fiction-alisation of the historian of the family an emblem or a miniature of Zola's own mammoth project (of the kind often referred to by critics as a *mise en abyme*). Of course, Pascal belongs to the family he analyses, but he fulfils the dual intellectual fantasy of intimacy with his subject and critical distance from it, and this is symbolised by his own genetic make-up, which is said to be 'innate' ['inné']; in other words, his individual characteristics seem to be innate because they cannot be traced to his ancestors in the Rougon family. Lay intuition of this separateness is expressed in the name he is given locally, Doctor Pascal, which erases the patronym. A bachelor, Pascal houses his niece, Clotilde, and in a fusion of romance and science, a sexual relationship slowly awakens.

Whereas *La Curée* articulates Parisian decadence in the step incest of Renée and Maxime, *Le Docteur Pascal* intensifies the taboo in the presentation of blood incest, but paradoxically idealises this uncle-niece love. If innateness distances Pascal from the family he studies, incest plunges him back into its core. The irony is that this incest is located on the legitimate Rougon side of the tree. But by 1893, the binary governance of sexual morality in terms of legitimacy (positive) and illegitimacy (negative) has been displaced by a cult of reproduction which stages the conflict between fertility (positive) and sterility (negative). This may have contradicted the conservative idolisation of the legitimate Family, articulated from the beginning of the century in the Napoleonic Code and Louis Bonald's conservative philosophy of family values, but it did fit the national desire for repopulation in the wake of the Franco-Prussian War (a refrain in French history which could still be heard when, in 1945, de Gaulle signalled *le baby boom* by announcing his desire to see 'twelve million bouncing babies for France in the space of ten years' ['en dix ans, douze millions de beaux bébés pour la France'].

For Zola, however, this cult of progeny (which would be amplified in his later fiction, not least in *Fécondité*) had a highly personal significance too. As Owen Morgan's chapter in this volume indicates, Zola is often acclaimed in the light of the Dreyfus Affair as the first modern public intellectual in France. No Sartre without Zola. Yet parallel to this public role ran the turmoil of Zola's personal history, which is encoded in euphoric terms in the *autofic-tion* of *Le Docteur Pascal*. Naturalism undoubtedly makes grand claims for its authors as 'hidden gods', and yet this very assertion of objectivity backgrounds authorial presence in the fantasy that such fictions resemble autonomous documents whose truths speak for themselves. It seems strange, then, to think of naturalism as *autofiction*, but in *Le Docteur Pascal* the projects of writing and fathering have themselves become the objects of mimesis.

In *Le Docteur Pascal*, however, reflexivity is not merely a dry, formal phenomenon. Zola's wife, Alexandrine, had stood by her husband as he rose from obscurity and poverty to notoriety and wealth, but theirs was a childless marriage. Here it is worth noting Zola's transcription from Lucas: 'Exaltation is . . . perhaps necessary in procreation, probably very influential. Intercourse forced upon the woman is, we believe, sterile' ['L'exaltation est . . . peut-être nécessaire à la procréation, elle y influe sans doute beaucoup. Le coït contraint chez la femme serait stérile' (RM v 1714)]. In fact, the conjugal sterility of the Zolas was haunted by the memory that in 1859, five years before meeting Zola, Alexandrine had given birth to an illegitimate daughter, Caroline, only to give her up to the Hôpital des Enfants-Trouvés. Three weeks later, Caroline would be dead.[9] This tale colours our perception of Zola's habit of referring to his family fictions as 'my children'. The national demand for procreation in any event and at all costs happened to dovetail with Zola's own experience of conjugal sterility and adulterous fertility. For it was by breaking the laws of wedlock that Zola discovered the pleasures of paternity.

Narrative closure and autofiction

One of the many virtues of Henri Mitterand's magisterial three-volume biography of Zola is that readers can now co-ordinate fiction and life with yet greater certainty, and this is a particularly powerful tool in the case of *Le Docteur Pascal*.[10] By the time Zola was preparing this terminal novel, he had taken a mistress, Jeanne Rozerot, who had been in the employ of the Zola household, and she had borne him two children, Denise in 1889 and Jacques in 1891. The official dedication of *Le Docteur Pascal* reads: 'To the memory of MY MOTHER and to MY DEAR WIFE I dedicate this novel which is the synthesis and conclusion of my entire work' ['A la mémoire de MA MÈRE et à MA CHÈRE FEMME je dédie ce roman qui est le résumé et la conclusion de toute mon oeuvre' (RM v 915)]. There exists in Paris, however, a rival copy in which Zola has torn out this ode to the official roles of legitimate women, and replaced it with a handwritten dedication intended solely for his mistress and illegitimate children. Here Zola places himself in the title role of Pascal, with Jeanne as his Clotilde:

> To my beloved Jeanne – to my Clotilde, who has given me the regal feast of her youth and taken me back to my thirties, by offering me the gift of my Denise and my Jacques, the two dear children for whom I have written this book, so

that they may know, by reading it one day, how much I adored their mother and what tender respect they will owe her for the happiness with which she consoled me, in my deepest despair.

[A ma bien-aimée Jeanne – à ma Clotilde, qui m'a donné le royal festin de sa jeunesse et qui m'a rendu mes trente ans, en me faisant le cadeau de ma Denise et de mon Jacques, les deux chers enfants pour qui j'ai écrit ce livre, afin qu'ils sachent, en le lisant un jour, combien j'ai adoré leur mère et de quelle respectueuse tendresse ils devront lui payer plus tard le bonheur dont elle m'a consolé, dans mes grands chagrins.   (RM v 1573)]

Hence Zola finds a highly personal and paradoxical analogy between the incest of Pascal and his niece, Clotilde (which keeps it in the family, so to speak) and his own adultery with Jeanne (which is testament to the porosity of the family unit).

This is matched by the textual resolution of the tension between enclosure and expansion. For *Le Docteur Pascal* unfolds across a divide between such contrary demands: the narrative desire for closure in classic 'well made' fiction versus the biological demand for unending perpetuation. This is resolved in the particular pattern of genealogy towards the end of the novel. Clotilde becomes pregnant by Pascal, which he learns of from a distance, only to die before he can see the birth of his son. This biological imbrication of death and birth is matched in the fate of Pascal's intellectual project. In one sense, Pascal's desire to write the history of his family is robbed of suspense, given that the preceding nineteen novels of the series have done precisely this already. Within the novel itself, however, Pascal's scientific project is undermined by the trio of women (Félicité, Martine and even Clotilde) who plot to destroy the embarrassing tales of the family which Pascal has collected.

The mimetic illogicality of writing in the past historic tense ('je mourus', I died) is second-guessed by Pascal's inscription on the family tree of his own imminent death and the birth of his unnamed son. It has seemed that his intellectual project (which has already been fulfilled in the near-completion of Zola's series) will fall far short, because Clotilde has betrayed his scientific ideals in favour of religious mysticism and the burning of Pascal's papers. In a final redemption, however, Clotilde is reunited intellectually with the father of her child, and saves the 'crumbs' ['miettes' (RM v 1215)] of his archive, in the hope that she and their son will reconstruct this fragile history of the family. It is fitting to recall that Zola had begun the series as the Second Empire was coming to a close, and in an aesthetically satisfying circularity *Le Docteur Pascal* gives the reader a fiction of the origins of the series as it comes to an end. And if, in some sense, any text can ultimately guarantee little but the fact of its own existence, there is a secure foundation to the hope represented in the final image of the entire series by the baby's outstretched arm 'like the rallying standard of Life' ['comme un drapeau d'appel à la vie' (RM v 1220)], as if to carry the flag of the new Republic, like the first heroine of the first novel in the series, *La Fortune des Rougon*, who bears the very name of incompletion, of the fragment, of work unfinished or eroded: Miette.

This hope born of the fresh shoots of the family tree echoes the broader humanism voiced in spite of defeat in the vision at the end of *La Débâcle* (a humanism which nevertheless post-modernity has since encouraged us to view ironically): 'This was the sure rejuvenation of eternal nature, of eternal humanity, the renewal of life promised to the man who hopes and toils, the tree which sends out a new, strong shoot after the rotten branch, whose poisonous sap has been turning the leaves yellow, has been cut off' ['C'était le rajeunissement certain de l'éternelle nature, le renouveau promis qui espère et travaille, l'arbre qui jette une nouvelle tige puissante, quand on en a coupé la branche pourrie, dont la sève empoisonnée jaunissait les feuilles' (RM v 912)]. And for all its transgressive danger and genetic risk, incest allows the legitimate Rougon bloodline to confirm its own identity, without the transplanting of other family trees, either by marriage or adultery. It is not only the narrative pleasure of conclusion but also the strange certainty that incest brings which explain the otherwise morally inappropriate euphoria of the final pages of *Le Docteur Pascal*. In the provocative and perturbing terms which, as we have already seen, Zola borrows from Lucas, if adultery is akin to interbreeding, incest bespeaks the racial purity of self-replicating endogamy (in the first category of that famous trio in naturalist analysis: 'race', 'milieu' and 'moment').

NOTES

1 Northrop Frye, *Anatomy of Criticism* (Princeton: Princeton University Press, 1957), p. 218.
2 Frank Kermode, *Romantic Image* (London: ARK, 1986), p. 94. See in particular Chapter 5, 'The Tree'.
3 Michel Charles, *L'Arbre et la source* (Paris: Seuil, 1985), p. 13.
4 Gilles Deleuze and Félix Guattari, *Mille Plateaux* (Paris: Minuit, 1985), p. 13.
5 Peter Brooks, *Reading for the Plot* (Oxford: Clarendon Press, 1984), p. 67. Julien Sorel, we may recall, is 'legitimized by illegitimacy' (p. 67).
6 Lynn Hunt, *The Family Romance of the French Revolution* (London: Routledge, 1992).
7 See Tony Tanner, *Adultery in the Novel* (Baltimore: Johns Hopkins University Press, 1979).
8 Emile Zola, *Pot Luck*, trans. Brian Nelson (Oxford: Oxford University Press, 1999), p. 144.
9 For an unproblematically readable account, see Evelyne Bloch-Dano, *Madame Zola* (Paris: Grasset, 1997).

10 See Henri Mitterand, *Zola* (Paris: Fayard, 1999–2002), vol. II: *L'homme de 'Germinal'*, Part 5, 'Les démons de midi (1888–93)', pp. 913–1129.

RECOMMENDED READING

Zola's preparatory material for the fabrication of the family tree and the shaping of the twenty-novel series is quoted at length in the current chapter and can be found in the appendices at the end of volume V of the Gallimard Pléiade edition of *Les Rougon-Macquart*. The 1878 and 1893 versions of the family tree are reproduced in volumes II and V of this edition. My account of the tree's growth argues that the role of Octave Mouret has been somewhat neglected by critics, and to redress the balance students might consult the following: Rachel Bowlby, *Just Looking: Consumer Culture in Dreiser, Gissing and Zola* (New York and London: Methuen,1985); Brian Nelson, *Zola and the Bourgeoisie* (London: Macmillan; Totowa, New Jersey: Barnes & Noble, 1983); Sharon Marcus, *Apartment Stories: City and Home in Nineteenth-Century Paris and London* (Berkeley: University of California Press, 1999); Nicholas White, *The Family in Crisis in Late Nineteenth-Century French Fiction* (Cambridge: Cambridge University Press, 1999). The chapter concludes with an analysis of the connections between Zola's private life and the culmination of the Rougon-Macquart series: amongst the number of biographies on Zola which have been published, such excavation can be best pursued via Henri Mitterand, *Zola*, 3 vols. (Paris: Fayard, 1999–2002) (the links to *Le Docteur Pascal* in particular can be traced in vol. II: *L'homme de 'Germinal'*).

3

SANDY PETREY

Zola and the representation of society

Background as foreground

The first words in Zola's planning notes for *L'Assommoir* memorably summarise the goals and achievements of his representation of society throughout *Les Rougon-Macquart*: 'Show the milieu of the lower classes, and explain lower-class behaviour through this milieu' ['Montrer le milieu peuple et expliquer par ce milieu les mœurs peuple' (RM ii 1544)]. The key words of that celebrated focal statement are 'explain' and 'milieu'. Zola's fiction makes the social milieu an active force instead of an inert setting, an explanatory background that interacts with everyone and everything in the foreground. In *L'Assommoir*, the milieu explains why workers act, look and smell like workers. In other novels, other milieus explain why the rich act and smell rich, why the members of the bourgeoisie act and look bourgeois. No matter what their socioeconomic status, Zola's individual characters are always part of a collectivity wielding monumental influence on their personality and biography. One consequence is that *Les Rougon-Macquart*'s delineation of characters is, invariably and imperatively, representation of society. Conversely, the cycle's representation of society explains, imperatively and invariably, how its characters become themselves. Zola's people exist in a social setting apart from which they would be someone else. That setting and the individuals within it constitute a whole. Neither is comprehensible without the other.

In fact, Zola and the representation of society are less a coupling than an identity, like 'Shakespeare and poetic power' or 'Sade and sexual perversity'. To consider the first part of the sequence, no matter what the reason, is immediately to introduce the second part. It is of course possible to approach certain topics – Zola's use of colour imagery, say, or his interest in what he and his contemporaries saw as laws of heredity – without paying the slightest attention to his representation of society. It is also possible to analyse Sade's arrangements of verb tenses without mentioning sexual perversity, or

Shakespeare's reliance on historical chronicles without pointing out that he had a flair for effective use of language. But to do so is to ignore what actually seduces readers into reading and critics into criticising. Why spend time with William Shakespeare? Because he came closer to realising the full poetic potential of the English language than any writer before or since. Why read Emile Zola? Because his representation of society's impact on the individuals within it memorably depicts what it means to be a human being in the modern world. Other reasons for reading Zola's works exist, of course, and they can readily be identified in the background of his fiction. The foreground is occupied by his representation of society.

Society takes up a dominant position in the opening words of *Les Rougon-Macquart*, the first clause in the preface to *La Fortune des Rougon*: 'I want to explain how a family, a small group of beings, acts in a society' ['Je veux expliquer comment une famille, un petit groupe d'êtres, se comporte dans une société' (RM i 3)]. The intriguing aspect of that foundational statement is its author's decision to explain that a 'family' is a small group of beings, in case some reader thought it was something else. On the other hand, the statement betrays no need at all to explain that society is a larger group of beings. The introductory sentence of *Les Rougon-Macquart* takes for granted that society's impact on the small groups of beings within it has no need to be articulated in order to be recognised. Zola's well-known desire to describe the genetic principles governing the members of his title family often led him to write reminders to himself, repeating throughout the compositional process that it was important not to forget to show heredity's mechanisms in action. He needed no such reminders about society, always foregrounded through the fundamental stylistic traits that together make him the novelist we know. Author and readers alike need to be reminded that a family is a small group of beings we ought to keep in mind. Neither author nor readers ever need reminding that every small group is itself because of a larger group known as society.

This definition of society as explaining the vices and virtues of the people within it sets Zola's novels squarely against the dominant ideology of the age during which he wrote. For that ideology, it is not the milieu that explains character but character that explains milieu. Members of the bourgeoisie live in a clean and healthy world because they understand that cleanliness is next to godliness and act accordingly. Workers live in a filthy and degraded environment because they have appalling habits that lead them to trash their surroundings and ruin their lives along with their neighbourhoods. In the view of Zola's contemporaries, how people live explains their milieu. In the view underlying his novels, people's milieu explains how they live. Who is Gervaise Macquart, the protagonist of *L'Assommoir*, in and of herself?

A gentle, loving woman dedicated to creating a better life for those close to her no matter how hard she must work to attain it. Who is Gervaise in the milieu society imposes on her and her fellows? A slatternly woman who sees her life get worse every day despite the virtues she deploys in her struggle against deterioration. 'Each of her qualities turns against her' ['Chacune de ses qualités tourne contre elle' (RM ii 1545)] not because her qualities are defective but because the organisation of her world is ghastly and inhuman. The fault is not in herself but in her society. In *L'Assommoir* as throughout *Les Rougon-Macquart*, representation of society is inseparable from indictment of it.

Because society weighs so heavily on characters' lives, its representation must always figure prominently in the novels' narrative, aesthetic and stylistic organisation. Zola responded to this creative necessity in several ways. His novels include a huge number of characters, and they and their interaction figure the multitude of ways society influences those living within it. At the same time, the novels' symbolic organisation constantly accords pride of place to figures for the crushing impact of a definite social system. When, in *Germinal*, Etienne Lantier looks at the mine where he hopes to work, he sees not only a physical space but also a mythic monster that appears to be the concrete form of an unjust socioeconomic system that condemns him and his fellow workers to starvation. 'This mine, its squat brick buildings jumbled at the bottom of a hollow, raising its smokestack like a threatening horn, appeared to him as the nightmarish dream of a greedy animal, crouching there to gobble up everyone near' ['Cette fosse, tassée au fond d'un creux, avec ses constructions trapues de briques, dressant sa cheminée comme une corne menaçante, lui semblait avoir un air mauvais de bête goulue, accroupie là pour manger le monde' (RM iii 1135)]. Representation of society takes the form of representing a monster because society's effects on those unfortunate enough to live under its dominion are monstrous. Etienne looks at a coal mine and sees a ravenous beast ready to devour him. Gervaise, his mother, looks at a tenement house and sees an immense weight ready to fall on her shoulders and crush her to death. 'Gervaise turned around, looked one last time at the tenement building. It seemed to have expanded under the moonless sky . . . Then it seemed to Gervaise that the house was on top of her, squashing her under its weight, frigid on her shoulders' ['Gervaise se retourna, regarda une dernière fois la maison. Elle paraissait grandie sous le ciel sans lune . . . Alors, il sembla à Gervaise que la maison était sur elle, écrasante, glaciale à ses épaules' (RM ii 431)]. Zola's two most celebrated novels are *Germinal* and *L'Assommoir*. Each owes much of its reputation to insistent representation of the weight of society as an overwhelming handicap for those unfortunate enough to be trapped under it.

Second Empire Paris

Novels with less celebrity are no less adamant in demonstrating that Zola's representation of society is basic to his representation of everything else, as *La Curée* memorably illustrates. This novel, the second episode of the Rougon-Macquart cycle, retells the Phaedra myth through narration of its protagonist's doomed desire for her stepson. According to the myth, Phaedra became infatuated with her stepson Hippolytus and made advances to him, but was rejected. In despair she hanged herself, but left a message accusing Hippolytus of having assaulted her. Her outraged husband, Theseus, without hearing Hippolytus' side of the story, appealed to Poseidon, god of the sea, for appropriate revenge. Poseidon sent a sea monster which terrified Hippolytus' horses so that they bolted and dragged their master to his death under the wheels of his own chariot. The novel thus inscribes itself in a timeless schema of personal relations, a schema so independent of the political and economic specificity identifying a particular society at a definite historical moment that it fits perfectly into the conventional pattern called 'the eternal triangle'. Renée, Maxime and Saccard play out roles in a sentimental drama that constantly evokes similar dramas in other societies and other times. In Zola's handling of the drama, however, representation of a specific society, that of Second Empire Paris, is so prominent that timeless interactions come across as thoroughly time-bound. The eternal triangle acquires a sociohistorical distinctiveness that moulds and inflects each phase of its development in accordance with the general configuration of society. Zola's Phaedra 'followed the fashions of the time, dressing and undressing according to the examples around her' ['suivait les modes de l'époque, elle s'habillait et se déshabillait à l'exemple des autres' (RM i 510–11)]. Even in the bedroom, representation of individuals is always also representation of society, of a corrupt world in a corrupt age. In ancient times, Phaedra's passion was grand. In modern society, Renée's passion is petty, a contrast that infuses every component of her story and every aspect of Zola's recounting of it. At one point, Renée and Maxime go to the theatre to see a visiting troupe perform Racine's *Phèdre*. The performance takes place in Italian, which neither Maxime nor Renée understands. Instead of an encounter with Racine's poetic genius, therefore, they perceive only babbling 'in that foreign language whose sounds struck them at times as a simple orchestral accompaniment supporting the actors' miming gestures' ['dans cette langue étrangère dont les sonorités leur semblaient, par moments, un simple accompagnement d'orchestre soutenant la mimique des acteurs' (RM i 508)]. The modern Phaedra and Hippolytus, sitting through hours of a drama with no means of grasping what they are hearing, are closed off from tragic grandeur as the blind are closed off from chromatic variations in great painting.

Renée and Maxime's distance from this theatrical performance figures their distance from tragic substance throughout their trivial affair. The text defines the gulf separating them from the intensity of *Phèdre* as a direct result of the society in which they live. In *La Curée*, representation of society and non-representation of tragedy are variant phrasings of the same message, the impact a large group of beings has on every smaller group of beings within it. From the moment the novel introduces its characters, they stand as members of a collectivity as important in delineating their personalities and defining their biographies as anything that comes from their individual makeup itself. Here, for example, is the first paragraph of *La Curée*, the sentences through which the text chooses to begin bringing its readers into contact with its human subjects: 'Coming back, in the congestion produced by all the carriages on the way home by the lake, the barouche slowed to a crawl. At one moment the jam was so bad that it even had to stop' ['Au retour, dans l'encombrement des voitures qui rentraient par le bord du lac, la calèche dut marcher au pas. Un moment, l'embarras devint tel, qu'il lui fallut même s'arrêter' (RM i 319)]. Here, even more than in the famous opening sentence of *Germinal*, the large group dominates all the smaller groups within it. Here, in fact, the human constituents of those groups never even appear. *La Curée* opens on carriages and immobility, begins its narrative on the information that nothing inhuman is moving and that nothing human matters enough to deserve mention. *Germinal* introduces Etienne as so small a presence that he has no name but is simply 'a man', alone on a straight road in an immense landscape under a towering sky. But he is at least deserving of a human designation and receives one; his status as a *man* acquires textual certification despite all the pressures assaulting his humanity. In the opening sentences of *La Curée*, however, Zola's protagonists do not even appear. They are absences, unnamed and undescribed, standing still in a line that cannot move because it has nowhere to go.

These and many more stylistic features derive from the novel's representation of society, its vision of Paris under Napoleon III as a stinking pit of corruption with toxic impact on the people within it. The novel's second page moves from a paragraph with no names to a paragraph with nothing but names: '*tout Paris* was there' ['tout Paris était là' (RM i 320)] in the traffic jam, and a surprising proportion of Paris is named. The text gives thirteen names in twelve lines, introducing a profusion of identities to complement the penury of identities on which it began. Yet the proliferating names have the same effect as the missing names. They too configure a society going nowhere because it has no purpose and no goals. An entire cast of characters and an absent cast of characters come together in a common assertion that society has become such that when *tout Paris* is there the effect is the same as if no one and nothing were there. In *La Curée*, representation of society as vacuous, inane and spiritually bankrupt has among other effects that of making all society's members repellent. They do more than dress alike, they undress alike too. Naked or clothed, their behaviour and appearance comment at every moment on the world in which they live.

The objects in that world are no less sociologically informative than the people in it. Statues, for instance, also appear dressed or undressed in conformity with social standards, which makes the Saccards' home a representation of society as revealing as the Saccards' infidelities. The house as a whole is 'a miniature version of the new Louvre, one of the most typical examples of the Napoleon III style, that opulent bastard of all styles' ['une réduction du nouveau Louvre, un des échantillons les plus caractéristiques du style Napoléon III, ce bâtard opulent de tous les styles' (RM i 332)]. In the Saccards' home, stone displays the same lush carnality as flesh, it too appears in elaborate connection to the explanatory milieu around it. 'The town house disappeared under its sculpture . . . there were balconies like baskets of greenery, supported by large nude women, their haunches twisted, their pointed breasts thrust forward' ['L'hôtel disparaissait sous les sculptures . . . il y avait des balcons pareils à des corbeilles de verdure, que soutenaient de grandes femmes nues, les hanches tordues, les pointes des seins en avant' (RM i 331)]. To see an era in its major buildings, in structures like Napoleon III's addition to the Louvre, is not at all unusual. What makes Zola himself is that he sees so many other buildings as exactly the same representation of society visible in its monuments. Small and large, equine and human, naked and clothed, material and spiritual, animate and inanimate, all that finds a place in society becomes in Zola's depiction a key to understanding society.

At times the dynamic link between everything the reader sees and the Second Empire's omnipresent influence is explicit, as when an enumeration of the Saccards' furnishings leads into a direct statement that they display the nature of the world around them as surely as they stand in the house around them.

> Within these princely rooms, along the gilded stairways, on the thick wool of the carpets, in this fairy-tale palace of a *parvenu*, hung the smell of the Club Mabille, while twisted bodies danced fashionable quadrilles and the entire era passed by with its insane and idiotic laughter, its eternal hunger and its eternal thirst.
>
> [Au milieu de ces appartements princiers, le long des rampes dorées, sur les tapis de haute laine, dans ce palais féerique de parvenu, l'odeur de Mabille

traînait, les déhanchements des quadrilles à la mode dansaient, toute l'époque passait, avec son rire fou et bête, son éternelle faim et son éternelle soif.

(RM i 437)]

In such passages, we know that the representation of society is part of every description because that is what the text tells us, in so many words. The era as a whole infuses all things within it, from a carpet's wool piling to the carriages standing still by a lake in the Bois de Boulogne. The entire era is always passing by, no matter what readers think they see before them.

The loving, sensuously alert method Zola adopted to describe the things that fill the settings he chooses for his novels has been much described, both admiringly and dismissively. Crucial to the naturalist vision associated with that descriptive method is the sensation that material objects count, that they receive textual prominence because they mould as well as fill the world chosen for textual narrative. One reason why objects count is their function in the novels' representation of society. Like people, things show the reader truths that extend far beyond the spaces in which the things actually figure, truths that hold throughout society as well as within the circumscribed area chosen as the narrative's setting. Whether Zola's novels describe a house or a session of parliament, a congestion of carriages or a confrontation of masses, the description always points to the general as well as to the particular. In *Les Rougon-Macquart*, representation of society inheres in everything counting as representation of any sort.

In *La Curée*, the sociohistorical resonance of physical and psychological representation becomes particularly resonant through the novel's attention to the transformation of Paris under the Second Empire, the public works associated with Baron Haussmann and his associates. It is not just in the Saccards' home that Renée and Maxime find an ideal material setting for their paltry incest. More importantly, all of Paris welcomes and encourages their affair. Physically, Paris became something new and different under Napoleon III. Morally, everything new and different condemned the inauthentic values of a despicable system. Zola painstakingly describes what changed in Paris' appearance not only for mimetic fidelity but also for thematic commentary on the world to which his characters respond. What Renée and Maxime see around them is both a city under radical reconstruction and a house of ill repute in which they can close the curtains whenever they choose.

The lovers were in love with the new Paris. They often took their carriage all over town . . . They would move about and keep moving, and it seemed to them that the carriage was riding on carpets, all along this straight and endless street, which had been created for the sole purpose of allowing them to avoid dark alleyways. Every boulevard became a hallway in their house.

[Les amants avaient l'amour du nouveau Paris. Ils couraient souvent la ville en voiture ... Ils roulaient toujours, et il leur semblait que la voiture roulait sur des tapis, le long de cette chaussée droite et sans fin, qu'on avait faite uniquement pour leur éviter les ruelles noires. Chaque boulevard devenait un couloir de leur hôtel. (RM i 496–7)]

As the entire era of Napoleon III's reign passes through the Saccards' home, so the Saccards' home occupies the entire city that Napoleon III constructed and reconstructed. Outdoor streets come indoors, indoor hallways appear out-doors. The microcosm recapitulates the macrocosm, the macrocosm meta-morphoses into the microcosm. The whole occupies each of its parts, the parts reappear throughout the whole. The large group of beings appears every time a smaller group of beings comes on stage, no smaller group of beings stands as independent of the larger group enclosing it.

Fashionable undress

Under the influence of Jacques Lacan and other psychoanalytic theorists, critics have in recent decades paid close attention to the nineteenth-century novel's propensity for reducing the human body, especially the female body, to its component parts. Zola's descriptions of Renée show the technique with exemplary clarity:

The charms of her head and breast were adorable ... With cleavage down to the points of her breasts, her arms bare and sprays of violets on her shoulders, the young woman seemed to be emerging nude from her tulle and satin garment, like a nymph whose bust comes up from a sacred oak; and her white breast, her lissome body, was already so happy with its half-freedom that the eyes riveted on her appeared to expect that her top and skirts would slide away bit by bit, like the covering of a bather crazy for her own flesh.

[Les grâces de la tête et du corsage étaient adorables ... Décolletée jusqu'à la pointe des seins, les bras découverts avec des touffes de violettes sur les épaules, la jeune femme semblait sortir toute nue de sa gaine de tulle et de satin, pareille à une de ces nymphes dont le buste se dégage des chênes sacrés; et sa gorge blanche, son corps souple, était déjà si heureux de sa demi-liberté, que le regard s'attendait toujours à voir peu à peu le corsage et les jupes glisser, comme le vêtement d'une baigneuse, folle de sa chair. (RM i 336)]

As her affair evokes the eternal triangle, Renée's breasts and arms, head and shoulders evoke the eternal feminine, especially as realist fiction has revelled in it. She walks through a ballroom as sections and pieces of herself, displayed for the delectation of the men watching her.

But in *La Curée* as in all the Rougon-Macquart novels it preceded and prepared, even transhistorical set pieces like description of a half-naked female body before an avid male gaze is also a historically precise representation of society. The eternal feminine is no more eternal than the eternal triangle. The gaze on Renée's breasts sees not only a naked body but also a political discourse, eloquent and persuasive.

> When she went through the rooms . . . men bumped into each other in their efforts to see her. And the intimate circle bowed and smiled, discreetly in the know, paying homage to those beautiful shoulders, so well known to the officialdom of *tout Paris*, which were among the Empire's firm supports. Her cleavage showed such contempt for watching eyes, she was so calm and tender in her nudity, that it almost stopped being indecent.

> [Quand elle traversait les salons . . . les hommes se bousculaient pour la voir. Et les intimes s'inclinaient, avec un discret sourire d'intelligence, rendant hommage à ces belles épaules, si connues du tout Paris officiel, et qui étaient les fermes colonnes de l'empire. Elle était décolletée avec un tel mépris des regards, elle marchait si calme et si tendre dans sa nudité, que cela n'était presque plus indécent. (RM i 475)]

The two descriptions of Renée under the lascivious gaze of men hungry for her are strikingly similar. Each foregrounds her *décolletage*, each lingers lovingly over her shoulders, each fetishistically details the interaction of her body and her clothes. The principal difference between the two descriptions is that only one announces the tight connection of this body and its accoutrements to its age, to the regime and the society around it.

The point of consequence, however, is that the connection is no less firm and no less important when not announced than when made primary. Renée's body parts work effectively with and for Second Empire Paris every time they are described. Saying so makes the social ramifications of her physical presence more obvious but not more significant. Whether made explicit or left implicit, representation is in Zola always a form of comment on society. *Les Rougon-Macquart* as a whole iterates and reiterates the social vision of *La Curée*, according to which textual designation of everything and everyone in society contributes tellingly to representation of society. Wherever Zola directs his readers' attention in his fiction, he is also showing them the social constitution of his vision of the world. The reason why social overtones and undertones dominate naturalist description in Zola's works is the importance of social influence in determining those works' moral message. The narrative of Renée and Maxime never rises above the squalid story of a bored couple looking for something to do because their society provides no access to tragic majesty. Gervaise destroys her life and her world because workers' lives cannot unfold as if workers' social condition did not matter. Throughout the Rougon-Macquart cycle, every small group of beings encounters and endures situations imposed by the larger group of beings around them. Naturalist descriptions cohere to delineate a milieu, and the milieu explains the behaviour of those it encloses.

The critical reaction

Given Zola's insistence on the sociohistorical, collective configuration of the human condition, one would expect Marxism's commitment to approaching people through the groups in which they figure to make *Les Rougon-Macquart* a favourite of Marxist criticism. The original meaning of 'socialism', after all, opposed the term to individualism rather than capitalism, and no novelist did more than Zola to highlight the inadequacies of a purely individualist approach to characters' narrative fortunes. It would seem logical that a body of fiction in which representation of anything is always also representation of society would have special appeal to a philosophy for which representation of society is fundamental to explanation of anything else. Logical perhaps, but not actual – for many years Marxist criticism roundly condemned Zola for representing society as *overly* monstrous, for failing to recognise that society is the creation of human subjects and can consequently be transformed by human action. The most influential Marxist condemnation of Zola is the essay Georg Lukács wrote in 1940, for the centenary of Zola's birth. Lukács argued that Zola's vision was corrupted by the ideology of his class and his time, the time when the Paris rebellion of June 1848 had made it impossible for the bourgeoisie not to sense its impending doom at the hands of the proletariat. Rather than showing the actual structure and impact of society, Lukács contends, Zola showed society as a panoply of objects independent of human activity and impervious to human will.

> Perhaps no one has painted more colourfully and suggestively the outer trappings of modern life. But only the *outer* trappings. They form a gigantic backdrop in front of which tiny, haphazard people move to and fro and live their haphazard lives. Zola could never achieve what the truly great realists Balzac, Tolstoy or Dickens accomplished: to present social institutions as human relationships and social objects as the vehicles of such relationships. Man and his surroundings are always sharply divided in all Zola's works.[1]

Despite the evidence in *La Curée* and the novels written after it that man and his surroundings form an indissoluble whole in Zola's works, Lukács' strictures held sway among left-leaning critics for a considerable period. Their influence is still visible among those for whom Zola's representation of society matters deeply, especially those who together make up the movement known as sociocriticism.

The term 'sociocriticism' is a perfect example of what Lewis Carroll called portmanteau words. According to Carroll, a portmanteau term packs two meanings into a single lexical unit. Carroll ought to be reliable on the subject. He invented the lexical sense of 'portmanteau', which he used to designate a word that combines two others because it incorporates both their meanings at once. To use Carroll's examples, 'slithy' means not just slimy and lithe but slimy-and-lithe at the same time. Something is slithy because slime is in its litheness, litheness in its slime. Borogroves are miserable, yes, that's correct. The important thing about them, however, is that they are always something else too. We should not speak of their misery in isolation because they are also flimsy. What they are is mimsy. Sociocritics address, constantly and attentively, the verbal structures that make literature literary. They consequently practise criticism of the most respectable and venerable sort. But they also, with no less attention and concern, address the multiple ways in which verbal structures intersect and interact with the social structures specific to a precise historical matrix. Sociocritics' basic tenet is that verbal structures not only make literature literary but also make society viable. Their textual perspective is always socialised, social concerns always inform their textual analysis. What they practise is sociocriticism.

Zola's works have been prominent among the texts discussed by sociocritics since this form of literary analysis gained prominence in the 1970s. The different episodes of *Les Rougon-Macquart* compellingly demonstrate the gains produced when readers are simultaneously concerned with verbal and social structures. Those gains were long hidden by the critical tendency to address either the stylistic form or the historical content of Zola's works, but not both. In the early days, readers interested in the social message of *Les Rougon-Macquart* confined their inquiry to content analysis, what the cycle's episodes showed of the social conditions in which they were set. *Germinal*, for example, contains compelling portraits of how miners in the north of France lived and worked in the last half of the nineteenth century, of how various forms of socialist and anarchist thought circulated among those miners, and of the explosive force created when workers' life, work and thought came together in a demand for rapid and extensive change. Like many of Zola's other novels, *Germinal* has been (and deserves to be) seen as containing reliable documentary information on a certain section of France's population at a certain moment in France's history.

But reading Zola's works for their documentary content necessarily ignores or slights much of what makes them masterpieces. *Germinal*, to continue with that example, elaborates stylistic patterns of the keenest literary interest that have no pertinence to the conditions inflicted on French miners in the area around Valenciennes during and after the Second Empire. One of the most celebrated examples is the novel's elaborate allusions to myths of death and rebirth, to the textual patterns that represent natural life as an endless renewal that is the very opposite of historical specificity. Death and rebirth characterise natural processes, not historical action arising from a social situation. *Germinal's* play with myths of death and rebirth must therefore be ignored by readers for whom only historical time and social organisation are of interest. For analogous motives, readers attentive to mythic and symbolic patterns in *Germinal* will look through, around, across and beyond the historical information the novel also contains. From one perspective, what germinates in *Germinal* is a series of symbolic and lexical configurations conveying the idea that what matters in human and natural life is precisely what human and natural life share, the eternal return of the eternally disappearing. Nothing could be farther from historical consciousness than such a naturalising vision, which makes the novel's title, *Germinal*, along with its proclamation that things germinate, into a resounding proclamation that historical specificity is trivial among the factors that constitute this novel as a work of literary art.

But here is where the sociocritical perspective quite obviously demonstrates its worth, for the title of *Germinal* refuses to let its meaning be limited to natural processes. At the same time that it evokes recurrent patterns of disappearance and return, of endlessly repeated germination, the title insists that history can rupture those patterns, can make them so irrelevant that time has to start over again in the Year One. 'Germinal' was the name of a month in the revolutionary calendar adopted by the Convention during the French Revolution to announce to the world that all patterns hitherto considered eternal had been annihilated, that human beings could and would actively shape their world rather than passively accept it. The novel's title, the word that begins it, also defines it. Everything in it that looks natural is also historical, all its stylistic and symbolic designs elaborate social and historical situations at the same time. 'This title is undoubtedly Zola's greatest verbal discovery' ['Ce titre est sans doute la plus belle découverte verbale de Zola' (RM iii 1184)], because it encapsulates Zola's mastery of compositional techniques capable of bringing stylistic and sociohistorial features together in such a way that both become more intense and alive. The judgment that 'germinal' is the greatest verbal discovery in all of Zola's immense literary output comes from Henri Mitterand, prominent both in the creation and development of sociocriticism and in the major scholarly editions of Zola published over the last four decades. Mitterand's dual identity, as a founder and spokesman for sociocriticism and as an editor and analyst of

Zola's literary output, is not accidental. Both the critical school and the novelistic corpus illustrate the necessity of considering literary form and social content together. Neither the novelistic corpus nor the critical school can remain itself unless the two are examined through the perspective of their constant interaction.

According to Mitterand, fictional form is 'a natural mediation between social, extra-textual substance, and the meaning acquired by novelistic enunciation. There is consequently no opposition but rather complementarity between a "materialist" criticism basically preoccupied with a work's historical determinants, and a "formalist" criticism. Sociocriticism can be nothing other than semiotic' ['une médiation naturelle entre la substance sociale, extra-textuelle, et le sens que prend l'énoncé romanesque. Il n'y a donc pas opposition, mais complémentarité, entre une critique "matérialiste", essentiellement préoccupée des déterminations historiques de l'œuvre, et la critique "formaliste". La sociocritique ne peut être autre chose que sémiotique'].[2] 'Sociocriticism' is a portmanteau word because practising it requires a portmanteau approach, one combining perspectives often set irredeemably apart. Sociocritics are acutely sensitive to the historical resonance of the textual patterns they address, but they are even more sensitive to the fact that those patterns are and will always be semiotic rather than material.

Although Mitterand furnishes the clearest indication of the vibrant interaction between sociocritical theory and practical criticism of Zola's work, the affinities between scholarly perspective and novelistic opus are salient in other thinkers as well. Claude Duchet and Philippe Hamon, for example, have joined Mitterand in providing important and consequential definitions of what sociocriticism is and how it can realise its potential. Both regularly turn to Zola to illustrate what their definitions mean and why they are important. The sociocritical perspective is in fact the ideal method for appreciating the extent to which Zola's fiction demonstrates that representation of society goes hand in hand with representation of every sort. To repeat, the first sentence of the first novel in *Les Rougon-Macquart* announces that this interpenetration will be crucial to the cycle's aesthetic and thematic organisation. More than a century and a quarter after Zola wrote that sentence, readers are developing the critical senses required to grasp just what he meant.

NOTES

1 Georg Lukács, *Studies in European Realism* (New York: Grosset and Dunlap, 1970), pp. 92–3.
2 Henri Mitterand, *Le Discours du roman* (Paris: Presses Universitaires de France, 1980), p. 17.

RECOMMENDED READING

Auerbach, Erich, *Mimesis: The Representation of Reality in Western Literature*, trans. Willard R. Trask (Princeton: Princeton University Press, 1953)

Baguley, David (ed.), *Critical Essays on Emile Zola* (Boston: G. K. Hall, 1986)

Hemmings, F. W. J., *Emile Zola*, second edition (Oxford: Oxford University Press, 1966)

Lukács, Georg, *Studies in European Realism* (New York: Grosset and Dunlap, 1970; London: The Merlin Press, 1972)

Mitterand, Henri, *Zola*, 3 vols. (Paris: Fayard, 1999–2002)

Nelson, Brian, *Zola and the Bourgeoisie* (London: Macmillan; Totowa, New Jersey: Barnes & Noble, 1983)

Petrey, Sandy, 'Stylistics and Society in *La Curée*', *Modern Language Notes*, 89 (1974), 626–40

Schor, Naomi, *Zola's Crowds* (Baltimore: Johns Hopkins University Press, 1978)

Wilson, Angus, *Emile Zola* (London: Secker and Warburg, 1952)

4

HANNAH THOMPSON

Questions of sexuality and gender

Questions of sexuality and gender occupy a pivotal place in Zola's understanding of the world, but it is only since the rise of feminism in the 1970s that Zola's surprisingly modern interest in these themes has attracted – and continues to attract – a great deal of critical attention. Indeed, when Zola's novels were first published, their often overtly sexual content was, along with his frank discussion of France's social and political problems, one of the principal reasons why they were at times greeted with indignation, even condemnation.

Zola's interest in questions of sexuality and gender can in part be explained by his commitment to close observation of even the most disturbing aspects of Second Empire society. One of the primary aims of Zola's naturalism was 'to see everything, know everything, say everything' ['tout voir, tout savoir, tout dire' (OC ix 351)], and it seemed that no subject was too scandalous for the novelist in his quest to document every aspect of society. Many of the details included in Zola's novels are drawn from his meticulous observation of reality and are fully documented in his extensive planning notes, but the range and manner of his observations were considered by many to represent a danger to the moral health of the nation. Although Zola was never successfully tried for obscenity in France, the translator and publisher of a number of English translations, Henry Vizetelly, was prosecuted twice under the Obscene Publications Act.[1] Like the realist novelists of the previous generation, Zola wanted to depict in novelistic language the hitherto unspeakable truths of the human condition. But Zola's naturalism, as evidenced in *Les Rougon-Macquart* in particular, is governed by scientific as well as representational aims. Zola is concerned with the ways in which certain inherited traits evolve from generation to generation as they, along with other factors such as environment and social standing, influence the behaviour of the Rougon-Macquart family members. Sex is a privileged topic in Zola's work not only because it is a central preoccupation of the Second Empire society he describes, but also because it is the means by which the Rougon-Macquart family, and thus the novel cycle, can progress. Like nineteenth-century French society, Zola's novel cycle depends for its advancement on a patriarchal model of sexuality in which a succession of fertile female heroines engage in heterosexual relationships to produce offspring who carry on the Rougon-Macquart family line. This patriarchal model relies in turn on traditional gender identities, whereby female characters displaying feminine characteristics are coupled with male characters displaying masculine characteristics. But to suggest that Zola's understanding of sexuality and gender is limited to this model is to misrepresent the complex and often contradictory nature of the novelist's vision of human desire. Indeed, it is precisely Zola's interest in those sexualities and genders that deviate from the patriarchal norm that explains the continuing appeal of his novels.

Zola's work contains some unflinchingly graphic descriptions of the most unpleasant aspects and passions of the human body, and such scenes scandalised a society which preferred to keep such sordid realities firmly hidden from view. The literate public felt that literature was not the place for the dissections of the human body of the kind that Zola was performing. His works posed a threat to the careful upbringing of bourgeois ladies and innocent young girls, who were protected from sexual and social truths and cocooned in the world of Romantic fantasy found in the novels of George Sand and Walter Scott. The caricaturists of the day variously depicted Zola as a depraved and bloodthirsty surgeon happily carving up the human body, or as an enormous pig revelling in the dirt he delighted in spreading. One example cited by Zola's adversaries is his depiction of peasant life in *La Terre* (1887), in which his unremittingly bleak analysis of bodily impulses was criticised for emphasising man's baseness and his animalistic interest in sexual pleasure. In one infamous scene, Buteau and Lise sadistically rape the latter's pregnant sister Françoise in an attempt to do away with her unborn child. The violence of the encounter leads to the murder of both mother and baby, though not before Françoise experiences a spasm of intense pleasure (RM iv 747). Buteau's behaviour may be animalistic, but this is due not only to the influence of the poverty-stricken rural environment in which he lives, but also to his passionate attachment to the land his family farms and his jealous hatred of Françoise's husband Jean. When taken out of context, this scene suggests that for Zola the impulses of the human body are as brutish and uncontrollable as those of the animals to which the protagonists of *La Terre* are ceaselessly compared. However, such a reading risks emulating Zola's nineteenth-century critics by holding up this particular portrayal of one man's desire as representative of Zola's view of human sexuality. Instead, this scene illustrates one aspect of a large and complex subject which Zola deals with in considerable detail throughout his work.

The dangers of desire

As well as describing the depths of violence and cruelty to which man is willing to sink, the scene in *La Terre* described above articulates an even more indigestible truth which threatens to undermine man's vision of his place in the world. Instead of being in control of his own thoughts, emotions, actions and destiny, man is constantly in thrall to his sexual desires, dominated by this terrifying yet irresistible force. The intensity of the sexual desire experienced by many of Zola's protagonists is all the more shocking because it is rarely translated into the kind of family-orientated heterosexual reproductive sexuality essential to both the development of the Rougon-Macquart family (and thus the novel series) and the healthy repopulation of a French nation ravaged by war and political crisis.[2] Instead, most of Zola's protagonists are driven by a quest for pleasure rather than procreation – a feature that reflects what Zola saw as the decadence of Second Empire society. For Zola, as for other nineteenth-century novelists such as Stendhal, Balzac and Flaubert, prostitution and adultery were the two most common manifestations of the selfish search for sexual gratification. Indeed, by the time Zola was writing the Rougon-Macquart novels, it had become something of a commonplace to base novelistic plots on adulterous intrigues.[3]

The world of the high-class courtesan is depicted at length in *Nana*, whilst the destructive power of adulterous desire is illustrated in *Thérèse Raquin*. *Thérèse Raquin* sketches out the shape of Zola's vision of sexual desire which will be honed throughout *Les Rougon-Macquart*. In *Thérèse Raquin*, the eponymous heroine's desire for Laurent, her husband Camille's friend and colleague, leads to Camille's murder. The horror of the non-procreative relationship of Thérèse and Laurent is encapsulated in the scene in which Thérèse engineers a miscarriage by presenting her belly to Laurent as he beats her. However, the novel's unflinching and apparently impartial treatment of sexually motivated adultery and murder is tempered by the fact that Thérèse and Laurent are punished for their actions. Not only do they fail to experience any real sexual fulfilment, but they are also tortured by an overwhelming sense of guilt that eventually drives them to a gruesome double suicide. The final message of *Thérèse Raquin* seems unequivocal: failure to control the 'human beast' brings about the protagonists' untimely and horrific demise (a demise which can be understood symbolically as well as literally). However, the novel also poses a question that recurs insistently throughout Zola's work: *can* desire ever be mastered? The liaison of Thérèse and Laurent seems natural and inevitable, something they were compelled to engage in by bodily impulses beyond their control.

The dangers of illicit sexual desire addressed in *Thérèse Raquin* are explored in a more sustained manner throughout the Rougon-Macquart novels. *La Curée* (1872) is a sustained examination of non-procreative sexuality in which Zola uses the perverse sexual excesses of the novel's protagonists as the basis of a broader criticism of Second Empire society's decadent morality. The novel is set amongst the newly rich capitalists whose wealth comes from the financial speculations encouraged by Haussmann's remodelling of Paris. The protagonists of *La Curée* have unlimited amounts of time and money, which they spend on increasingly hedonistic activities. For Zola, non-procreative sexuality is the most frivolous of pleasures, and the instances of male and female homosexuality in the novel function as allegories of the moral degeneration of Second Empire society. Zola extends the discussion of adultery begun in *Thérèse Raquin* in his depiction of the semi-incestuous affair between Renée Saccard and her stepson Maxime, a foppish and effeminate figure whose pleasure-seeking lifestyle is the image of the corrupt society in which he flourishes.[4] Maxime and Renée are doubly perverse for Zola. Not only do they engage in sexual acts that privilege pleasure over procreation, their relationship breaks the laws of gender difference on which the continuation of the family depends. As well as mothering Maxime, Renée dominates him as she assumes the masculine role in their sexual encounters. For Zola (and this was a commonly held view in the nineteenth century), any departure from traditional gender assignations, even within a heterosexual pairing, signals a latent homosexual desire which leads to the corruption and ultimate annihilation of the race. Zola's point is clear: a society that encourages the kind of decadent lifestyle embodied not only by Renée and Maxime but by all the protagonists in the novel is courting its own destruction.

La Faute de l'abbé Mouret offers a powerful illustration of the fact that in Zola's world the repression of sexual desire can be as detrimental as its misdirection, since no one can remain immune from the irrepressible pull of his or her sexuality. Serge Mouret is a devout priest whose strict Catholic beliefs leave him unequipped to deal with the awakening of his sexuality, obliging him to live a life of celibacy during which he attempts to repress any sexual desire he may feel. In the second part of the novel, Serge succumbs to a fever which results in a state of prelapsarian amnesia during which he engages in a passionate relationship with Albine. In *La Faute de l'abbé Mouret*, Zola not only strongly criticises the Catholic Church's repressive approach to sexuality, he also nuances the questions raised by *Thérèse Raquin*. By asking not only whether desire *can* but *should* be controlled, Zola suggests that, despite the Catholic Church's teaching to the contrary, sexuality is a necessary – albeit sometimes negative – aspect of the human condition, and something which must be openly acknowledged and understood rather than repressed.

In all the examples examined thus far, the presence of a seductive female protagonist is intrinsic to Zola's vision of the destructive force of human desire. Indeed, it is impossible to understand Zola's approach to sexuality without examining his vision of woman. In *Nana*, the novel most overtly concerned with sexual desire in all its manifestations, the eponymous heroine is a ferociously sexual being whose body captivates her male admirers. Nana is destructive, selfish and morally corrupt. Yet she is also endearingly naive and surprisingly vulnerable. Readers of *Nana* are unable to decide whether to love or hate the novel's central protagonist, and it is precisely this irreconcilable duality in Nana's character that renders her emblematic of Zola's complex and frequently contradictory vision of female sexuality. On the one hand Zola's novels celebrate the feminine qualities associated with the mother figure and epitomised in the character of Denise Baudu (*Au Bonheur des Dames*). Denise is modest, hard-working and caring; she nurtures and protects her brothers whilst remaining uncorrupted by the illicit desires of those around her. Clotilde (*Le Docteur Pascal*) is another female protagonist who is celebrated for her maternity. Clotilde may be a sexual being who engages in an incestuous relationship with her uncle Pascal, but she is primarily a mother; and it is this aspect of her character that is most extensively celebrated in the novel. In the final pages of *Le Docteur Pascal*, which also represent the conclusion of the Rougon-Macquart series, Zola uses the figures of Clotilde and her newborn son to paint an idealised picture of the archetypal feminine attribute of maternity. Indeed, Clotilde is the last in a succession of intelligent, capable and caring young women (such as Miette in *La Fortune des Rougon*, Angélique in *Le Rêve*, and Pauline in *La Joie de vivre*) who appear at intervals throughout the Rougon-Macquart novels and who are at once beguilingly attractive and yet touchingly unaware of the impact their charms have on their male admirers.

Zola's vision of idealised femininity, which is embodied by these women, is balanced by a fascination with the darker side of female sexuality which sits uneasily with the novelist's celebration of family values. Zola's novels feature a number of eroticised female heroines who exert a frequently devastating influence on the men they encounter. The appeal of women such as Lisa Quenu (*Le Ventre de Paris*) and Clorinde Balbi (*Son Excellence Eugène Rougon*) is heightened by Zola's detailed descriptions of their physical appearance, descriptions which are intended to seduce the (male) reader in the same way as the characters themselves are seduced. Christine

(*L'Œuvre*) is one example of a female protagonist whose naked body is described repeatedly and at length by Zola. Christine's erotically attractive body is a source of artistic inspiration for her lover, the painter Claude Lantier. However, her sexuality also exerts a pernicious influence over him as it distracts him from the work of artistic creation. It is Christine's body, coupled with Claude's inability to control his own desires, that ultimately leads to his artistic failure and eventual self-destruction.

The pull of dangerous female sexuality reaches its height in *La Bête humaine*. Like all members of the Rougon-Macquart family, Jacques Lantier is afflicted by a hereditary taint inherited from the family's original matriarch, Tante Dide. Jacques suffers from an uncontrollable desire to kill, which is triggered by sexual contact with the desired female body. Zola's description of Jacques' murder of his lover Séverine demonstrates that it is the troubling eroticism of the woman, coupled with Jacques' fatal flaw, that is responsible for the murder:

> Soon his hands would cease to be his own amidst the overwhelming intoxication of this female nudity. The bare breasts crushed against his clothes, the bare neck stretched up, so white and delicate, irresistibly tempting; and the sovereign sway of her sharp, warm scent finally reduced him to a state of wild dizziness, an endless, giddy oscillation, in which his independent will, torn from him and destroyed, was vanishing without trace.[5]

> [Ses mains n'allaient plus être à lui, dans l'ivresse trop forte de cette nudité de femme. Ses seins nus s'écrasaient contre ses vêtements, le cou nu se tendait, si blanc, si délicat, d'une irrésistible tentation; et l'odeur chaude et âpre, souveraine, achevait de le jeter à un furieux vertige, un balancement sans fin, où sombrait sa volonté, arrachée, anéantie. (RM iv 1296)]

The sexualised female body is a destructive force which Zola holds at least partly responsible for the downfall of his male characters, and it is this view of female sexuality that has frequently led readers to condemn the novelist as irredeemably misogynistic. However, such a charge fails to acknowledge the sophisticated nature of Zola's understanding of female sexuality. By presenting his reader with women who embody a range of seemingly irreconcilable characteristics, Zola demonstrates that female sexuality is a mysterious notion which evades simple categorisation.

Sex and the survival of the species

Zola's condemnation of sterile sexuality contrasts with his glorification of procreative, heterosexual desire in the final Rougon-Macquart novel, *Le Docteur Pascal* (1893), and the first of his *Quatre Evangiles, Fécondité*

(1899). Both novels illustrate Zola's view that France could only overcome her population crisis through a sustained attempt to increase the number of healthy children born each year. In *Fécondité*, the figure of Marianne Froment celebrates what Zola sees as woman's duty to create and nourish life. Marianne's selfless devotion to her twelve children epitomises Zola's vision of maternity, and her sexuality exists only as a means of reproduction. Alongside the mythic figure of the Mother is a warning against any attempt to interfere with female fertility. The practices of abstinence, abortion, contraception, hysterectomy, adoption and the use of wet-nurses are examined with Zola's characteristic attention to the goriest of details. Zola's commitment to the celebration of fertility is so strong that the novel becomes a frequently repetitive didactic tool which idealistically plots the inevitable demise of those who selfishly attempt to interrupt woman's natural propensity to procreate.

Still more pernicious in Zola's eyes than the self-serving couples who refuse to contribute to the good of the French nation are individuals, such as those depicted in *La Curée*, who depart altogether from the heterosexual model. The figure of the *inverti* or effeminate male homosexual fascinated Zola, and a letter to Dr Laupts outlines his understanding of the *inverti*'s destructive influence on attempts to repopulate France[6]: 'The invert is responsible for the disintegration of the family, of the nation, and of humanity. Men and women were surely only put on this earth to have children, and they kill life itself the moment that they no longer do what is necessary in order to have them' ['Un inverti est un désorganisateur de la famille, de la nation, de l'humanité. L'homme et la femme ne sont certainement ici-bas que pour faire des enfants, et ils tuent la vie le jour où ils ne font plus ce qu'il faut pour en faire'].[7] Zola lists the characteristics of these creatures, who threaten the stability of the French nation: 'the effeminate, delicate, weak man; the masculine, violent, heartless woman' ['l'homme efféminé, délicat, lâche; la femme masculine, violente, sans tendresse'].[8] Not only do they refuse the responsibilities of procreation, they also blur the difference between the sexes which is the basis for procreation. As we have seen, Zola's depiction of the decadent relationship between the effeminate Maxime and his stepmother Renée illustrates his belief that such characters and their perverse activities represent a selfish and sterile quest for pleasure: the antithesis of the natural drive to procreate championed in *Fécondité*.

Sex and society

Even as they condemned the novelist for the sexual excesses depicted throughout his novels, Zola's nineteenth-century critics failed to understand that it was the Second Empire society depicted by him, rather than the author himself, which should be the object of their censure. Zola was attempting, through an examination of the more shameful types of behaviour which the bourgeoisie preferred to keep hidden from view, to analyse a society in which such behaviour was allowed to flourish. In *Pot-Bouille* he explores the effects of society's hypocritical refusal to acknowledge the existence of unruly sexual desire. In nineteenth-century French society, sexuality was only publicly acceptable when employed in the service of procreation. The bourgeois protagonists of the novel understand the importance of appearing to endorse this belief by maintaining a veneer of irreproachable morality. They regularly attend church and openly criticise those who fail to meet their strict behavioural standards; but, behind the well-polished doors of their apartment building, the novel's protagonists indulge in a range of illicit sexual relationships whose existence undermines their proclaimed moral stance. Berthe Josserand's behaviour is emblematic of the moral bankruptcy that characterises this society. Berthe's desperate quest for a husband is motivated not by love but by a need for social status and financial security. This necessitates an endless round of evening engagements during which her charms are displayed to the assembled males in a process described by Zola as a bourgeois kind of prostitution. Her eventual marriage to Auguste Vabre is only enabled when the young man is trapped into making a pass at Berthe at one such gathering. The code of honour to which the bourgeoisie subscribes dictates that their marriage contract be drawn up immediately. Unhappy in a loveless marriage, Berthe is soon seduced by the rakish charms of Octave Mouret. Her husband's dramatic discovery of their affair results in widespread condemnation of Berthe's actions. It is indicative of the hypocrisy of bourgeois society that it is Berthe, rather than Octave, who receives most criticism. Even if unhappy and unfulfilled, married women were expected to remain unquestioningly faithful to their husbands, whilst the sexual needs of young unmarried men, if not indulged, were at least tolerated.

Despite (or perhaps because of) its refusal openly to acknowledge the truths of human desire, the society depicted by Zola is permeated by a repressed yet insistent obsession with sexuality. In the world of bohemian artists evoked first in *Le Ventre de Paris* and later, in more detail, in *L'Œuvre*, the painters, sculptors and writers depicted by Zola are engaged in an endless struggle to represent Paris' ever-changing modernity. Yet in their attempts to represent the modernity of the capital, they return again and again to depictions of the female body. Claude Lantier in particular is haunted by his insatiable desire to capture the enigma of female sexuality on canvas. Each picture he creates is less an image of Paris than a further attempt to represent his ideal woman. Claude's obsession testifies to the insistent presence of sexual desire even in those areas not readily associated with it.

The frequently pernicious influence of sexual desire permeates all aspects of a society motivated not only by pleasure, but also by the desire for financial gain and the promise of improved social status. Throughout the Rougon-Macquart novels, Zola uses depictions of the female body to illustrate the commodification of sexual desire that characterised Second Empire society. In the food market of *Le Ventre de Paris*, the success of the female stall-holders is gauged not only by the appearance of their wares but also by their own attractiveness. In this economy-driven environment women are not valued as aesthetically beautiful love-objects or as the means of procreation; instead, they are mere tokens exchanged by men for sex, money and status. In *La Curée* Renée is only valuable to her husband Saccard as a means of showing off his financial status. He uses her body like a clothes-horse, adorning it with expensive jewels in a dazzling display of his buying power (RM i 337).

Au Bonheur des Dames (1883) represents the novelist's most sustained examination of this commodification of the female body.[9] Octave Mouret is typical of the new breed of Second Empire entrepreneur who both terrifies and fascinates Zola. He gradually transforms his department store into a monstrous machine whose success depends on its manipulation of the female clientèle's seemingly inexhaustible appetite for new clothes. For Zola's women understand that it is only by making themselves attractive to men that they retain any value in this sexually driven society. Mouret's mannequins announce the symbolic fate of the women whom they entice into the shop: 'The dummies' round bosoms swelled out the material, their wide hips exaggerated the narrow waists, and their missing heads were replaced by price tags with pins stuck through them into the red bunting around the collars'[10] ['La gorge ronde des mannequins gonflait l'étoffe, les hanches fortes exagéraient la finesse de la taille, la tête absente était remplacée par une grande étiquette, piquée avec une épingle dans le molleton rouge du col' (RM iii 392)]. The women who shop in the 'Bonheur des Dames' have lost their individuality. They are faceless consumers whose value is measured as much by the money they spend as by their physical attractiveness. As well as serving as the means by which female shoppers increase their value in the eyes of men, Mouret's department store also functions as an emblem of the place sexuality occupies in society. Mouret's breathtaking window displays use the female clothes, accessories and toiletries sold in the shop to create erotically charged evocations of half-dressed female bodies. The shop, like Bordenave's theatre in *Nana*, becomes a kind of brothel, a giant *boudoir* which moves sexuality from the privacy of the bedroom into the public domain. It represents a society obsessed with the conspicuous display of wealth, and in which sexuality is one more commodity to be bought and sold.

Sexuality and gender: the critical perspective

The single most intriguing aspect of Zola's approach to questions of sexuality and gender is the inconsistency with which he discusses these issues. We have seen how Zola argues that procreative sexuality and the concomitant insistence on traditional patriarchal structures are essential to the healthy repopulation of the French nation. In addition, Zola's privileging of the family is central to the structure of his novelistic project. However, Zola's novels are full of protagonists who depart from this model without being condemned by the novelist. In particular, Zola portrays a number of female characters who are praised for their masculine characteristics. Caroline (*L'Argent*, 1891) and Henriette (*La Débâcle*, 1892) are caring and maternal whilst exhibiting what nineteenth-century society saw as the archetypal masculine traits of leadership, decisiveness and bravery. Unlike many of Zola's female protagonists, neither Caroline nor Henriette is described in overtly sexual terms. By showing how the actions of these women override the dictates of their biological sex, Zola suggests that gender identity is not necessarily related to biological sex. In *La Débâcle* Zola further nuances his earlier vision of the desirability of rigidly delineated gender differences by evoking in a positive light male characters who display traditionally feminine characteristics. In his depiction of the relationship between Maurice and Jean, Zola explores the impact of traditionally feminine characteristics on male behaviour. Jean is a competent and respected soldier and yet the tenderness and consideration he shows his compatriot Maurice sit uneasily alongside conventional notions of masculinity usually associated with the military. Even as Zola emphasises the importance of clearly delineated gender differences, he creates characters whose combination of masculine and feminine traits belies his own statements. This inconsistency allows modern critics to re-present Zola as a writer whose interest in non-traditional gender assignments prefigures twenty-first-century conceptions of gender identity.

Nana is the character most frequently held up as an example of this enlightened vision. Nana is able to use her sexuality to manipulate those around her. As such she is reclaimed by feminist critics as a woman who is not subject to the constraints of patriarchy and who uses her body to dominate her male oppressors in an affirmation of her own identity.[11] Nana's relationship with her lesbian lover Satin is further evidence of Zola's interest in non-traditional relationships. By allowing Nana to experience with Satin a pleasure she does not experience with her male lovers, Zola not only acknowledges the possibility of female sexual pleasure, but also allows his most celebrated female protagonist privileged access to it. In so doing he has been seen as celebrating, or at least acknowledging, woman's right to an autonomous sexuality. As well as attracting the attention of the first wave of feminist literary critics, Zola's Nana has also become the focus of the subsequent generation of post-feminists. Nana's relationship with the young Georges Hugon is an emblematic example of Zola's progressive view of gender identity.[12] In this scene (RM ii 1236–9) Nana dresses Georges up in some of her clothes whilst his own clothes dry. Nana, who has hitherto had exclusively maternal feelings towards the adolescent Georges, finds herself attracted to the boy when she sees him dressed in women's clothes. Rather than forming an essential, natural and unchangeable part of Georges' identity, his gender, and thus his attractiveness to Nana, seems to change according to what he wears. By implying that a character's gender identity can fluctuate, this scene seems to undermine Zola's belief in fixed gender identities, which forms the basis of his faith in the natural predominance of the heterosexual procreative relationship. Nana and Georges are not the only couple for whom desire is sparked by transvestite disguise. In *Germinal*, Etienne first encounters Catherine in the murky depths of the mine. In her miner's outfit, Catherine is indistinguishable from her male comrades, and Etienne naturally mistakes her for a man. The incident is a lighthearted respite from the drudgery of life down the mine, but it has serious implications for an understanding of Zola's vision of sexuality and gender. By rooting Etienne's desire for Catherine in this instance of gender confusion, Zola suggests that Etienne, like Nana, is attracted to the combination of masculine and feminine mapped on Catherine's body. These readings reveal that Zola's understanding of gender is a complex and frequently contradictory one. Consequently, the question of whether Zola should be condemned as a misogynist or reclaimed as a proto-feminist continues to intrigue contemporary critics.

If Zola's representations of woman's place in patriarchal society and his related conception of how gender identity is constructed have recently attracted much interest, his vision of sexuality is no less perplexing to the modern reader. On the one hand, his novels are a clear celebration of procreation. However, this puritanical stance is undermined by the detail with which the perverse non-procreative desires of his protagonists are described. Zola's depictions of sexual excess are evidence of a fascination with transgressive practices which is not entirely in keeping with the novelist's proclaimed moral stance. *Au Bonheur des Dames* encapsulates some of the contradictions discernible in Zola's approach to sexuality. On the one hand, the image of the department store replicates the patriarchal sexual structure of both the bourgeois home and Second Empire society. Octave Mouret is an accomplished lady-killer, enticing women into his shop with elaborate displays of appealing fabrics before seducing them into spending ever-increasing amounts of money. Yet on the other hand, the sexual metaphors used by Zola to describe the shop emphasise the overtly erotic nature of the shopping experience and the heightened sexuality of the shoppers, neither of which is related to procreation.

> The customers, who were suffocating, were pale-faced and shiny-eyed. It seemed as if all the seductions of the shop had been leading up to this supreme temptation, that this was the hidden alcove where the customers were doomed to fall, the place of perdition where even the strongest succumbed. Hands were being plunged into the overflowing piles of lace, quivering with excitement from touching them. (pp. 63–4)

> [Les clientes, qui s'y étouffaient, avaient des visages pâles aux yeux luisants. On eût dit que toutes les séductions des magasins aboutissaient à cette tentation suprême, que c'était là l'alcôve reculée de la chute, le coin de perdition où les plus fortes succombaient. Les mains s'enfonçaient parmi les pièces débordantes, et elles en gardaient un tremblement d'ivresse. (RM iii 640)]

However seductive Mouret's charms prove to be, the department store also hosts a number of female figures who resist the attraction of this Don Juan figure. The shoplifters, exemplified by Mme de Boves, undermine the patriarchal structure of the shop by bypassing the cash registers and indulging their passion for fabrics with no intention of paying for them. Although these figures exist at the margins of the novel's narrative, they nonetheless demonstrate that alternatives to patriarchal sexuality are posited within Zola's work. *Au Bonheur des Dames* is not the only novel revealing the novelist's fascination with non-procreative sexuality. The detail with which Zola evokes the painter Claude's obsession with the impossible depiction of the ideal female body (*L'Œuvre*), Renée's and Maxime's liaison amidst the exotic plants of the hothouse (*La Curée*), and Albine's and Serge's passionate affair amidst the wild Paradou (*La Faute de l'abbé Mouret*) suggests that, alongside his belief in the importance of procreative relationships, Zola harboured an interest in the decadent sexuality more readily associated with the writers and artists of the *fin de siècle* and epitomised by J.-K. Huysmans.

The paradoxes discussed above lend additional depth to Zola's vision of sexuality and gender. Although these intriguing inconsistencies were not noticed by Zola's contemporaries, who tended either to condemn his interest in the obscene or to praise his commitment to an unflinching portrayal of the darker side of human nature, modern critics have focused at length on issues of sexuality and gender in his work. Indeed, this interest, which corresponds to a wider critical interest in questions of sexuality and gender discernible in literary studies since the rise of feminist criticism in the 1970s, has powerfully enhanced Zola's popularity today.

NOTES

1 See Graham King, *Garden of Zola: Emile Zola and his Novels for English Readers* (London: Barrie and Jenkins, 1978) for an analysis of Zola's reception in England.

2 See Robert A. Nye, 'The Medical Origins of Sexual Fetishism', in Emily Apter and William Pietz (eds.), *Fetishism and Cultural Discourse* (Ithaca: Cornell University Press, 1993), pp. 13–30, for an analysis of France's post Franco-Prussian war population anxiety and its impact on late nineteenth-century notions of sexuality.

3 An investigation of the place of adultery in nineteenth-century fiction can be found in Tony Tanner, *Adultery in the Novel: Contract and Transgression* (Baltimore: Johns Hopkins University Press, 1979).

4 For an analysis of Maxime's significance, see Robert Lethbridge, 'Zola: Decadence and Autobiography in the Genesis of a Fictional Character', *Nottingham French Studies*, 17 (1978), 39–52, and Susan Harrow, *Zola: 'La Curée'* (Glasgow: University of Glasgow French and German Publications, 1998), pp. 56–60.

5 Emile Zola, *La Bête humaine*, trans. Roger Pearson (Oxford: Oxford University Press, 1999), p. 329.

6 See Jennifer Birkett, *The Sins of the Fathers: Decadence in France 1870–1914* (London: Quartet Books, 1986) and Vernon A. Rosario, *The Erotic Imagination: French Histories of Perversion* (Oxford: Oxford University Press, 1997) for overviews of the late nineteenth-century interest in sexual perversion which Zola shared.

7 Emile Zola, 'Préface au *Roman d'un inverti-né*', in Pierre Hahn, *Nos ancêtres les pervers: la vie des homosexuels au dix-neuvième siècle* (Paris: Olivier Orban, 1979), pp. 231–5 (p. 235).

8 Ibid., p. 234.

9 Both Rachel Bowlby, *Just Looking: Consumer Culture in Dreiser, Gissing and Zola* (London: Methuen, 1989), pp. 66–83, and Peter Brooks, *Body Work: Objects of Desire in Modern Narrative* (Cambridge, Mass.: Harvard University Press, 1993), pp. 149–54, examine the commodification of the female body in *Au Bonheur des Dames*.

10 Emile Zola, *The Ladies' Paradise*, trans. Brian Nelson (Oxford: Oxford University Press, 1998), p. 6.

11 Bernice Chitnis, *Reflecting on 'Nana'* (New York & London: Routledge, 1991) is one example of a study which seeks to reclaim *Nana*. Naomi Schor's chapter on *Nana* in *Zola's Crowds* (Baltimore: Johns Hopkins University Press, 1978) provides another feminist perspective.

12 See Janet L. Beizer, *Ventriloquized Bodies: Narratives of Hysteria in Nineteenth-Century France* (Ithaca: Cornell University Press, 1994), pp. 182–3, and Sandy Petrey, 'Anna-Nana-Nana: identité sexuelle, écriture naturaliste, lectures lesbiennes', *Les Cahiers naturalistes*, 69 (1995), 69–80.

RECOMMENDED READING

Baguley, David, 'Fécondité' d'Emile Zola: roman à thèse, évangile, mythe (Toronto: University of Toronto Press, 1973)

Beizer, Janet L., 'Uncovering Nana: The Courtesan's New Clothes', L'Esprit créateur, 25, 2 (1985), 45–56

Beizer, Janet L., 'The Body in Question: Anatomy, Textuality and Fetishism in Zola', L'Esprit créateur, 29, 1 (1989), 50–61

Bertrand-Jennings, Chantal, 'Zola féministe? (1)', Les Cahiers naturalistes, 44 (1972), 172–87

Bertrand-Jennings, Chantal, 'Zola féministe? (2)', Les Cahiers naturalistes, 45 (1972), 1–22

Bertrand-Jennings, Chantal, L'Eros et la femme chez Zola: de la chute au paradis retrouvé (Paris: Klincksieck, 1977)

Borie, Jean, Zola et les mythes, ou de la nausée au salut (Paris: Seuil, 1971)

Brooks, Peter, 'Storied Bodies, or Nana at last Unveil'd', Critical Inquiry, 16, 1 (1989), 1–32

Chitnis, Bernice, Reflecting on 'Nana' (New York & London: Routledge, 1991)

Nelson, Brian, 'Nana: Uses of the Female Body', Australian Journal of French Studies, 38, 3 (2001), 407–30

Schor, Naomi, Zola's Crowds (Baltimore: Johns Hopkins University Press, 1978)

Thompson, Hannah, Naturalism Redressed: Identity and Clothing in the Novels of Emile Zola (Oxford: Legenda, 2004)

5

ROBERT LETHBRIDGE

Zola and contemporary painting

It is often said of Zola that, with the possible exception of Baudelaire, no other nineteenth-century French writer enjoyed a closer or more extended relationship with the painters of his time. By virtue of timing, precisely, and in support of Zola's own modernist credentials, the biographical, critical and creative dimensions of that relationship are largely organised, in our cultural histories, around the Impressionists. This over-simplification relegates to the margins an engagement, on the writer's part, which finds expression in an early enthusiasm for Ary Scheffer and Bastien-Lepage and which ranges, in his work as an art critic over thirty years (either as points of reference or in more substantive reflection), from Ingres to Gustave Moreau. The privileged status of the avant-garde of the 1860s and 1870s, however, is certainly reinforced in the oft-cited remarks made by Zola himself shortly before his death in 1902:

> I didn't merely support the Impressionists. Through the brush-strokes, tonalities and colour-values of my own descriptive palette, I brought them into the literary domain. Every one of my books . . . is evidence of contact and interchange with the painters . . . For they helped me paint in a new way, in literary terms.[1]

> [Je n'ai pas seulement soutenu les Impressionnistes. Je les ai traduits en littérature, par les touches, notes, colorations, par la palette de beaucoup de mes descriptions. Dans tous mes livres . . . j'ai été en contact et échange avec les peintres . . . Les peintres m'ont aidé à peindre d'une manière neuve, 'littérairement'.]

Yet such a generalisation also brings into sharper relief some of the more problematic aspects of the relationship between Zola and contemporary painting, requiring us to explore the nature of those interchanges and what is implied by the apparently straightforward trans-generic pictorialism of 'en littérature'.

At a biographical level, the closeness of personal friendships and a shared professional milieu is certainly not beside the point. That the novelist and Cézanne were childhood friends, for example, arguably over-determines the identification of the man and his work in both Zola's intermittent writing on the painter and his partial portrait of him in *L'Œuvre* (1886). And, as far as the future Impressionists are concerned, Zola's presence in their midst in the late 1860s, at the same café Guerbois in the Batignolles district, is not merely of anecdotal interest. Coinciding with his own apprenticeship as a journalist, his first published fiction and his early reflections on artistic practice, Zola's familiarity with Manet and his circle has far-reaching consequences. Not only does his championing of Manet in the period 1866–8 occupy a deservedly celebrated chapter in the history of nineteenth-century French art; it also opens up a perspective which moves too seamlessly, perhaps, from biographical intersection to a *fraternité des arts* at odds with the tensions and conflicts of competing artistic fields.

Much the same could be said of those kinds of 'contact and interchange' visible at the level of common subjects. Emblematic in this respect is Manet's *Nana* (1877), originally inspired in part by the Nana who appears in the last chapters of Zola's *L'Assommoir* (serialised in the autumn of 1876) prior to her re-presentation in the scene in Zola's *Nana* (1880) in which the courtesan transfixes Count Muffat's obsessive gaze while admiring herself in the mirror. *Thérèse Raquin* (1867) has parallels with *Olympia* which are both significant in themselves and allow us to qualify some of Zola's more doctrinaire statements about both his own and Manet's art.[2] But Manet's are not the only apparently corresponding pictures. To read Zola's novels with one eye on contemporary painting (often explicitly illustrating the covers of modern paperback editions of his work) is to be tempted into assumed transpositions of prostitutes, absinthe drinkers, laundresses, iconic urban sites and railway stations based on similar aesthetic principles. And this can be extended from common subjects to descriptive technique. To compare Renoir's *La Balançoire* (1877) to a similar scene in Zola's *Une page d'amour* (1878), for instance, is to highlight precise corresponding textual and pictorial effects.[3]

But that is not to subscribe uncritically to the celebratory perspective which continues to inform so many assessments of the relationship between Zola and the artists of his time. For the painters and their work also provide a mirror in which he can see himself reflected, lodged between uniqueness and similarities, the site of the related staging of an individual and artistic originality. And these more problematic dimensions of Zola's relationship with the visual arts are at least opened up by the cases of Cézanne and

Manet – to choose the two most famous and the most contrary of Zola's encounters with contemporary painting.

In the case of the former, a process of negative definition is marked on Zola's part by the straining desire of a possessive self-identification. This runs through the two young men's mawkish correspondence of the 1850s and 1860s, and the repeated advice given to Cézanne to adopt the writer's own habits of work and mind, an idealised projection frustrated by, and superimposed on, a barely contained resistance to the painter's often provocatively eccentric persona. Against such a backdrop, Zola's advice speaks of an absolute differentiation from Cézanne, and a perception of both the painter and his art as volatile, impatient, stubbornly inconsistent and infuriatingly illogical. Zola, in other words, is so close to Cézanne that he never gets away from confusing the painter and the man. At one level, this can be explained in the juxtaposition of the latter as Zola first knew him and the increasing divergence of initially parallel lives; in the shifting position from which the established Parisian writer *perceives* Cézanne mostly out of sight (down there in Provence), remembered as he *was*, trapped in the mythologies of the past and of his personality as surely as both Cézanne and his painting, for Zola, are perceived once and for all as he had seen the work and known the man up close, too close to the intensity and vicissitudes of his life, in the context of their personal friendship.

It is that same temporal freeze-frame and inordinate biographical focus that informs Zola's partial portraits of Cézanne in his own fiction. These are to be found, essentially, in three works. First, in the portrait of Laurent, the neurotic painter of *Thérèse Raquin* struggling with his demons and producing works that are repulsive, ill-composed and murky, but nevertheless intensely powerful. Secondly, in the case of *Le Ventre de Paris* (1873), it is clear from Zola's notes for the novel that, both physically and in relation to his fictional painter's apprenticeship – and in his early reliance on the Old Masters in particular – Cézanne is indeed the model for the character of Claude Lantier. Once again Zola refers to a painter's vain efforts to get it right, his extravagant visions, his imaginative excess and, as in *Thérèse Raquin*, his repeated destruction of his canvases. And then, thirdly, and most notoriously of all, there is the Cézanne visible within the composite figure of the same Lantier in *L'Œuvre*, in which the recognisable pen-portrait of him in *Le Ventre de Paris* is used again, almost word-for-word, more than a decade later. Without wanting to dwell on the mannered and variously interpretable 'Thank you very much' with which Cézanne responds to the gift of his own signed copy of *L'Œuvre*, it remains instructive that, in his planning notes for the latter, Zola says at one point that his fictional painter will be, at least in part, 'a dramatised Cézanne' ['un Cézanne dramatisé'], further underlining the extent to which Zola conceives the artist as an individual psychology and almost a ready-made character for a drama or a novel, assessing him, it seems, from an essentially literary perspective.

If we remain concerned less with the story of a friendship and its tensions than with Zola's critical writing on Cézanne, that biographical reflection is merely a starting-point for what such writing ultimately tells us about the very nature of Zola's art criticism and the possibilities and limits of its engagement with contemporary painting. For the process of negative self-definition means that the work of Cézanne, in particular, cannot be accommodated within, or appropriated by, its discursive strategies and aesthetic assumptions. At an earlier stage, long before Zola's journalistic education as an art critic in the late 1860s, we find a seldom-quoted admission to Cézanne that he really knew nothing at all about painting: 'when I look at a painting, given that my competence is limited to being able to distinguish white from black, it's obvious that I'm not qualified to pass judgment on it' ['lorsque je vois un tableau, moi qui sais tout au plus distinguer le blanc du noir, il est évident que je ne puis me permettre de juger des coups de pinceau' (Cor. i 149)]. By the time of the distorted transpositions of *Thérèse Raquin*, by contrast, Zola has at his disposal a lexicon and a set of emerging presuppositions into which Cézanne does not fit by virtue, precisely, of what Zola calls his 'strangeness' ['étrangeté'], making it perhaps less curious that nowhere in his art criticism is there any substantive reference to Cézanne himself.

In his 1866 articles in *L'Evénement*, his stress on 'le tempérament', related to his oft-repeated definition of a work of art as 'a corner of nature seen through a temperament' ['un coin de la nature vue à travers un tempérament'] has sometimes been seen as gesturing towards Cézanne's forceful individuality. And when he collected those articles in volume form later in the same year (under the title *Mon Salon*), Zola did publicly dedicate the volume to Cézanne, as he would dedicate, a few months later, his first (and largely autobiographical) novel, *La Confession de Claude*. But the *dédicace* to the volume of art criticism did come with something of a double edge, with Zola explaining to Cézanne that although (of course) he remained his best friend, he had not actually mentioned him in his art criticism because he was reserving judgment on him *as a painter*, a judgment deferred because Zola felt that Cézanne's experimentation in technique and subject was itself a deferral, or a procrastination, endlessly postponing the adoption of a recognisable aesthetic or a personal style. In a letter of May 1870, Zola writes of Cézanne's continuing 'phase of trial and error' ['période de tâtonnements']: 'Let's wait until he's found himself' ['Attendez qu'il se soit trouvé lui-même' (Cor. ii 219)], thereby inscribing in the mirror of his own newly fashioned self-assurance the problematised self of Cézanne's unfinished quest for identity. For it is that notion of Cézanne not yet having found himself, or not yet having become more like the novelist, which at least partly explains Zola's differentiating *fictional* representations of Cézanne and the virtual absence of his name in Zola's art criticism. The references to him are notoriously few and far between. Over three decades, to be more precise, from Zola's first writing on painting in 1866 up until 1896 (when he does so for the last time) there are only six such references, a paucity put in more acute perspective by the fact that this is as few as to a relatively forgotten artist like Bonnat, while, by comparison, there are over one hundred references to Manet, and almost thirty to Corot or Monet. What is more, they are barely passing mentions at that, amounting to a few isolated comments on a painter still in the process of becoming one, with not a single one of Cézanne's paintings the subject of analysis or detailed appreciation.

Zola's apparent failure to accord Cézanne the same pre-eminence, in the development of modern painting, as he so intuitively recognised in Manet, remains a subject of debate. We might better make sense of that infamous critical silence not so much in terms of incomprehension or lack of insight, but rather in Zola's inability to *write* about Cézanne, to the extent that his work is unamenable not only to Zola's aesthetic principles and priorities, but also to the semantic configurations and discursive practices of Zola's art-historical rhetoric. What *L'Œuvre* underlines, extrapolating from its composite portraits, is that Zola's Cézanne is a failure on aesthetic grounds too. For the painter's residual Romanticism and assertive subjectivity are at odds with Zola's own mimetic imperatives, not least in the writer's strategic reconciliation (symptomatically identifiable in his writing on Manet) of individuated vision and truth, and of technical mastery and the appearance of the spontaneity of the real. Judged against such criteria, it is no wonder that Zola has nothing to say about Cézanne other than to stress that he is an artist in the making, still emerging in Zola's own looking-glass through the blur of indistinction.

For it has often been shown that the novelist's art criticism, however challenging and intelligent in its own right, is the testing-ground for the development of his own theoretical positioning. This is equally visible, in the adjoining literary domain, in his teleological cultural history interrupted by the aberrations of Romanticism and spaced by precursors (Stendhal, Flaubert, Balzac) – in which the fixed end-point, the apex, is naturalism and Zola himself. So too, as far as the visual arts are concerned, the writer recruits this or that painter or sculptor in the very *terms* of his own emerging aesthetic, territorially gathering, under the naturalist banner, each and every modernist tendency from Delacroix to Impressionism. It is within that forward-looking dynamic too that Cézanne does not fit – in his case so deliberately re-working the art of the past (as this dimension of the fictional painter in *Le Ventre de Paris* already suggests) that Zola would have found it impossible to effect so strategic a suppression of that past which Manet's modern subject matter, by contrast, inherently allowed him to do, and as Manet knew. And if, at a purely rhetorical level, much of Zola's art criticism works by analogy, comparison and conflation, by equivalents, metaphorical substitutions and superimpositions eroding the distinctions between differentiated artistic practices in the service of his own naturalist project and, crucially, on the assumption that the literary is inherently superior to the pictorial, here again Cézanne does not fit, simply by virtue of refusing to offer the writer the necessary fixed point in any such rhetorical move.

Moreover, Zola's *contrary* positioning (contrary, not least, to a perpetual motion on Cézanne's part) is stabilised by his own ordering propensities and, as is evident from the planning notes for *L'Œuvre*, by characterising the surrogate figure of Sandoz, the novelist, as 'immobile'. The fixed point in the mirror is thereby self-defining *in opposition to* the painter partly modelled on Cézanne, while it simultaneously asserts a defiant conservative positioning in relation to what Zola calls the contemporary 'anarchy' in the shape of the extraordinary proliferation of painters and paintings liberated from institutional control: 'an artistic Babel' ['une Babel de l'art'] (as Zola puts it in his art criticism contemporary to the writing of *L'Œuvre*), which is also the hyperbolic 'crisis' of indirection, absent geniuses, generic illegibility and transitional disorder, which is a crisis less of the time *in* the novel (the 1860s) than in the time *of* the novel (the 1880s), which is also reflected in Zola's critical writing at that time. Cézanne, by contrast to Zola's positioning and almost confirming his worst fears, does not stand still. This is evident in both the serial indeterminacy of his own self-portraits and in the creative re-inventions of his artistic styles, never fixed within an identifiable school or a movement, a development or an evolution, or even a tendency. He is impossible to *place*, in Zola's terms and lexicon, to situate or classify, to explain or define, to include or leave out, other than in the interstices and silent margins of transition. In Zola's looking-glass, Cézanne can never be more than an inverted image of himself, but more usually figures the far more sinister absence of any reflection at all.

This is not the case with Manet, of course. Indeed, if Manet is Zola's favourite painter, it is surely, within the above dialectic, because he is not Cézanne. As Fantin-Latour's 1867 portrait of him also projects, this worldly, well-dressed, stylish gentleman was not at all, as Zola stressed in his championing, the 'dishevelled' revolutionary of polemical caricature and popular mythology: as Zola recalled him, in 1884, 'a Parisian passionately enjoying high society, with his subtle and sophisticated elegance' ['un Parisien adorant le monde, d'une élégance fine et spirituelle'].[4] The creative relationship between the two men has many mirroring dimensions to it: an identification, in the 1860s and early 1870s, which pervades the language of Zola's self-definition as a critic and as a novelist; common themes and sources elaborated in analogous techniques and descriptive fabrics; the pre-emptive relegation, by Zola, of subject matter to formalist concerns, thereby effecting the necessary separation between scandalous realism and artistic integrity; those positive valencies ascribed to various fictional painters, compensating for Cézanne-like aberrations, by the writer intermittently mapping their practice on to Manet's own; the *verbatim* cannibalisation of his journalistic discourse on Manet retranscribed within dialogue or authorial commentary in *L'Œuvre*; a posited shared martyrdom at the hands of the philistines; sincere solidarity neatly coinciding with self-interest in the superimposition of the image of one modernist on another. These dimensions add up, in every sense (sartorial, moral, optical), to *distinction*.

To approach the relationship between Zola and contemporary painting from such angles is thus to take issue with the orthodoxy exemplified by the very title of Henri Mitterand's *Zola journaliste: de l'affaire Manet à l'affaire Dreyfus* (1962). That is not to question, of course, the sincerity of Zola's positioning in either 'affaire'; but the alignment of those two 'badges of courage' might imply an unproblematic solidarity. It may be provocative enough simply to note that the converse notion of competing artistic spaces (as exemplified in the work of Pierre Bourdieu) seldom informs analysis of Zola's relationship with the visual arts of his time. To argue that this inherent rivalry culminates in the writing of *L'Œuvre* is to consider Cézanne's breaking off of a forty-year friendship after reading it as something other than a tantrum. It explains why a notorious 1886 dinner-party, attended by Pissarro, Monet, Duret and Mallarmé, resulted in Huysmans being substituted as the painters' champion. The former, the guests agreed, had a more sensitive understanding of modern painting and would write more sympathetically on their behalf than Zola. And it makes of Degas' bitter 'with a single brush-stroke we can say more than can be expressed in an entire volume of words' ['en un trait nous en disons plus long qu'un littérateur en un volume'] less an expression of personal animosity than a symptomatic response to the perception that Zola had written *L'Œuvre* 'to demonstrate the clear superiority of the writer over the painter' ['pour prouver la grande supériorité de l'homme de lettres sur l'artiste'].[5]

By way of illustrating a more uneasy positioning than is usually retailed by heroic surveys, one could return to three pictures in which Zola and painting are placed, literally, side by side. We might need to take another look, for example, at that most familiar of pictorial statements of mutual support and common purpose, namely Fantin-Latour's *L'Atelier des Batignolles* of 1870. For even spatially, precisely, Zola is self-contained, with his own agenda perhaps, but clearly not gazing at Manet at his easel nor at any of his so-called 'disciples'. If Zola's inclusion is polemical in intent, he remains at odds with its compositional planes, not aligned within its structural focus, and not integrated into its collective design. This is even more true of Bazille's *Mon Atelier* (1869–70). Here again, the disposition of the figures is far from arbitrary, as is obvious from Bazille's centrality and the disproportionate stature with which Manet endowed him – while giving him a helping hand – when painting him in. Nor can there be any doubt that Bazille himself is engaged in a fruitful interchange with both Manet and Monet (standing behind him) around the work in progress. Zola, by contrast, really is (literally) a marginal figure, even if one resists the temptation to make too much of the fact that the writer is talking down to Renoir while making his own way up potentially symbolic stairs at the left-hand edge of the canvas.

The painting most visibly marked by such spatial tensions is Manet's 1868 portrait of Zola himself. This is often seen as another celebration, testimony not only to a friendship but also, like the Fantin-Latour, to a shared commitment to a new aesthetic programme. A more equivocal reading of the painting might start with Manet's own signature, the ludic possibilities of which are also exploited in his portraits of Duret and Mallarmé, as well as in *Le Fifre* (1866). At one level the highlighting, with its distinctive blue cover, of Zola's 1867 study of him (republished in brochure form to coincide with the opening, on 24 May, of Manet's private exhibition in the Place de l'Alma) repays a genuine debt. But it has also been shown that if many of the portrait's internal references gratefully respond to Zola's admiring commentary on the painter's early work, others reassert those creative contacts with tradition which Zola had missed, or dismissed, in all his writing on Manet since 1866. What is certain is that its extraordinarily rich allusive texture makes the portrait as a whole the most eloquent refutation of the novelist's unwillingness to grant Manet a degree of intentionality; and those multiple inscriptions contradict a formalism the implications of which are that only writing can articulate meaning.[6]

It is in the wider context of that argument, rather than in relation to this particular dialogue, that positioning is telling. It was a journalist writing about the portrait in 1868 who remarked that Zola's glance was turned away in non-recognition from every single visual influence on display. Indeed, the fact that he is surrounded by the signs of Manet's activities and tastes, rather than his own, adds to that sense of his being awkwardly misplaced. And dangling eye-glasses suggest the perceptual blank of Zola's gaze, oblivious not only of pictures in hand and around him, but also of the portrait-painter. What is more, there seems to be a calculated inversion of the literary and the pictorial in the transformation of Zola's books into a decorative fan, and the juxtaposition of the *image* of the writer and the *name* of the painter. If that signature is framed by texts, both Zola and his writing about the artist are firmly within Manet's interlocking frames of Japanese screen, angled chair and cropped reproductions. Where the painter himself ultimately stands can be gauged by following the diagonals to an originality writ large, in the lettering dwarfing Zola's authorship. For resistance to textual appropriation is indexed by an exuberant quill pen which fails to obscure the marker of his achievement, overlaid by the ironies of a Zola captured in contemplation rather than the act of writing, while Manet's creative presence manifests itself (literally) in print.[7] As well as evidence of a characteristic visual wit, such paradoxes inform the contemporary debate about the relative autonomy of literature and painting.

What Manet can be seen to resist, it can be argued, are Zola's strategic analogies mentioned earlier. Those erosions are so pervasive, in Zola's art criticism, that progressive pictorial tendencies are often reduced to an illustrative function within a hierarchy which privileges the verbal. For his conflations speak of a quasi-territorial imperative. Just as Zola himself reclaims the centrality vacated by Balzac; and as his own fiction resembles the work of a military cartographer, with its compartments and departments (and department stores), and its inner dynamic generated by the conflictual juxtapositions of city *quartiers*, garden plots and adjoining rooms. Doubtless reflecting the preoccupations of the period as well as those of competitive cultural fields, this antagonistic topology is equally visible in Zola's writing about the visual arts, without being incompatible (it is worth repeating) with the sincerity with which he adopts unpopular causes.

His writing on contemporary painting relies on the same evolutionary model which legitimises naturalism's status as the fullest realisation of literary tendencies thereby validated in retrospect. The modernist pictorial alignment works back from Manet to Courbet and Delacroix. The Impressionists are thus situated as 'following on from Courbet and our great landscape artists [who] have devoted themselves to the study of nature' ['à la suite de Courbet et de nos grands paysagistes [qui] se sont voués à l'étude de la nature'], while 'in his wake, this direction was maintained as is the case in literature, in the footsteps of Stendhal, Balzac and Flaubert' ['derrière lui, le mouvement a continué, comme il continue en littérature, derrière Stendhal,

Balzac et Flaubert' (p. 419)]. With this kind of wisdom of hindsight, even an artist as reliant on classical mythology as Puvis de Chavannes (1824–98) becomes 'a precursor'. Indeed, through the slippage between 'natural' and 'naturalist', virtually no painter escapes Zola's annexation. It is entirely logical that Manet should be 'a realist and a positivist' ['un réaliste, un positiviste'] and 'the only painter since Courbet distinguished by a truly original talent heralding the naturalist school in which I place all my hopes for the renewal of art' ['le seul depuis Courbet qui se soit distingué par des traits vraiment originaux annonçant cette école naturaliste que je rêve pour le renouveau de l'art' (p. 296)]. Such exclusivity, however, is less an absolute judgment than a reflection of a revisionism inseparable from Zola's sense of (and dissatisfaction with, by 1875) unmistakably new directions. As early as 1868, Corot too had been defined as 'one of the masters of modern naturalism' ['un des maîtres du naturalisme moderne' (p. 215)]. Four years later, 'among the naturalists who have been able to give expression to nature in an original and dynamic language, one of the most interesting figures is certainly the painter Jongkind' ['parmi les naturalistes qui ont su parler de la nature en une langue vivante et originale, une des plus curieuses figures est certainement le peintre Jongkind' (p. 252)]. Notwithstanding Manet's 1875 status as 'the only painter since Courbet', merely a couple of weeks later Fantin-Latour is also 'one of the painters of the young naturalist school' ['un des peintres de la jeune école naturaliste' (pp. 227–8)]. Sculpture's representative is Philippe Solari, yet another artist unambiguously working in Balzac's footsteps. Corrective advice is freely given. Sometimes this is merely implicit, as in Corot's 'elevation' to the rank of 'the leader of the naturalists in spite of his predilection for misty effects' ['le doyen des naturalistes, malgré ses prédilections pour les effets de brouillard' (p. 216)]. At others, admiration is overtly qualified: 'M. Gervex remains nevertheless, along with M. Bastien-Lepage, at the head of that group of artists who have distanced themselves from the Academy in order to come over to naturalism' ['M. Gervex n'en reste pas moins, avec M. Bastien-Lepage, à la tête du groupe des artistes qui se sont détachés de l'Ecole pour venir au naturalisme']; for their work does not exactly conform to 'the perfect unity of a naturalist subject' ['la belle unité naturaliste du sujet' (pp. 428–30)]. Jules Breton and Jean-Paul Laurens are hopeless anachronisms. A minor figure like Duez, on the other hand, is to be encouraged. For, in spite of Zola's intermittent misgivings and the oblique paths taken by misguided individuals, painting itself is moving along lines as predetermined as any other organic development. And if critical appropriation is gradual, relentless and inevitable, it reaches its spatial apogee in the triumphalist semantics of *Le Naturalisme au Salon* of 1880.

Simultaneously, however, there is a paradoxically contrary strain in Zola's art criticism which castigates within the space of *painting* the conflation of the visual and the verbal. Artists guilty of this transgression are 'using a brush as if it were a pen' ['ils se servent d'un pinceau comme d'une plume' (p. 202)]. Only Bastien-Lepage's immaturity excuses his 'literary intentions' ['intentions littéraires' (p. 286)] and saves him from the contempt more generally reserved for all forms of illustrated narrative. This disdain for 'philosophical painting' ['la peinture à idées'] can be traced back to *Mes Haines* (1866), in which Zola caricatures Proudhon's 'literary' interpretation of Courbet. So too, his association of textual approximation simply with an outdated Romanticism is not wholly convincing. Given his own discursive strategies, we cannot but be struck by the irony of Zola's lament in respect of literature's domination of the artistic field ['la littérature a tout envahi']. But where this is elaborated as 'our painters have tried to write epics or novels' ['nos peintres ont voulu écrire des pages d'épopée ou de roman' (p. 428)], the necessity of separate artistic spheres becomes an insistent theme.

Such concerns clearly underlie Zola's apparently perverse disassociation of Manet's Baudelairean affinities:

I want to use this opportunity to reject the relationship which is supposed to exist between the paintings of Edouard Manet and the poetry of Charles Baudelaire. I know that their friendship was a close one, but I can categorically state that the painter never committed the widespread error of putting ideas into his canvases.

[Et je profite de l'occasion pour protester contre la parenté qu'on a voulu établir entre les tableaux d'Edouard Manet et les vers de Charles Baudelaire. Je sais qu'une vive sympathie a rapproché le poète et le peintre, mais je crois pouvoir affirmer que ce dernier n'a jamais fait la sottise, commise par tant d'autres, de vouloir mettre des idées dans sa peinture. (p. 152)]

That is not to deny that there were urgent polemical reasons too, in 1867, for deflecting attention away from Manet's subject matter and towards pictorial values. But it is in Zola's confrontation with early Symbolist art, notably in his writing on Moreau after 1876, that he reacts most violently against painting's incursion into the literary domain. That he sees Moreau's work within a dialectic ultimately reinforcing his own aesthetic is only to be expected. But, once again, it is such painting's intellectual claims, as much as its retrograde symbolism, which are the source of Zola's irritation. It is little wonder that, for Zola, Moreau's artistic theories are the very opposite of his own ['diamétralement opposées aux miennes' (p. 390)]. Manet, by contrast, 'knows how to paint, and that's all there is to it, and it is such a rare gift that it is sufficient to have made him the most original artist of the last fifteen years' ['sait peindre, et voilà tout, et c'est un don si rare qu'il suffit pour faire de [lui] l'artiste le plus original des quinze dernières années' (p. 345)]. To juxtapose 'la peinture à idées' and such purity is to better understand the extent to which Zola's formalist stance seeks to define, as well as to reassert, the inherently differentiated limits of painting itself.

Behind this, one can occasionally discern the normal professional jealousies: the amazement that, with a single painting, an artist could achieve the fame and fortune it would take a novelist a lifetime to match; outrage at the financial distortions of the art market; irony at the expense of Degas' self-seeking exhibition strategies. Yet even these asides point, more significantly, to Zola's 'disorientation' faced with the confusion of the break-up of coherent groupings and 'schools'; the emergence of a Moreau 'whose talent is so bewildering that one has no idea how to categorise him' ['dont le talent est si étourdissant qu'on ne sait où le caser' (p. 390)] defies the very principles of taxonomy. What Zola refers to, in 1875, as 'the complete anarchy of tendencies' ['l'anarchie complète des tendances' (p. 285)] is repeated word for word six years later (p. 443). While a Huysmans may delight in such transitional disorder, Zola's almost obsessive *need* for order leads him to revert to a hierarchy long since abandoned. As he puts it, in a preamble to the third instalment of his Salon of 1875:

> Although nowadays there is, in painting, a confusion of genres, for the sake of clarity I am going to stick with the old system of classification; it is difficult to give a clear picture of our exhibitions without having recourse to some sort of logic. So I shall begin with traditional historical and religious painting.
>
> [Bien que tous les genres de la peinture soient aujourd'hui confondus, je m'en tiendrai pour plus de simplicité à l'ancienne classification; il n'est pas aisé de donner une idée claire de nos expositions à moins de suivre un système logique. Donc, je commencerai par la grande peinture, la peinture historique et religieuse. (p. 288)]

It is in a similar perspective that one might consider the necessity, from Zola's point of view, of the spatial distinction of literature and painting, while at the same time relating his cultural imperialism to an anxiety about the absence of hierarchy which might undermine his own authority.

To isolate such underlying patterns in Zola's critical discourse is to be able to re-read *L'Œuvre* at several removes from its status as a *roman à clef*, and to amplify Degas' intuitive sense of its demonstration of textual superiority beyond the transparently plotted opposition between failed painter and successful writer. The necessity of separate spheres, for example, illuminates that otherwise enigmatic reflection in the novel's *Ebauche*: 'One art consumed by another and producing nothing' ['Un art mangé par l'autre et ne produisant rien']. Though it also has to be said that the subsequently encoded taboo on such voracity applies mainly to pictorial encroachment, rather than the other way round; and, to extend the metaphor, one could almost describe *L'Œuvre* as a cannibalistic novel which, far from respecting the spatial autonomy of painting, appropriates the pictorial in many different ways.

There are, of course, numerous echoes in the novel of Zola's earlier critical texts, sometimes repeated *verbatim*. But there is also a hardening of his position, even to the extent of a discreet irony at his own expense, a virtual disclaimer generated by a profound uneasiness with the unforeseen directions taken by contemporary painting during the twenty years since he had recruited Manet in the very terms of his emerging literary aesthetic. Thus, amongst *L'Œuvre*'s many self-portraits, not the least uncomfortable is that of Jory:

> One of his articles, a study of a picture of Claude's exhibited by old Malgras, had just stirred up a terrific scandal by praising his friend at the expense of 'the public's favourites' and proclaiming him the leader of a new school, the 'open-air' school. Fundamentally extremely practical, he had no use for anything which was not to his own advantage and simply repeated the theories he heard the others expound.[8]

> [Même un de ces articles, une étude sur un tableau de Claude, exposé chez le père Malgras, venait de soulever un scandale énorme, car il y sacrifiait à son ami les peintres 'aimés du public', et il le posait comme chef d'une école nouvelle, l'école du plein air. Au fond, très pratique, il se moquait de tout ce qui n'était pas sa jouissance, il répétait simplement les théories entendues dans le groupe.   (RM iv 69)]

We are left unsure whether to refer to a hack journalism very different from his own championing of Manet in 1866–7, or to the entry in the Goncourt journal recording Zola's self-deprecating mockery of schools and labels such as naturalism 'because things need a new name, so that the public thinks they are new' ['parce qu'il faut un baptême aux choses, pour que le public les croie neuves'].[9]

If in silhouette, at least, the experience of the café Guerbois seems to be somewhat demystified (Jory's article is treated as a 'joke') in a discussion between Sandoz and Claude about the fictional *Plein air*, there is no mistaking Zola's own confession of transgression:

> 'Tell me,' said Sandoz, 'what are you going to call it?'
> '"Open Air",' was the curt reply.
> Such a title sounded over-technical to Sandoz who, being a writer, often found himself being tempted to introduce literature into painting.

'"Open Air"! But it doesn't mean anything!'
'It doesn't need to mean anything.'

['Décidément, comment appelles-tu ça?' demanda Sandoz.
– *'Plein air'*, répondit Claude d'une voix brève.
Mais ce titre parut bien technique à l'écrivain, qui, malgré lui, était parfois
tenté d'introduire de la littérature, dans la peinture.
'Plein-air', ça ne dit rien.'
– Ça n'a besoin de rien dire.   (RM iv 47)]

And what also needs to be underlined, perhaps, is how Christine's point of
view functions as another critical voice, Claude's handling of tonalities upset-
ting 'her firm ideas about colouring' ['toutes ses idées arrêtées de coloration']:

> One day, when she ventured to criticise him for painting in a blue poplar, he
> showed her on the spot the delicate blue cast of the leaves, and she had to agree
> with him that the tree really did look blue. In her heart of hearts, however, she
> refused to accept the fact. She was convinced that, in nature, there was no such
> thing as a blue tree.

> [Un jour qu'elle osait se permettre une critique, précisément à cause d'un peu-
> plier lavé d'azur, il lui avait fait constater, sur la nature même, ce bleuissement
> des feuilles. C'était vrai pourtant, l'arbre était bleu; mais, au fond, elle ne se
> rendait pas, condamnait la réalité: il ne pouvait y avoir des arbres bleus dans
> la nature.   (RM iv 155)]

If her reservations about Claude's impressionism are exactly Zola's own, so
too, in the conventional rivalry between Art and the Feminine, there may be
the sub-text of a more fundamental opposition: 'She could not understand
such painting; she thought it was abominable; she hated it instinctively, as an
enemy' ['Cette peinture, elle ne la comprenait pas, elle la jugeait exécrable,
elle se sentait contre elle une haine, la haine instinctive d'une ennemie' (RM
iv 93)].

More revealing still, however, are the ways in which the fabric of *L'Œuvre*
is itself invested with the competitive tensions between word and image. At
an elementary level, this can be seen in the following descriptive segments:

> ... the bright blue sky above the rust-red earth. One sketch showed a stretch of
> plain with wave after wave of little grey olive trees rolling back to the irregular
> line of rosy hills on the skyline. Another showed the dried-up bed of the Viorne
> crossed by an ancient bridge white with dust, joining two sun-baked hillsides
> red as terra-cotta, on which all green things had withered in the drought.

> [... l'ardent ciel bleu sur la campagne rousse. Là, une plaine s'étendait, avec
> le moutonnement des petits oliviers grisâtres, jusqu'aux dentelures roses de

collines lointaines. Ici, entre des coteaux brûlés, couleur de rouille, l'eau tarie de la Viorne se desséchait sous l'arche d'un vieux pont, enfariné de poussière, sans autre verdure que des buissons morts de soif. (RM iv 41)]

Her flesh was faintly golden and silk-like in its texture, her firm little breasts, tipped with palest rose-colour, thrust upwards with all the freshness of spring. Her sleepy head lay back upon the pillow, her right arm folded under it, thus displaying her bosom in a line of trusting, delicious abandon, clothed only in the dark mantle of her loose black hair.

[C'était une chair dorée, d'une finesse de soie, le printemps de la chair, deux petits seins rigides, gonflés de sève, où pointaient deux roses pâles. Elle avait passé le bras droit sous sa nuque, sa tête ensommeillée se renversait, sa poitrine confiante s'offrait, dans une adorable ligne d'abandon; tandis que ses cheveux noirs, dénoués, la vêtaient encore d'un manteau sombre. (RM iv 19)]

. . . a view of the Place du Carrousel at midday, when the sun beats down without mercy. He showed a cab ambling across in the quivering heat, the driver drowsing on his box, and the horse, head down, perspiring between the shafts, while the passers-by were apparently staggering along on the pavements, all except one young woman who, all fresh and rosy under her parasol, swept with the ease of a queen through the fiery air . . . In the background, the Tuileries melted away into a golden mist; the pavements were blood-red and the passers-by were merely indicated by a number of darker patches, swallowed up by the overbright sunshine.

[. . . un coin de la place du Carrousel, à une heure, lorsque l'astre tape d'aplomb. Un fiacre cahotait, au cocher somnolent, au cheval en eau, la tête basse, vague dans la vibration de la chaleur; des passants semblaient ivres, pendant que seule, une jeune femme, rose et gaillarde sous son ombrelle, marchait à l'aise d'un pas de reine . . . Les Tuileries, au fond s'évanouissaient en nuée d'or; les pavés saignaient, les passants n'étaient plus que des indications, des taches sombres mangées par la clarté trop vive. (RM iv 206)]

Whether or not these are transpositions of identifiable works by Cézanne, Renoir and Monet (or Pissarro) respectively, it is the permutations of narrative exploitation which refer us to the writer's imaginative prowess: the first 'picture' is used for flashback purposes, mediated through the sketches with which the hero returns from the Midi; the second is Zola's description offered to Claude who subsequently undertakes his own unsuccessful version of it; and the third is a textual visualisation even more resonant than the painter's cityscape it evokes. While Claude moves fitfully through an impossibly incongruous range of styles, Zola himself masterfully assimilates them all.

That demonstration often takes the shape of verbal pictures autonomously cast, as at the very beginning of the novel:

On the far bank of the Seine the irregular roofs of the row of little grey houses on the Quai des Ormes stood out against the sky, while their doors and the shutters of the little shops made their lower half a patchwork of bright colours. On the left a wider horizon opened up as far as the blue slate gables of the Hôtel de Ville, and on the right to the lead-covered dome of Saint Paul's church.

[De l'autre côté de la Seine, le quai des Ormes alignait ses petites maisons grises, bariolées en bas par les boiseries des boutiques, découpant en haut leurs toitures inégales; tandis que l'horizon élargi s'éclairait, à gauche, jusqu'aux ardoises bleues des combles de l'Hôtel de Ville, à droite jusqu'à la coupole plombée de Saint-Paul.   (RM iv 12)]

At other moments, they are juxtaposed; thus, in Chapter 8, we have Zola's picturing ('In the foreground . . . the whole background was framed . . . What occupied the centre of this vast picture' ['D'abord au premier plan . . . Tout le fond s'encadrait là . . . Mais ce qui tenait le centre de l'immense tableau'], pp. 212–13), immediately followed by Claude's only partially realised painting of the same scene ('Well, in the background, I have the two vistas of river, with the embankments' ['Enfin, j'ai le fond, les deux trouées de la rivière avec les quais'], p. 216). And, in many of those juxtapositions, there is also the sense of Zola revising and, ultimately, correcting the pictorial:

'That,' he declared as he looked around him, 'is not bad at all.'
    It was four o'clock, and the day was just beginning to wane in a golden haze of glorious sunshine. To right and left, towards the Madeleine and the Corps Législatif, the lines of *buildings* stretched far into the distance, their rooftops cutting clean against the sky. Between them the Tuileries gardens piled up wave upon wave of round-topped *chestnut trees*, while between the two green borders *of its side avenues* the Champs-Elysées climbed up and up, as far as the eye could see, up to the gigantic gateway of the Arc de Triomphe, which opened on to infinity. The Avenue itself was filled with a double stream of traffic, rolling on like twin rivers, with eddies and waves of moving carriages tipped *like* foam with the sparkle of a *lamp-glass* or the glint of a *polished panel*, down to the Place de la Concorde with its enormous pavements and roadways like big, broad lakes, crossed in every direction by the flash of *wheels*, peopled by black specks *which were really human beings*, and its two splashing fountains breathing coolness over all its feverish activity.

['Ça, finit par déclarer Claude, ça, ce n'est pas bête du tout'.
    Il était quatre heures, la belle journée s'achevait dans un poudroiement glorieux du soleil. A droite et à gauche, vers la Madeleine et vers le Corps législatif, des lignes *d'édifices* filaient en lointaines perspectives, se découpaient nettement au ras du ciel; tandis que le jardin des Tuileries étageait les cimes rondes *de ses grands marronniers*. Et, entre les deux bordures vertes

des contre-allées, l'avenue des Champs-Elysées montait tout là-haut, à perte de vue, terminée par la porte colossale de l'Arc de Triomphe, béante sur l'infini. Un double courant de foule, un double fleuve y roulait, avec les remous vivants des attelages, les vagues fuyantes des voitures, que le reflet *d'un panneau*, l'étincelle *d'une vitre* de lanterne *semblaient* blanchir d'une écume. En bas, la place, aux trottoirs immenses, aux chaussées larges comme des lacs, s'emplissait de ce flot continuel, traversée en tous sens du rayonnement *des roues*, peuplée de points noirs *qui étaient des hommes*; et les deux fontaines ruisselaient, exhalaient une fraîcheur, dans cette vie ardente. (RM iv 74–75, my emphases)]

Not content with the translation of Claude's gaze into an admirable panorama, Zola incorporates impressionistic effects while simultaneously restoring the delineations, the geometry and the perspectival co-ordinates Impressionism had erased. But he also goes one stage further, recuperatively signalling (as my italics underline) the material realities it seemed to have lost from sight.

L'Œuvre is a novel organised, even thematically, by the tensions between this kind of spatial stability and its insidious erosions; between, on the one hand, the symmetries of Sandoz's professional and private life energised by unity around the family table, and, on the other, the 'unmaking' ['la déroute . . . la débâcle' (RM iv 331)] of harmonious dinner-parties, coherent menus and cohesive groupings overlaid on Claude's ever-changing styles correlated to his meandering *flâneries* across the spaces of the city. Of Sandoz, by contrast, we are told that he 'was immobilised in a dream' ['un rêve . . . l'immobilisait' (RM iv 193)]; and however double-edged that immobility may be, it precisely defines Zola's positioning within what he calls the artistic 'disequilibrium' ['déséquilibrements'] of the moment. Spatially, as readers will know, *L'Œuvre* embraces and contains Claude's efforts and failures, including his own 'peinture à idées' of symbolist pretensions whereby he too inserts 'the literary into his work' ['de la littérature dans son affaire']; it does so by triumphantly asserting a completeness which the painter's unfinished projects can never hope to rival. And not the least telling of Zola's appropriating metaphors, but only in the French original, is the one superimposed on the painter's ultimately inarticulate expression: 'As he walked about Paris he discovered pictures everywhere . . . He would return home . . . in the evening, in the lamplight, he would sketch on bits of paper, but without ever being able to make up his mind how or where he would set to work on the series of great works he so often dreamed of' ['Quand il traversait Paris, il découvrait des tableaux partout . . . rentrait . . . jetant des croquis sur les bouts de papier, le soir, à la lampe, sans pouvoir décider par où il entamerait *la série des grandes pages* qu'il rêvait' (RM iv 203)].

NOTES

1 Cited by F. W. J. Hemmings, 'Zola, Manet and the Impressionists', *PMLA*, 73 (1958), 416–17.
2 See Robert Lethbridge, 'Zola, Manet and *Thérèse Raquin*', *French Studies*, 34 (1980), 278–99.
3 See Joy Newton, 'Emile Zola impressionniste', *Les Cahiers naturalistes*, 33 (1967), 39–52, and 34 (1967), 124–38.
4 *Ecrits sur l'art*, ed. Jean-Pierre Leduc-Adine (Paris: Gallimard, 1991), p. 452. All subsequent interpolated page references are, unless otherwise indicated, to this most comprehensive edition of Zola's art criticism.
5 Cited by Theodore Reff, 'Degas and the Literature of his Time', in Ulrich Finke (ed.), *French Nineteenth-Century Painting and Literature* (Manchester: Manchester University Press, 1972), p. 203; Cézanne is reported by Emile Bernard to have said of the 'mensonge' of *L'Œuvre* that the distorted image of the painter had, as its rationale, the corrective self-glorifying image of the novelist; see *Conversations avec Cézanne*, ed. P. M. Doran (Paris: Macula, 1986), p. 56.
6 See both the classic study by Theodore Reff, 'Manet's Portrait of Zola', *Burlington Magazine*, 117 (1975), 35–44, and the persuasive revisionist critique by Nicole Savy, 'Un étranger vu par Manet: Emile Zola', *Les Cahiers naturalistes*, 66 (1992), 109–15.
7 See Robert Lethbridge, 'Manet's Textual Frames', in Peter Collier and Robert Lethbridge (eds.), *Artistic Relations. Literature and the Visual Arts in Nineteenth-Century France* (London: Yale University Press, 1994), pp. 144–58.
8 All translations of the text of *L'Œuvre* are those of Roger Pearson in his 'Oxford World's Classics' edition of the novel as *The Masterpiece* (Oxford: Oxford University Press, 1993).
9 Edmond et Jules de Goncourt, *Journal. Mémoires de la vie littéraire*, 3 vols., ed. Robert Ricatte (Paris: Laffont, 1989), vol. II, pp. 728–9 (entry for 19 February 1877).

RECOMMENDED READING

Berg, William J., *Emile Zola and the Art of His Times* (University Park, Pennsylvania: Pennsylvania State University Press, 1992)
Brady, Patrick, '*L'Œuvre' d'Emile Zola: Roman sur les arts, manifeste, autobiographie, roman à clef* (Geneva: Droz, 1967)
Butler, Ronnie, 'Zola's Art Criticism (1865–1868)', *Forum for Modern Language Studies*, 10 (1974), 334–47
Guieu, J.-M. and Alison Hilton (eds.), *Emile Zola and the Arts* (Georgetown: Georgetown University Press, 1988)
Hamon, Philippe, 'A propos de l'impressionnisme de Zola', *Les Cahiers naturalistes*, 34 (1967), 139–47
Hemmings, F. W. J., 'Zola, Manet and the Impressionists', *PMLA*, 73 (1958), 407–17
Leduc-Adine, Jean-Pierre (ed.), *Emile Zola: Ecrits sur l'art* (Paris: Gallimard, 1991)
Lethbridge, Robert, 'Zola, Manet and *Thérèse Raquin*', *French Studies*, 34 (1980), 278–99

Mitterand, Henri, 'Le Regard d'Emile Zola', *Europe*, 468–9 (1968), 182–99

Newton, Joy, 'Emile Zola impressionniste', *Les Cahiers naturalistes*, 33 (1967), 39–52 and 34 (1967), 124–38

Niess, Robert, *Zola, Cézanne and Manet: A Study of 'L'Œuvre'* (Ann Arbor: University of Michigan Press, 1968)

Reff, Theodore, 'Manet's Portrait of Zola', *Burlington Magazine*, 117 (1975), 35–44

Savy, Nicole, 'Un étranger vu par Manet: Emile Zola', *Les Cahiers naturalistes*, 66 (1992), 109–15

6

CHANTAL PIERRE-GNASSOUNOU

Zola and the art of fiction

Behind the scenes of fiction: Zola's planning notes

Zola left to posterity a substantial collection of texts linked to the genesis of his novels. Commonly called the 'dossiers préparatoires' ['planning notes'], they provide direct insight into the creative process. It is highly likely that the novelist intended these files to be an exemplary illustration of the naturalist method. There was no desire on his part to keep the notes secret; on the contrary, he revealed the existence of some of them during his lifetime, so that some of his admirers, including Edmondo de Amicis and Jan Van Santen Kolff, found themselves in possession of the notes for *L'Assommoir* and *Le Docteur Pascal*. Zola no doubt intended to bolster his image as a serious novelist with little use for improvisation or imaginative invention. Beginning with *Le Ventre de Paris*, all the planning notes are composed in the same way, in four large sections. In a section entitled 'Outline' ['Ebauche'], the novelist gives a broad-brush indication of the setting, the plot, and the principal characters. In a section entitled 'Characters' he draws up a file on each of his characters, giving their main biographical, physical and psychological particulars. A section entitled 'Plans' usually includes a brief summary and two series of detailed plans in which Zola organises the narrative and descriptive material chapter by chapter. Finally, there is a section containing documentation based either on his reading-notes or the results of his field-work. This homogeneous set of documents gives the impression of a perfectly controlled process of creation founded on genuine knowledge. The planning notes seem to illustrate to perfection the two great principles of naturalist fiction enunciated in *Le Roman expérimental*: observation (as in the Notes) and experimentation (as in the Outline, in which the story is invented). The development of the work seems to coincide with the substance of the theory. This provided the basis for the legend of the naturalist writer.

However, careful examination of the planning notes, as undertaken by contemporary genetic criticism, reveals the extent to which, in his narrative practice, Zola went well beyond the supposed naturalist method. The facts which, according to *Le Roman expérimental*, must precede novelistic invention, rarely come first in the actual creative process. Zola generally seeks documentation when his Outline is already well under way. The story and the characters exist independently of any documentary research, and the novelist's imagination, in full control of the game, is unconstrained by any pre-existent data. The first part of the Outline for *Germinal*, for example, was written before Zola's trip to Anzin. Zola invented his story of the workers' uprising without the benefit of any local research whatsoever. The Outline of *Le Ventre de Paris*, in which the two opposing figures of Lisa, the amply built *charcutière*, and Florent, the thin deportee, appear, was drafted before the novelist undertook his reportage on Les Halles. As Henri Mitterand has pointed out,[1] Zola's novelistic invention is pre-shaped by a corpus of acquired knowledge, received ideas, stereotypes and literary models, which impose narrative patterns (such as the battle of the Fat and the Thin in *Le Ventre de Paris*), certain roles (the good workman versus the bad workman in *L'Assommoir*), and some dramatic scenes (the knife fight planned for the end of *L'Assommoir*). We are far from the scientific rigour vaunted by Zola. The Outlines of Zola's novels manifestly bear the imprint of the cultural and ideological codes that formed the author.

The most striking of these models is no doubt that of melodrama,[2] the imprint of which often characterises the author's first attempts at a story-line: betrayal, revenge, exaggeratedly villainous characters, and stark contrasts of good and evil are the apparently acceptable order of the day. Zola imagines a particularly violent ending for *L'Assommoir*, including revenge by vitriol with which Gervaise, overcome with jealousy, was to attempt to disfigure Virginie, and a knife fight between Coupeau and Lantier. Lisa, the *charcutière* of *Le Ventre de Paris*, appears in the first sketches of the story as a particularly Machiavellian character, falsely accusing Florent of murder in order to destroy him, even fabricating 'compromising letters' for this purpose. Christine, Claude's partner in *L'Œuvre*, is initially a girl of easy virtue who falls deeply in love with the painter. These initial configurations reproduce at every possible opportunity the paroxysms and complications of plot that Zola never tired of condemning in his critical writings. However, the 'superego' of the naturalist generally intervenes in the end to repress the melodramatic drives of the author, imposing greater simplicity on the story and making the characters more ordinary. Zola thus gives up (rather belatedly, it's true) his violent dénouement for *L'Assommoir*, writing the following comment in the margin of a manuscript sheet: 'Absolutely no drama' ['Non pas de drame'].[3] Lisa is also brought back into line, and loses her position as a dangerous manipulator: 'She must not be so intent on doing evil. She is also its victim' ['Il ne faut pas la faire si agissante dans le mal. Elle subit plutôt'].[4] As for Christine, when Zola realises he is reproducing in her the eternal 'good-time girl', she is made to become a mere 'bourgeoise'. So it is that the naturalist retaliates against the excesses of the first outlines of the plot.

Documentary investigation often contributes to this corrective process. Local fieldwork can, in fact, substantially modify the pre-formed visions of the author, who discovers, *in situ*, a reality quite different from the one he rather hastily imagined. Before his trip to Anzin, Zola had thought of giving young Jeanlin syphilis, as well as an old mistress, 'a half-mad beggarwoman' ['une mendiante à moitié folle']; on his return, he decided to abandon these exaggeratedly sordid touches, as the mining villages he was able to visit were not the slums he had imagined. It is clear, however, that documentary evidence is not endowed with a determining status in the creative process. Indeed the novelist at times maintains his phantasms even at the expense of factual reality, as the former seem to him ultimately both more plastic and more logical than the latter. In *La Bête humaine*, Zola refused to abandon his plan for a fantastic ending (the runaway train with neither driver nor stoker, hurtling into the night), although his consultant, a railway engineer, had pointed out to him that such an incident was, for technical reasons, highly unlikely. The novelist *wants* his insane engine, as it makes a magnificent conclusion for this disaster-novel about the fall of humanity; and he gets it, despite expert advice to the contrary.

This means that, contrary to naturalist mythology, Zola's fiction is far from being solidly grounded in documentary evidence. The imagination constantly asserts itself against the claims of documentation. The author of *Une page d'amour* will not hesitate, for example, to alter a map of Paris, transforming into a square, in the fiction, the triangle formed by two streets in the actual topography.[5] The novelist idealises the actual form of the streets by giving it an orthogonal structure that no doubt corresponds better to his visual imagination. The notes Zola takes sometimes exist merely to be bypassed. In his documentary file for *Germinal*, for example, Zola notes an ethnological fact which does not agree *a priori* with the dramatic character he wants to impart to his fictional strike. Immediately, without any further worry about this fact that does not fit his plans, the author thinks of how he might deny in his novel the acknowledged good nature of the Northern miners: 'In Anzin, the miners are peaceful, slow, proper, Flemish. Strikes there are quiet. But I think they could be made to degenerate into violence because of some great anger, or by a particular wound which *remains to be found*' ['A Anzin, les mineurs sont donc paisibles, lents, propres, des Flamands. Les grèves y ont le caractère tranquille. Mais je crois qu'on pourrait les faire dégénérer en violence, sous le coup d'une grande colère, d'une blessure particulière *à trouver*'].[6]

The investigator's work is in fact generally dictated by the needs of the story. When Zola visits a location or consults a book, he already knows what he is looking for and to what end. The real places Zola surveyed were seen as so many potential settings for his fictional characters. When planning *Le Ventre de Paris*, he followed the convoy of market gardeners entering Paris at night, noting: 'Avenue de Neuilly, I'll have Florent fall down after the bridge, up by the rue de Longchamp on the edge of a footpath (wide footpaths, big trees, low houses)' ['Avenue de Neuilly, je ferai tomber Florent après le pont, à la hauteur de la rue de Longchamp au bord d'un trottoir (larges trottoirs, grands arbres, maisons basses)'].[7] Real space is already seen through the prism of fiction; it is immediately inhabited by the story, as in this observation carried out for *L'Assommoir*, in which the heroine of the story, Gervaise, appears as if by magic: 'On the right, a vast wine-shop, with bars for the workers; on the left, the coalmerchant's shop, painted, an umbrella shop, and what will be Gervaise's shop, where there was a fruiterer' ['A droite, une vaste boutique de marchand de vin, avec salles pour les ouvriers; à gauche la boutique du charbonnier, peinte, une boutique de parapluies, et la boutique que tiendra Gervaise et où se trouvait une fruitière'].[8] Following this procedure, which consists of transforming reality into a setting for fiction, Zola's note-taking is highly selective, and in consequence, highly profitable. There is little waste in Zola's creative process; the assembled documents are in fact injected into the fiction almost integrally – the real world, in short, never goes beyond the bounds of the fiction, since it has been selected according to the needs of the fiction.

There are some decidedly unorthodox methods at work behind the scenes of Zola's fiction, and these certainly allow us not to take at face value the edicts of the theoretical doctrine he officially espouses.

Narrate or describe?

Description was Zola's major preoccupation, as he himself recognised in an article in *Le Roman expérimental* entitled 'On Description' ['De la description']. Since the aim of the naturalist novel is to set human beings in their environment and explain its effects upon them, descriptive writing is obviously of decisive importance:

> We consider that man cannot be separated from his milieu, that he is shaped
> by his clothing, his house, his town and his province; this being the case, we
> will not refer to one single phenomenon of his brain or heart without searching

for its causes and consequences in his milieu. This explains what people call our interminable descriptions.

[Nous estimons que l'homme ne peut être séparé de son milieu, qu'il est complété par son vêtement, par sa maison, par sa ville, par sa province; et dès lors, nous ne noterons pas un seul phénomène de son cerveau ou de son coeur, sans en chercher les causes et le contrecoup dans le milieu. De là ce qu'on appelle nos éternelles descriptions.   (OC x 1300)]

Description seems, for Zola, even to take precedence over narration. The plot is secondary, he often repeats, as if he had basically lost interest in the narrative dimension of his work and preferred to devote himself to the diffusion of documentary knowledge through the medium of description. In his fiction, the descriptive imperative effectively dictates both the division of the novels into chapters and the actions of the characters. As the chapters unfold, the novelist very carefully distributes among them the documentation amassed in the notes; Zola chooses, for instance, to divide his notes on the Théâtre des Variétés between two different chapters of *Nana*. The first chapter shows the world of the stage and auditorium, while Chapter 5 reveals life backstage. Similarly, Zola entrusts three types of character, described by Philippe Hamon as 'watcher-voyeurs' ['regardeurs-voyeurs'], 'voluble chatterboxes' ['bavards volubiles'] and 'busy technicians' ['techniciens affairés'],[9] with the diffusion of the documentary notes from the files. In the fiction, this produces scenes of high pedagogical tenor, which have been much mocked by the enemies of naturalism – for example, the encyclopaedic inventory of cheeses in *Le Ventre de Paris*, or the exposition of the blacksmith's trade which takes place before the dumbfounded Gervaise in Chapter 6 of *L'Assommoir*. Clearly, in this strategy of delegating to the characters the author's practical and lexicographical knowledge, there is a desire to legitimise the descriptions as much as possible by effacing the presence of the narrator, who, unlike Balzac's narrators, is not omniscient. The documentation is thus not imposed on the reader but seems, on the contrary, to emerge naturally from the fiction itself. This does sometimes stretch credibility, for certain pauses for description are in truth quite improbable – as when the engineer Négrel, in the midst of revolutionary rioting, takes the time to explain to his companions the strange geology of the Côte verte and the Tartaret. The circumstances of the narrative call for action – flight, or at least prudence – but the pedagogical imperative, which always takes priority, demands a 'detour' to hear the lecture of the knowledgeable engineer (RM iii 1395–6).[10] Once the account is finished, Négrel's companions are permitted to feel anxiety about what is about to happen, and the narrative, suspended for a moment, can resume.

It is important, however, to qualify this idea of an encyclopaedic description controlling and even exhausting the diversity of the world with lists, explanations and classifications. Critics have pointed out the 'ontological drama'[11] enacted in Zola's descriptive passages, in which the descriptor is confronted with the inevitable dissolution of form and matter. Patient and scrupulous naming cannot avert ever re-emergent chaos – as in the opening of *Le Ventre de Paris*, in which the splendid still lifes described through the eyes of the painter Claude Lantier disintegrate under the gaze of the starving Florent, around whom everything oscillates and dissolves. The foreigner he has become *refuses to see* the grandiose panoramas of vegetables and other victuals that the painter, a native, unfolds before his eyes: 'Claude . . . forced his companion to admire the sun rising over the vegetables . . . Florent was suffering. He felt that he was the victim of some superhuman temptation. He wished he could no longer see' ['Claude . . . força son compagnon à admirer le jour se levant sur les légumes . . . Florent souffrait. Il croyait à quelque tentation surhumaine. Il ne voulait plus voir' (RM i 626–8)]. This is a strange posture of avoidance and withdrawal for a novel that is meant to spread its world in all its detail before the reader's eyes. The enthusiastic painter, who creates imaginary pictures, no doubt goes a little too far, as if Zola recognised in him the illusion of mastery on which his own naturalist descriptions are founded,[12] which suggests that this author, so often reproached for his descriptive excesses, is mistrustful of description, and capable of calling it into question.

If Zola manifestly wished to explain the role of description in his writing, he was, on the other hand, less than forthcoming about his narrative art – except to say that he basically cared little for it. From the beginning of his career as a literary critic, Zola systematically took against the writers of serial novels, whose consummate narrative art is the source of their implausible fictions. Their taste for complication and their grasp on plot development certainly hold the reader in suspense, but this is to the detriment of truth, which for Zola is inevitably simple. Hence the idea, on the part of the author of *Les Rougon-Macquart*, that plot should be reduced to its essentials and not be the object of special study. This is why, in planning *Son Excellence Eugène Rougon*, he notes: 'I will avoid a tremendous dénouement. The book's dénouement will not be a drama. It will stop when I am finished. But it could still go on . . . I will try less than ever to tell a story. I will lay out a simple picture of characters and facts' ['J'éviterai un dénouement terrible. Le livre ne se dénouera pas par un drame. Il s'arrêtera quand j'aurai fini. Mais il pourrait continuer encore . . . Je chercherai moins que jamais à raconter une histoire. J'étalerai une simple peinture de caractères et de faits'].[13] If fiction is to correspond to life, it cannot be contrived and must even assume the unfinished quality of lived experience itself. In this way, Zola places himself in the tradition of the Flaubertian novel, which, with *Madame Bovary*, would begin the slow erosion of plot that would be completed in the twentieth century.[14]

This is why Zola's novels are so often at pains to 'fix things up' ['arranger les choses']. He rarely makes situations, even the most perilous, worse than they might be, preferring to tone down catastrophe rather than play it up as a serial novelist would, stressing the dramatic repercussion of events. Thus in *L'Assommoir*, the return of Lantier in Chapter 7 does not produce the stabbings promised by the gossip of the Goutte-d'Or. When, at the end of *La Curée*, Saccard surprises his wife Renée and his son Maxime *in flagrante delicto*, the scene does not end in physical violence, as would have been the case in a melodrama. Saccard, the humiliated husband and father, is content to make his guilty spouse sign a legal document by which she surrenders her fortune to him. The business is discreetly concluded by a simple signature, rather than by the spilling of blood. And if blood there must be, if a murder must be committed (and this is not uncommon in Zola, especially in the last novels of *Les Rougon-Macquart* – *La Terre*, *La Bête humaine* and *La Débâcle* – in which violent deaths abound), it might as well take place quite simply, rather than as the result of some dramatic paroxysm. As Zola reflects, while planning the scene in *La Terre* in which Buteau disembowels Françoise: 'I'm very keen to have one last act of violence . . . when he gets hold of her again with the scythe playing a role, but how? A fight would be rather Romantic' ['Je tiens à une dernière violence . . . lorsqu'il la reprend et la faux jouant un rôle, mais comment. Un combat serait bien romantique'].[15] The novelist is quick to see the risk of running off the rails and immediately finds a way of integrating the episode into ordinary life, attributing it to a quarrel between neighbours: 'The two are scything, cutting towards each other, harvesting a second crop . . . Then the quarrel (the problem of having adjacent fields, she accuses him of cutting on her patch)' ['Les deux fauchent, allant l'un vers l'autre, pour du regain . . . Puis la querelle (les misères de champ à champ, elle l'accuse de faucher chez eux)'].[16] The murder becomes nothing more than an incident of everyday life in a rural community.

If Zola, like many of his contemporaries, worked to destroy the conventional novelistic plot, and if it pleased him to underline this aspect of his writing, he nevertheless continued to be interested in composition. It is not because his novels were no longer contrived as they were in the good old days that they lack organising principles; these remain, certainly more abstract but nonetheless decisively important. But Zola says nothing (or almost nothing) about this in his theoretical writings, as if it were preferable to ignore the *semiosis* of the novel and concentrate on *mimesis* alone. Zola's narrative is, however, quite obviously tightly organised, not so much cunningly contrived as solidly balanced, in a harmonious ensemble, in which chapters echo each other across the text, thematic variations interlink at regular intervals, characters are distributed in such a way as to avoid any risk of dispersion or disproportion, and, finally, in which space is rendered narratively productive.

The last chapter of *Nana* is a magisterially ironic rewriting of the opening chapter. For Nana's death scene at the Grand Hotel, the novelist brings back all the characters (at least those who have survived), who saw the actress's first appearance in *The Blonde Venus* in the first chapter of the novel. However, in the final scene, the men, previously so powerfully attracted to Nana's glorious body, turn away from her, afraid of being contaminated by the smallpox from which she is dying. They prefer to stay below, outside the hotel, vaguely bored, their minds already elsewhere – very far now from the erotic ecstasy which opened the narrative. 'Venus was decomposing' ['Vénus se décomposait'], Zola wrote in the last lines of the novel, as if to ensure that the reader would recall Venus' past triumph on the stage of the Théâtre des Variétés. In *Germinal*, the chapter devoted to the cosy awakening of the bourgeois Grégoire family at La Piolaine is closely correlated to the chapter that describes the painful awakening of the Maheus, before they leave for the mine. The chapters of *L'Assommoir*, the number of which – thirteen – exactly figures misfortune, are organised according to a very clear pyramidal structure. This consists of two series of six chapters each – the first relating Gervaise's rise, and the second, her fall – both linked together by Chapter 7, which describes the feast for Gervaise's saint's day. In this pivotal chapter at the centre of the novel, the heroine's glory, celebrated by the whole neighbourhood, ends, and her Calvary begins, with the fateful return of Lantier. This dynamic, harmonious and meaning-laden structure was obtained by a considerable rearrangement of the original division into chapters, which had the drawback of unnecessarily multiplying the genre scenes and weakening the novel's form. In this way Zola's novel of Parisian working class life avoided becoming a flat juxtaposition of tableaux.[17]

Just as he knows how to build a solid structure, Zola is a past master of the art of thematic variation. Like the Impressionist painters, he repeats the same motif. Of *Une page d'amour*, he notes: 'I want to place the characters in a beautiful setting, simple yet always the same, consisting of five or six great landscape effects, which recur like a melody, always the same' ['Je veux mettre les personnages dans un beau décor, simple et toujours le même, avec cinq ou six grands effets de paysage, revenant comme un chant, toujours le même'].[18] This produces the five long descriptions of Paris that conclude each of the five parts of the novel. The panoramic views of the city, captured at different seasons or times of day, provide a range of tones and lighting which the writing tries to capture. These modulated reprises are not simply the effect of an artistic whim; they allow, on the basis of a permanent feature regularly reinscribed in the narrative (a landscape, for instance), a measuring of the gradual development of a character or of a relationship between characters. The three great dinner scenes at the writer Sandoz's house in *L'Œuvre* crystallise the deterioration of relations within the group of artists, even as they mark the young writer's pitiful lack of material success. Repetition of the same motif in Zola's novels always signals an irresistible degradation. Returning to the same place, recommencing the same scene, is to observe the ineluctable process of decomposition of life and things. Repetition, an internal factor of regularity and continuity, produces formal cohesion but ultimately reveals a world in which entropy is always at work.

Zola marshals his characters with an iron hand, so that they also participate in the general equilibrium which he never ceases to pursue. Consequently, there are, in Zola's novels, no characters who get lost, disappear halfway, or turn up in the closing stages. This would be a crime against the principle of harmony. The reader quickly gets to know the principal characters, and stays with them until the end of the story, and the group will not be disturbed by unexpected newcomers. In this way, most of the characters in *Le Ventre de Paris* are named and sketched out in the first chapter of the novel; given their number, this is something of a *tour de force*. The novelist has them return later on, either in isolation (a whole chapter is devoted to Cadine and Marjolin) or as a choral gathering (the swarming market scenes). Zola takes care always to alternate mass scenes (society receptions, crowds on the move) with more intimate ones (idylls, or solitary work). Even an intimate novel like *Une page d'amour* includes communal scenes, such as the children's ball, in which the principal characters are lost in a mass of extras. This of course imitates the intermittences of existence, divided as it is between public and private life, but above all, first and foremost, it takes the characters into a contrapuntal system in which opposites – movement and stillness, multitude and solitude, inside and outside – are happily balanced.

Finally, space is made to serve the purposes of narrative. It translates in an exemplary manner the concern for configuration that animates Zola's fiction. In fact, the space of the novel (even when taken from the real world) is never a mere setting for the activity of the characters, but clearly plays a part in the economy of the narrative. This can be seen in *L'Assommoir*, in which the tenement building has a particularly evident function: it permits the novelist to house together most of his characters, thus facilitating their circulation, the encounters and conflicts between them, which take place without troublesome plotting problems. The communal building contributes to the ineluctable centralisation of the novel, which is not dispersed over multiple locations. Space can even constitute the main issue in the conflict being related. Darwinism has often been invoked in relation to Zola, and it is true that his narratives frequently concern territorial rivalries and conflicts that are measured mainly in terms of terrain won or lost. One has only to recall the symbolic importance of Gervaise's shop in *L'Assommoir* and its loss to Virginie, which definitively marks the heroine's defeat. In a novel that remains little known even today, *La Conquête de Plassans*, space is entirely structured in the manner of a sort of provincial war-game[19] exposing the small town rivalries and political intrigues in the wake of the *coup d'état* and the proclamation of the Second Empire. The Abbé Faujas, sent from Paris, settles in the Mouret household with the mission of reconciling the two opposed parties of Bonapartists and Legitimists, and eliminating the Republican opposition. As if by chance, Mouret's house (Mouret himself is a Republican) is ideally placed between the two worlds of the Bonapartists and the Legitimists. Faujas is thus able to manoeuvre as he pleases, bringing together on neutral ground, in an alley bordering all three territories, the two previously hostile conservative forces. This reconciliation is accompanied by the expulsion of the owner of the strategic residence; Mouret, the undesirable Republican, is interned in the asylum where he eventually goes mad. In this way a new political space, that of the Imperial order, is created on the basis of three houses and an alley.

It is clear then that Zola's narratives in no way entail the dissolution of form. They are, rather, the product of 'a solid, architectural, monumental, pyramidal vision' ['une vision maçonne, architecturale, monumentale, pyramidale'],[20] founded on the principle of cohesion. As a result, the reader is made subject to firm direction. As Zola painstakingly builds up the elements of his narration so that each makes sense in relation to the others, he fully intends that this patient work of construction should not go unnoticed, and to this end, he puts up signposts for the reader's benefit. This, for instance, is how the various flashbacks and anticipations deployed in the novels should be understood. They oblige the reader to interpret a certain number of precursory signs, and to verify, at the end of the story, the accuracy of the author's desired interpretations. In this respect, *La Curée* is exemplary. When Renée, in the first chapter, contemplates the Parc Monceau from her bedroom, she feels a premonitory shiver: 'And one morning, she would awaken from the dream of pleasure she had lived in for the last ten years, mad, soiled by one of her husband's speculations, in which he himself would go under. It came to her as a sudden foreboding. The trees sighed even louder' ['Et quelque matin, elle s'éveillerait du rêve de jouissance qu'elle faisait depuis dix ans, folle, salie par une des spéculations de son mari, dans laquelle il se noierait lui-même.

Ce fut comme un pressentiment rapide. Les arbres se lamentaient à voix plus haute' (RM i 334)]. The reader is invited to imagine the worst for the heroine, and in Chapter 6 of the novel this inevitably takes place. Renée, abandoned by Maxime and robbed by Saccard, takes stock of her life and recalls 'the one occasion when she had been able to read the future, on the day when, gazing at the murmuring shadows in the Parc Monceau, the thought that her husband would corrupt her and one day drive her mad had come to her and disturbed her growing desires' ['une seule fois elle avait lu l'avenir, le jour où, devant les ombres murmurantes du parc Monceau, la pensée que son mari la salirait et la jetterait un jour à la folie, était venue effrayer ses désirs grandissants' (RM i 575)]. Not only is the prediction borne out – which would suffice – but it is deliberately recalled, as if the novelist, tying his narrative into a loop, were forcing his readers to retrace their steps to find the earlier passage. By imposing such a regime of redundancy on the reader, Zola makes sure that nothing is lost in the course of literary communication and, in this case, that the determinist message of his fiction is clearly received.

In making the last novel of *Les Rougon-Macquart*, *Le Docteur Pascal*, a monumental *mise en abyme* of the series, Zola seems to have wished to provide his reader with the necessary user's manual to his work. 'I would like to summarise the whole philosophical meaning of the series with *Le Docteur Pascal*' ['Je voudrais, avec *Le Docteur Pascal*, résumer toute la signification philosophique de la série'],[21] he wrote while planning his concluding volume. The scientist-scholar Pascal Rougon will be given the task of expounding the meaning of the preceding nineteen novels, for Zola, making him his double, entrusts him with the memory of the whole series. Doctor Pascal keeps files on all the main characters – members of the Rougon-Macquart family – locked in a cupboard in his house. One by one, he reads them out and comments on them to his niece, recalling in a single sitting the facts that Zola took twenty years to write, and outlining the ultimate significance of this vast history: 'Ah! . . . a whole world, a society, a civilisation, life itself, are in there, with their good and evil manifestations, in the fire and the work of the smithy's forge which carries off everything' ['Ah! . . . c'est un monde, une société, une civilisation, et la vie entière est là, avec ses manifestations bonnes et mauvaises, dans le feu et le travail de la forge qui emporte tout' (RM v 1015)]. In this strange text, which unrolls like the closing credits of a film, Pascal-Zola hands down the correct reading of his work, intent, above all, on responding to those who could see nothing but darkness and morbidity in *Les Rougon-Macquart*: 'What a frightening mass has here been stirred, so many adventures, pleasant or terrible, such joy and such suffering scattered throughout this huge conglomeration of events' ['Quelle masse effroyable remuée, que d'aventures douces ou terribles, que de joies, que de souffrances jetées à la pelle, dans cet amas colossal de faits!' (ibid.)]. Zola wants it understood that the series is not the work of a misanthropist and pessimist, but that it was written 'out of a love for life, out of admiration for its vital forces' ['par amour de la vie, par admiration des forces vitales'], as he says in the Outline for *Le Docteur Pascal*. The strict guidance of the reader overtly undertaken in the last novel of the series has no doubt done Zola's reputation as a novelist no good; for in this perspective at least, the novelist seems to place himself very far from the modern (or postmodern) narrative, always so ready to confuse and puzzle the reader.

Zola's characters: construction and deconstruction

For Zola, characters must be readable, and readability is without doubt their most distinctive attribute.[22] This is required not only by Zola's positivism, according to which each individual is the product of the interaction of heredity and environment, but also by a poetics of the novel which has no truck with mystery and confusion. The novelist strives to make his heroes easily identifiable, providing them with a sort of identity document that elucidates them perfectly; just as Pascal Rougon does in *Le Docteur Pascal*, keeping the roll of his terrible family, compiling invaluable files on each of its members, the heroes of the different novels of the cycle. The different hereditary features to which the characters are subject, and the deeds and actions which proceed from them, are all duly recorded. Doctor Pascal's knowledge is not, however, absolute. Despite his research, he lacks information about some of the protagonists (as in the case of Etienne, the hero of *Germinal*: Pascal does not know what became of him after his deportation to New Caledonia). These 'holes' in characters' biographies are Pascal's despair, since where there is incompleteness, phantasm and myth take over. Against such uncertainty, the character portrait will be a high point of readability in Zola's novels. Everything begins with the character's name, which is the foundation of this ideal of transparency. The novelist expressed his views very clearly on this point: 'I am putting all sorts of literary intentions into the names. I am being quite fastidious, I want a certain consonance, I often see a whole character in a collection of a few syllables . . . to the point where it becomes in my eyes the very soul of the character . . .; to change the name of a character is to kill the character' ['Nous mettons toutes sortes d'intentions littéraires dans les noms. Nous nous montrons très difficiles, nous voulons une certaine consonance, nous voyons souvent tout un caractère dans l'assemblage de quelques syllabes . . . au point qu'il devient à nos yeux l'âme même du personnage . . .; changer le nom d'un personnage c'est tuer le personnage' (Cor. iv 260, letter to Elie de Cyon dated 29 January 1882)]. This is why in *La Terre* the name of an old peasant, passionately attached to the soil he cultivates, Fouan, seems so precisely derived from the verbs 'fouir' and 'enfouir' ('to dig' and 'to bury'), and why Maigrat, the grocer in *Germinal*, combines in his name his state of prosperity, 'gras' (fat), and the reason for this, the 'maigreur' (thinness) of the miners. Physical description, focused on the characters' faces, also provides an efficient template for the reading of the character. Zola's faces have something of the oxymoron about them, that figure which makes contradictions visible. The face of Christine in *L'Œuvre* is endowed with an 'upper part . . . of great kindness and great sweetness' ['[un] haut . . . d'une grande bonté et d'une grande douceur'] and a 'lower part' ['bas'] which is more carnivorous, characterised by a 'passionate jaw' ['mâchoire passionnée'] and a 'bloody mouth' ['bouche saignante' (RM iv 20)]. The reader, alerted by this description that brings into play a common physiognomic trope, naturally deduces a certain bipolar aspect to the character. In Zola's portraits, inessential details are omitted, and everything is significant.

If we turn from the *being* of the characters to the *doing* that characterises them, the personnel of Zola's novels proves to be varied and complex, allowing multiple readings, structuralist as much as mythographic. Philippe Hamon's analyses have shown that Zola's characters are in large part 'functionaries' ['fonctionnaires'] delegated to the task of describing the world: Gervaise has to *give* (to use the term that Zola uses repeatedly in his files, *donner*) the universe of the laundry, Etienne Lantier must *give* the mine, etc. They are, on principle, auxiliaries of the naturalist descriptive project, to the point that their actions are largely determined by this service. If Gervaise, in the first chapter of *L'Assommoir*, waits at her window for Lantier, it is so that her gaze can give the description of the working-class area of Paris that she inhabits, and if Muffat waits for Nana at the exit of the theatre, it is to allow the description of the Passage des Panoramas.

If, however, Zola's characters were merely a convenient means of transmitting the novelist's documentation, it is unlikely that the fiction would leave any trace whatsoever in the reader's imagination. The fictional beings invented by Zola are creatures not just of function but also of passion; they have been endowed by their creator with a strength of desire, often frustrated by circumstance, which provokes the reader's sympathy. In this sense, Zola's character invention remains indebted to well-tested novelistic models. Even if he renounces the classic hero, that exceptional character in whom desire and capacity miraculously coincide, Zola still plays on the well-known mechanism of the sympathetic character, the one for whom the public, touched by 'all that suffers and struggles' ['tout ce qui souffre et combat'] feels 'a compassionate fraternity' ['une fraternité émue'].[23] This is why, as the Outline of *L'Assommoir* would have it, Gervaise 'must be a sympathetic figure [all of whose] good qualities turn against her' ['doit être une figure sympathique [dont] chacune [des] qualités tourne contre elle'],[24] and why, in general, Zola's heroes are often powerless creatures who do not have the means to realise their dreams: Etienne Lantier suffers from his lack of the qualities necessary for his role as leader of the workers; and Claude, the artist, from his inability to achieve the chimerical work that haunts him. In an even more elementary manner, Zola will not hesitate to use the melodramatic figure of the innocent victim, which is sure to capture the reader's sympathy: the fragile Denise, for instance, in *Au Bonheur des Dames*, persecuted by the customers and her superiors at the store, or the sacrificial children, like Lalie Bijard, the young martyr of *L'Assommoir*, or Alzire Maheu, the young cripple in *Germinal*. Zola never totally departs from this concern for the sympathetic character in his works, as he knows only too well that the interest of the novel depends on it. Thus, when he conceives his murderer for *La Bête humaine*, he is careful not to model him entirely on the 'born criminal' as defined by the Italian scientist, Cesare Lombroso,[25] for if this were the case, Jacques Lantier would be too monstrous to identify with. Zola's need for a sympathetic character thus requires that his source material be somewhat reworked.

While attending to the 'humanity' of his characters, Zola endows some of them with another dimension, that of myth, which radically demarcates his fiction from the realist-naturalist current.[26] Zola is not only a remarkable manipulator of fictional personnel, directing his characters according to his descriptive needs, nor merely a skilled illusionist who promotes the reader's sympathetic identification with his paper heroes; he is also a primitive visionary, whose characters revive stories from the dawn of time. This is why Zola's characters, though anchored in the historical reality of the Second Empire, are often marked by a real allegorical excessiveness, through which primordial desires, sufferings and conflicts are materialised. Is not Adélaïde Fouque, the mad ancestress who transgressed every law by loving the tramp Macquart, the founder of an accursed tribe comparable to the Atridae in its familial violence? Zola is not afraid to use these lofty and disproportionate figures with their crushing symbolism. Nana is not just a successful prostitute, she is 'the ferment, nudity, sex, which leads to the decomposition of our society . . . she is the central flesh' ['le ferment, la nudité, le cul, qui amène la décomposition de notre société . . . elle est la chair centrale'].[27] Flore, who, Zola indicates in his Outline for *La Bête humaine*, is an 'original creation', is a virgin warrior and, like the Diana of antiquity, a killer of men; Etienne, hurled at Le Voreux, is clearly a modern Theseus fighting the Minotaur of the mine. Goujet, the giant blacksmith of *L'Assommoir*, and Cabuche, the

Herculean quarryman of *La Bête humaine*, handsome rough-edged brutes working iron and stone, are like primitive Titans astray in the modern world.

Many of Zola's characters originate not from a familiar modernity but from a sort of original chaos, in which sex, blood and murder – Eros and Thanatos – intermingle. In this sense, the character of Jacques Lantier, the murderer in *La Bête humaine*, haunted by obsessive images of rape and murder, brings to the surface the archaic substratum that is the basis of most of Zola's heroes. His heredity links him, beyond the generations of alcoholics, with the primal horde, and the Dionysian era Nietzsche speaks of in *The Birth of Tragedy* (1872). In another register, less tragic but just as fantastic, one must point out Zola's taste for carnivalesque characters: extraordinary physiologies and sensational bodies offer themselves up as spectacle, anchoring Zola's world in that of François Rabelais, the French humanist writer of the Renaissance. Mes-Bottes in *L'Assommoir* and Jésus-Christ in *La Terre* exceed naturalist normality by their corporeal exploits. In a similar vein, the town drunk ingests live mayflies and dead cat, and the country drunk swallows coins. Zola is also enchanted by these excesses.

These lofty mythical figures who haunt Zola's fiction do not, however, exclude characters who are very much of their time, and display an undeniable naturalist stamp. Even if energy and impulsions fascinate Zola above all else, he does not ignore the 'woodlice' ['cloportes'], as Flaubert would have said. The world of *Les Rougon-Macquart* includes a good number of such greyish figures, mere nonentities: characters with small private incomes, junior employees and small shopkeepers, whose well-ordered lives are doomed to insignificance. If all of Zola's narratives include this type of character, scattered here and there (*La Bête humaine*, a novel of murderous passion, also recounts the petty quarrels and cares that govern the lives of the employees at the railway station in Le Havre), *Pot-Bouille* is the novel devoted entirely to them, the one in which they become a true object of study. We find in *Pot-Bouille* an apathetic young married woman who half-heartedly deceives her equally apathetic spouse, a hypochondriac who spends her life in bed reading sentimental novels, a bourgeois gentleman who has the bad taste to attempt suicide – unsuccessfully – in the toilet, an old landlord whose obsessive occupation is tearing the pages out of the official catalogue of the Salon to make them into index cards – a rather dismal passion, like Poisson's devotion to making little boxes in *L'Assommoir*. Thus Zola's characters do not escape the generalised entropy that reigns in French realism and naturalism; wear and tear, monotony and insignificance affect some of them quite badly.

If Zola's fiction has long been seen as a basically referential form of writing, modern criticism has re-read Zola in the light of the reflexivity that characterises literary modernity. In this reading, Zola's novels reveal his strong propensity for *mise en abyme*, to the point of presenting themselves not only as 'the writing of an adventure but also the adventure of a writing' ['l'écriture d'une aventure mais aussi l'aventure d'une écriture'].[28] Without making Zola a precursor of the literary avant-garde of the 1950s and 60s (those who were then called the 'new novelists'), it is apparent that the narratives of *Les Rougon-Macquart* contain portraits of the Zola hero as novelist. The numerous entrepreneurs and adventurers portrayed in *Les Rougon-Macquart*, whether their enterprise is commercial, industrial, financial or even political, are all born 'story builders' ['bâtisseurs d'histoires'].[29] To found a bank, like Saccard in *L'Argent*, to create a department store like Octave Mouret in *Au Bonheur des Dames*, to rebel against the powers that be like Lantier in *Germinal*, or Florent in *Le Ventre de Paris*, or to exercise power like Eugène Rougon in *Son Excellence Eugène Rougon*, implies a *savoir faire* and a questioning spirit appropriate for the profession of novelist. The shop owner in *Au Bonheur des Dames*, Octave Mouret, who decides on a whim to change completely the rational classification of his merchandise, becomes the equivalent of a serial novelist who prefers complication to simplicity. His intentions are to lay out his store like a serial novel, full of sudden changes and detours, in which the female customer would become a captivated reader. Similarly, Zola's revolutionaries show themselves to be accomplished plotters – which generally augurs ill for the outcome of their plans. Florent writes down his plan for an insurgency with the guilty pleasure of a pamphleteer: 'This plan, which Florent went back to every night, as if to the scenario of a drama which relieved his nervous overexcitement, was as yet written only on scraps of paper covered in crossings-out, showing the author's gropings, and allowing one to follow this at once childish and scientific conception' ['Ce plan, auquel Florent revenait chaque soir, comme à un scénario de drame qui soulageait sa surexcitation nerveuse, n'était encore qu'écrit sur des bouts de papier, raturés, montrant les tâtonnements de l'auteur, permettant de suivre les phases de cette conception à la fois enfantine et scientifique' (RM i 813)]. In terms of figures of authority, the salient characters are equally marked by the practice of fiction. In the novel that bears his name, *Son Excellence Eugène Rougon*, the minister Eugène Rougon is at the head of a whole network of minor figures to whom he doles out positions and roles in the various plots he weaves and unravels. He is the very image of a busy novelist in charge of a large cast. Other characters quite obviously incarnate the investigative, or indeed inquisitorial, calling of the Zolian novel. The remarkable conspirators, Sidonie Rougon and Clorinde Balbi, for instance, go about with bags stuffed with documents; Judge Denizet in *La Bête humaine*, charged with investigating the murder of Grandmorin, assembles a monumental file containing 'three hundred and ten items', and Mademoiselle Saget, the gossip of Les Halles, spends her time spying on her neighbours, drawing up files on all of them. What makes a reappearance here, though materialised and sometimes ridiculed, is all the novelist's work of documentary preparation. Capitalists, revolutionaries, gossips – all these characters, rather than being strictly sociological figures, are the doubles of the novelist at work, a zealous observer and an uncontainable demiurge.

* * *

Zola never really explained his 'art of fiction', often preferring to promote his art of truth.[30] However, it is now well established that Zola's writing, far from being a simple consignment of documents, is an undeniably powerful exercise in configuration, in which the imaginary plays its part. If the author of *Les Rougon-Macquart* succeeded in perpetuating the image of the documentary novelist, whose descriptions could be considered to constitute the core of his writing, his planning notes betray him by revealing the extent to which his novels are marked by the temptations of fiction, to the point of his sometimes ignoring the constraints of his source material. Knowing this, it is not surprising that his characters show a pronounced taste for plotting, planning and, when all is said and done, illusion. They reveal what Zola intended to suppress.

Translated by Mark McCann and Brian Nelson

NOTES

1 See Henri Mitterand, *Le Regard et le signe* (Paris: Presses Universitaires de France, 1987), pp. 75–91.
2 See Colette Becker, 'Zola et le mélodrame', in Robert Lethbridge and Terry Keefe (eds.), *Zola and the Craft of Fiction* (Leicester, London and New York: Leicester University Press, 1990), pp. 53–66.
3 BNF, NAF, Ms 10271, fol. 86.
4 BNF, NAF, Ms 10338, fol. 69.
5 These analyses are taken from Olivier Lumbroso's 'Les métamorphoses du cadre', in Jean-Pierre Leduc-Adine (ed.), *Zola. Genèse de l'œuvre* (Paris: CNRS Editions, 2003), p. 116.
6 BNF, NAF, Ms 10308, fol. 304 (Notes Lévy).
7 BNF, NAF, Ms 10338, fol. 245.
8 BNF, NAF, Ms 10271, fol. 105.
9 Philippe Hamon, *Le Personnel du roman* (Paris: Droz, 1983).
10 The description begins significantly as follows: 'So we made a detour. Le Tartaret, at the edge of the wood, was uncultivated ground, of volcanic sterility, beneath

which a mine had been burning for centuries' ['Alors, on fit un détour. Le Tartaret, à la lisière du bois, était une lande inculte, d'une stérilité volcanique, sous laquelle brûlait depuis des siècles une mine incendiée'].

11 The expression is taken from David Baguley, *Naturalist Fiction: The Entropic Vision* (Cambridge: Cambridge University Press, 1990), pp. 184–203.

12 See Christopher Prendergast, *Paris and the Nineteenth Century* (Oxford: Blackwell, 1992), pp. 66–73.

13 BNF, NAF, Ms 10292, fol. 118.

14 See the comments with which Zola greeted Flaubert's *Madame Bovary*: 'There are no more children marked at birth here, then lost only to be found again at the dénouement. No more furniture with secret drawers, no more papers to be used, at the right moment, to save persecuted innocence. Even the simplest of plots is missing' ['On n'y rencontre plus des enfants marqués à la naissance, puis perdus pour être retrouvés au dénouement. Il n'y est plus question de meubles à secret, de papiers qui servent, au bon moment, à sauver l'innocence persécutée. Même toute intrigue manque, si simple qu'elle soit' (*Les Romanciers naturalistes*, OC xii 98)].

15 BNF, NAF, Ms 10328, fol. 436.

16 Ibid., fol. 437.

17 For a precise study of this redivision of the chapters of *L'Assommoir*, see Henri Mitterand, 'Programme et préconstruit génétique: le dossier de *L'Assommoir*', *Essais de critique génétique* (Paris: Flammarion, 1979), pp. 195–225.

18 BNF, NAF, Ms 10318, fol. 491.

19 See Henri Mitterand's analysis of this novel: 'It is always advisable to pay attention to Zola's use of space; but nowhere more so than in *La Conquête de Plassans* does it appear as something entirely other than a geographical and social setting: it is a closed field of forces, of tactics, of countershocks and perverse effects, which make it both the object of the action and its agent, as important as the hero, and a central configuration of the novel' ['Il convient toujours d'être attentif à l'espace zolien; mais nulle part mieux que dans *La Conquête de Plassans* il n'apparaît comme autre chose qu'un décor géographique et social: comme un champ clos de forces, de tactiques, de chocs en retours et d'effets pervers, qui en font tout à la fois l'objet et l'agent de l'action, et à égalité avec le héros, une configuration centrale du roman' (*Le Regard et le signe*, p. 131)].

20 Henri Mitterand, *Le Roman à l'œuvre. Genèse et valeurs* (Paris: Presses Universitaires de France, 1999), p. 67.

21 Bibliothèque Bodmer (Cologny, Switzerland), fol. 1.

22 On Zola's technique of the portrait, see *Le Personnel du roman*, pp. 107–84.

23 These are the terms Zola uses to describe the sympathetic character (*Théâtre et poèmes*, OC xv 358).

24 BNF, NAF, Ms 10271, fol. 160.

25 'I should keep the physical type of the born criminal and embellish it' ['Il faudrait garder le type physique des criminels-nés et l'embellir'] notes Zola in the 'Characters' file of *La Bête humaine* (BNF, NAF, Ms 10274, fol. 540).

26 On this question, which has been extensively explored by contemporary criticism, see for example Henri Mitterand, 'Zola, le Grec', *Le Roman à l'œuvre*, pp. 84–96.

27 BNF, NAF, Ms 10313, fol. 212 (Outline for *Nana*).

28 This is the famous expression used by the novelist and theoretician of the Nouveau Roman Jean Ricardou, to define the predominant reflexivity of literary modernity (*Problèmes du nouveau roman* (Paris: Seuil, 1967)).

29 The expression comes from Robert Lethbridge, 'Le Miroir et ses textes', *Les Cahiers naturalistes*, 67 (1993), 157–67.

30 See, for example, the Preface to *L'Assommoir*: 'This is a work of truth, the first novel about the common people which does not tell lies but has the authentic smell of the people' ['C'est une œuvre de vérité, le premier roman sur le peuple, qui ne mente pas et qui ait l'odeur du peuple' (RM ii 373)].

RECOMMENDED READING

Baguley, David, *Naturalist Fiction: The Entropic Vision* (Cambridge: Cambridge University Press, 1990; reprinted 2005)

Zola et les genres (Glasgow: University of Glasgow French & German Publications, 1993)

Hamon, Philippe, *Le Personnel du roman. Le système des personnages dans 'Les Rougon-Macquart'* (Geneva: Droz, 1983)

Lethbridge, Robert and Keefe, Terry (eds.), *Zola and the Craft of Fiction: Essays in Honour of F. W. J. Hemmings* (Leicester, London and New York: Leicester University Press, 1990)

Lumbroso, Olivier and Mitterand, Henri (eds.), *Les Manuscrits et les dessins de Zola. Notes préparatoires et dessins des 'Rougon-Macquart'* (Paris: Textuel, 2002)

Mitterand, Henri, *Zola: l'histoire et la fiction* (Paris: Presses Universitaires de France, 1990)

Pierre-Gnassounou, Chantal, *Zola. Les Fortunes de la fiction* (Paris: Nathan, 1999)

Thompson, Hannah, *Naturalism Redressed: Identity and Clothing in the Novels of Emile Zola* (Oxford: Legenda, 2004)

7

SUSAN HARROW

Thérèse Raquin: animal passion and the brutality of reading

Controversy greeted *Thérèse Raquin*, Zola's major pre-Rougon-Macquart novel, when it was published in December 1867. Writing in *Le Figaro* in January 1868, 'Ferragus' (Louis Ulbach) blasted the novel as 'a pool of mud and blood' and a wholly representative example of 'the utter filth that is contemporary literature'.[1] Edmond and Jules de Goncourt, whose work encouraged Zola's interest in heredity and hysteria, countered such critical vitriol with copious praise for the novel's 'admirable autopsy of remorse'. Polemic would prove a highly effective marketing tool, stirring keen public interest and generating impressive sales figures, as Zola anticipated when he launched a vigorous self-defence in the form of a preface to the novel's second edition (April 1868). (I shall return to the preface, for this statement of naturalist intent relates in complex and ambivalent ways to Zola's narrative craft.)

Zola's earliest commercial success has become an enduringly popular novel, one that has inspired related projects in a variety of media: Zola's own stage adaptation was first performed in 1873; Jacques Feyder made a silent movie based on the novel in 1928; Marcel Carné's 1953 film adaptation with Simone Signoret became a classic; and versions for television emerged in 1965 and, in mini-series format, in 1980 and 2002. Tobias Picker's opera *Thérèse Raquin* was premiered by the Dallas Opera in 2001 and reprised by opera companies in Montreal, San Diego and London (in March 2006), and, at the time of writing, a new film version with Kate Winslet in the role of Thérèse and Judi Dench as Madame Raquin is in pre-production.

What has attracted dramatists, film-makers, librettists, composers, translators and, above all, readers?[2] First, there is Zola's potent mix of themes: feminine desire and family dysfunction, cynical passion and criminal plotting, adultery and murder, guilt and retribution, gothic horror and everyday 'naturalism'. The novel's appeal owes much to the sheer vividness of Zola's writing, which ranges from the incisive depiction of Thérèse's hysteria (inspired by the Goncourts' *Germinie Lacerteux* of 1864) to the visionary description of the hallucinations suffered by Laurent. The inexorable forward thrust of the plot takes us from the tense drama of the murder scene – the faked drowning of Camille – through the grisly 'tales from the morgue' episode, to the unflinching brutality of Laurent and Thérèse's marital relations. Zola's powerful storytelling and daring manipulations of narrative time ensure the steady escalation of plot tension that reaches its climax with the intolerable mental agony of the two culprits. The architectural rigour of Zola's composition builds from the wearing banality of *petit bourgeois* family shopkeeping, through a plot of sexual transgression and murder, to its culmination in remorse and madness, and their resolution in the double suicide of the novel's dénouement. Particularly compelling is Zola's mixing of realism and popular romance, melodrama and naturalist 'analysis', tragedy and banality, facticity and fantasy, in a novel which is more distinctively modern (equivocal, hybrid, oscillating) than one might assume from a novelist subscribing (at least in his theoretical pronouncements) to naturalist tenets.

Thérèse Raquin reveals the prodigious skills that will come to maturity in the Rougon-Macquart cycle. Zola's atmospheric description of the lugubrious Passage du Pont-Neuf betokens his evocation of the squalid tenement building of *L'Assommoir* (1877) and the miasmic courtyard of *Pot-Bouille* (1882). His dissection of characters who are cynical, predatory, terminally bored and divided against themselves offers acute insights into the mind of the human individual under extreme pressure. His analysis of Thérèse and Laurent (described by the Goncourts as 'meticulously detailed' ['fouillé']) anticipates the portraits of such complex figures as Renée Saccard (*La Curée*, 1872), the eponymous Nana (1880), and Jacques Lantier (*La Bête humaine*, 1890). Zola's *plein air* description of the Seine at Saint-Ouen (Chapter 11) unveils his powers as a creator of landscapes and a verbal colourist in thrall to the new Impressionist movement in painting. The same talent for 'visual writing' will produce shimmering descriptions of a sunset over the Bois de Boulogne in the opening pages of *La Curée* and the series of stunning depictions of Paris viewed from the heights of Passy in *Une page d'amour* (1878).

Triangular desire and the Tainean plot

Thérèse Raquin is, indisputably, a product of the intellectual and scientific climate of the 1850s and 1860s: the preface to the second edition makes clear Zola's debt to the theories of natural determinism. In particular, Hippolyte Taine's model, based on the related criteria of heredity (*race*), environment (*milieu*) and historical context (*moment*), will inform Zola's writing throughout *Les Rougon-Macquart* as the historical and fictional fresco of Napoleon III's regime is progressively constructed. Whilst the question of heredity surfaces in the analysis of Thérèse, Taine's third determinant, 'moment', is less marked here than in the subsequent Rougon-Macquart series. In *Thérèse Raquin* the characters seem somewhat abstracted from the historical context; the lugubrious arcade and the successive set-piece locations (the Morgue, the Seine at Saint-Ouen, Laurent's studio) are self-contained spaces. The absence of references to capital projects (Haussmannisation) and to the retail revolution reinforces the compelling interiority of the narrative. On the other hand, both male characters work for the railway company, and the demise of the arcade signals, indirectly, the structural shift in consumerism produced by the development of the department stores. The prime determinant of motivations and actions in the novel is environment (upbringing, family mores, social pressures). The Tainean model, focused through aspects of nurture and culture, inflects the plot of adulterous desire, and provides a framework for the tensions and complexities of the narrative.

Central to *Thérèse Raquin* is a failed project of desire founded on a variant of the romance archetype where a woman is the object of desire for two rivals: here, the female protagonist is the exasperated, resentful wife of an indifferent husband, and the object coveted by his acquisitive rival.[3] Trying to possess Thérèse – in order to acquire the benefits of domestic comfort and sexual gratification – drives Laurent, the intruder into the Raquin family, to overcome the obstacle represented by the gullible Camille, who is both Thérèse's husband (and cousin) and Laurent's present-day colleague (and his friend from their childhood in Vernon).

In Zola's reworking of the Tainean model, the differences (instinctual, attitudinal and behavioural) between the self-absorbed husband and the active, calculating lover represent the insuperable conflict of temperaments. The virile Laurent ('le sanguin') triggers the narrative action, whilst Camille ('le lymphatique') is passive and unseeing. In *Thérèse Raquin*, temperament emerges as a function, primarily, of upbringing and social environment: Camille has been mollycoddled by an indulgent and manipulative widowed mother; Laurent has been made rapacious in his desperation to escape the rural toil and poverty represented by his peasant father. The more complex Thérèse embodies the *interrelation* of environment and predisposition. The repressive atmosphere of the Raquin household has nourished in her a mixture of bitterness and apathy ('disdain and indifference' (10) ['une indifférence dédaigneuse' (36)]). In Thérèse ('la nerveuse') emotional atrophy and sexual frustration combine with a sense of proto-existentialist nausea ('she felt as if she were dropping into the clinging earth of a grave. A sense of revulsion seized her throat' (19) ['il lui sembla qu'elle descendait dans la terre grasse d'une fosse. Une sorte d'écœurement la prit à la gorge' (47)]). The tedium of Raquin family life stifles – but does not extinguish – the passionate, sensual disposition which Thérèse has inherited from her North African mother, who died when she was an infant (this 'fatal' transmission is hinted at in Chapter 2 and elaborated on by Thérèse herself in Chapter 7). The eruption of Laurent into her life acts as a catalyst for Thérèse's volatile, passionate side.

As Camille becomes an increasingly exasperating obstacle between Chapters 7 and 10, so opportunities for adultery diminish, sexual (and narrative) tension mounts, and the murderous plot is hatched. Zola stages the boating 'accident' on the Seine at Saint-Ouen (Chapter 11) in a superbly tense scene, full of false starts and taut with indecision:

> [Laurent] was going to stamp on Camille's face once and for all. Thérèse stifled a cry ... She turned her head away as if to avoid being spattered with blood. And, for a few seconds, Laurent's foot hovered above the sleeping Camille's face. Then, slowly, he brought his leg down and moved a few paces further away. He had realized that to murder him like that would be utterly stupid; if he stove in Camille's head, he would soon have the whole police force after him. (60)

> [[Laurent] allait, d'un coup, lui écraser la face. Thérèse retint un cri ... Elle tourna la tête, comme pour éviter les éclaboussures du sang. Et Laurent, pendant quelques secondes, resta, le talon en l'air, au-dessus du visage de Camille. Puis, lentement, il replia la jambe, il s'éloigna de quelques pas. Il s'était dit que ce serait là un assassinat d'imbécile. Cette tête broyée lui aurait mis toute la police sur les bras.] (105–6)

The pressure is heightened by Camille's frantic efforts to resist drowning and culminates with his decisive 'branding' of the principal culprit when he bites deep into Laurent's neck. The material elimination of Camille produces the structuring irony of the novel, for when the adulterous lovers are physically free of Camille and can marry, they find themselves unbearably more constrained by the *memory* of Camille and by the materialisation of that memory in the form of terrifying hallucinations. As the hallucinations intensify, trapping the culprits in an intersubjective hell, so the successive configurations of the defining triangular plot are fully revealed.

The original family triangle, composed of Thérèse, Camille and Madame Raquin, is challenged by the adulterous triangle (Thérèse, Camille and Laurent), which is then reconfigured as the infernal triangle (Thérèse, Laurent and the ghost of Camille), which is, in turn, supplemented by the punitive triangle (Thérèse, Laurent and Madame Raquin). The project of desire is blocked, first by a living man, then by a dead man whose memory (or ghost) haunts the guilty couple in a narrative where the sex drive and the death drive are fated to merge ('[Laurent] was constantly rushing towards Thérèse, only to come up against the corpse of Laurent' (96) ['toujours [Laurent] allait vers Thérèse, toujours il se heurtait contre le corps de Camille' (155)]). The desire of Thérèse and Laurent is destroyed finally by the probing, paralysed stare of Madame Raquin, who becomes the avenging representative of her dead son, and whose condemnation is doubled by the electrifying presence of her cat, François.[4]

Thérèse Raquin tracks the thwarted desire of each of the protagonists. The conflict originates in the family triangle where Madame Raquin's desire to preserve her authority has turned her sickly son Camille into a lethargic, egotistical individual and constrained her niece, Thérèse, in an arid marriage with Camille. Thérèse craves passion and adventure, but ends up complicit in murder, capitulating to vice, and trapped in self-contempt and hatred. Laurent thirsts for uncomplicated material and sexual satisfaction, but turns to killing, wife-beating, elder abuse, animal cruelty (he hurls the cat against the wall, breaking its spine), and – together with Thérèse – is driven to suicide by poisoning. Camille is the only character without a defining project of desire; he lacks motivation and critical insight, and is quite oblivious to the motivations of others. Yet, Camille's unreflective passivity and his own lack of desire are crucial to the desire of others: a frustrated wife, a scheming friend and a fearful, controlling mother.

How, then, does the narrative plot of *Thérèse Raquin* connect with Zola's naturalist project? To answer this, we need to consider more fully the preface to the novel's second edition, for as well as a counter-blast against charges of crudeness and obscenity, the preface presents a fragmentary manifesto of literary naturalism.

'Human beasts, no more than that' ['Brutes humaines, rien de plus'] is Zola's unequivocal definition of Thérèse and Laurent in his preface. Zola makes clear that his focus is not the psychology of his protagonists but their instincts and base passions ('their fated flesh' ['les fatalités de leur chair']). He emphasises the physiology of characters who are the product of their nerves and their blood. Explaining his novelistic intentions in the discourse of experimental objectivity, Zola affirms the importance of scientific theories of determinism to his writerly project: 'my aim was primarily scientific' ['mon but a été un but scientifique avant tout' (24)]; 'each chapter analyses a curious physiological case' ['chaque chapitre est l'étude d'un cas curieux de physiologie' (25)]; 'I simply performed the analytical work on two living bodies that pathologists typically carry out on cadavers' ['j'ai simplement fait sur deux corps vivants le travail analytique que les chirurgiens font sur des cadavres' (25)].

The careful reader is alert to the differences, contradictions even, between the programmatic position Zola asserts in the preface and his novelistic practice, infinitely more equivocal and pliant. Where Zola, in his preface, rejected explanations founded in psychology or pertaining to the 'soul', throughout their long torment Thérèse and Laurent are presented as sharing body *and* soul ('They now had but one body and one soul with which to feel pleasure and pain' (99) ['Ils eurent dès lors un seul corps et une seule âme pour jouir et pour souffrir' (159)]). Thrown together by nervous trauma, their reciprocal 'pénétration' is both physiological and psychological (160), affirms the narrator in further contradiction of the preface. Where the preface insists on heredity, the question of transmission down the bloodline recedes in the narrative as environmental pressures, combined with urges and instincts, determine plot development. These differences notwithstanding, the discourse of the preface provides a theoretical frame for the novel's powerful figurative writing as it draws on the language of the experimental sciences, and gives particular emphasis to the body as a signifying surface. Take the microscopic analysis by the narrator-turned-pathologist in Chapter 10 and the astonishing close-up vision it provides of the sweat beads appearing at the root of Thérèse's hair and the shivers traversing Laurent's skin as absurd stories of unsolved murders and miscarriages of justice are traded by the Raquins' Thursday evening guests (100). This is a thrilling and timely reminder that Zola's defining role (although he largely elides this in the preface) is that of a storyteller, a writer of fiction. It is at these crucial points that we can see most clearly how naturalist theory and narrative imperatives coincide: in the representation of the body.

The body is the site criss-crossed by the tensions between culture (social norms, family expectations) and instinct (the 'natural' self). Zola's complex study of Thérèse reveals this conflict and the resulting split persona: Her outward appearance signals docility whilst her inner self is ardent and eruptive (41). Feelings of cowardice and exasperation seethe within Thérèse in response to Laurent's entry into her grindingly tedious life. If her innate wildness is initially checked by internalised family values, her repressed sexual desire soon begins to surface in nervous gestures, twitchiness, restiveness, and alternating pallor and blushing.

Zola's vision of characters driven by brute passion translates into recurrent metaphors of animality that structure the figurative world of *Thérèse Raquin* in terms of exchanges and migrations (between human life and animality, between taming and 'unleashing', between interior and exterior). That we have entered a bestiary of instincts and drives is suggested from the beginning.

Femme-fauve

In the flashback in Chapter 2, the young Thérèse is described as having the strength of an ox, but, forced to share her cousin's invalid existence, she has been stilled. She may be anaesthetised by her upbringing in the Raquin household, but the narrator alerts us to her feline suppleness (40), her ready energy and her unpredictable passion. Lying on her stomach in the grass, the young Thérèse was 'like an animal, her black eyes wide open, her body twisted in readiness to pounce', 14 ['comme une bête, les yeux noirs et agrandis, le corps tordu, près de bondir', 41]. Her aunt has taught Thérèse to restrain her passionate temperament, but the language of controlling and taming animals (*domptage*) hints that the mastery gained over instinct is provisional and precarious. This is confirmed by her eruptions of wildness, for example, when during a mock fight, her 'sauvagerie de bête' had frightened Camille (43). As Thérèse reflects on her fractured self – her outward, 'learned' calm and her inner, instinctual turmoil – she evokes the animal passion and the urge to lash out and to bite that will energise the developing plot (75).

The animal instincts of Thérèse find their complement in the ardent, if sexually anxious Laurent, whose dark fleshiness ('nature sanguine') mesmerises her. The perspectivist subjectivity of Chapter 5 reveals Thérèse's dormant passions quickened by her perception of Laurent's animal power and sexual potency. As Thérèse contemplates hands capable of killing an ox, there is a premonitory sign of the violence that will be unleashed against Camille, and ultimately turned on Thérèse herself. At this point, the focus is on the taurine virility (58) of the first *real* man Thérèse has ever seen.

In a narrative that will focus increasingly on acute sensory perception and its distortions, it is the pungent scent of sexual allure that arouses and disturbs Thérèse (63). Aggravated rather than relieved by their first act of adultery (Chapter 6), Thérèse's surges of feline desire, stirred by male pheromones, will lead her to stalk her prey (76).[5] The fatal attraction of each for the other is expressed in the reciprocity of animal metaphors. Deprived of Thérèse's caresses for two weeks provokes a primitive need in Laurent ('une obstination d'animal affamé', 88), and his jealous urge to possess Thérèse will lead to his watching with hungry desire ('yeux fauves', 103) the swaying hips of his mistress at Saint-Ouen.

The conflict between cultural norms and instinctual behaviour surfaces quickly in the novel: in front of the Thursday guests, Thérèse and Laurent invest all their passion in a sociable handshake, but hunger to rip each other's flesh (98). This launches the biting plot that originates as a symbol of their shared desire to inflict a sexual wound, but is fated to become a nexus of erotic and punitive energy when the drowning Camille, defending himself like a stricken animal, will make his retributive rip in Laurent's flesh (Chapter 11). Already the midday sun at Saint-Ouen biting into the neck of Laurent in the build-up to the drowning prefigures Camille's actual bite, which then becomes the catalyst of a series of imaginary holes, punctures and gashes, the symptoms of Laurent's mental torture.

To be bitten is to be branded, but Laurent's guilt is not visible to society: it goes unsuspected by his friends and undetected by the authorities. His guilt is wholly internalised and, in the absence of external pressure and sanction, tension builds up on the inside ('the burning sensation in his neck' (73) ['la cuisson ardente qui le brûlait au cou' (123)]). His reproachful flesh acts as a perpetual reminder of his guilt, stressed by multiple metaphors of torture ('the cold air . . . quickened [*lit*. whipped up] his sluggish blood', 'it felt like a dozen needles slowly penetrating his skin' (73) ['l'air froid . . . fouettait son sang alourdi', 'une douzaine d'aiguilles pénétraient peu à peu dans sa chair' (123)]). This suffering on the inside prompts a crucial instance of self-viewing when Laurent inspects the bite in a mirror; the mesmeric experience is captured by the colourist, abstractive charge of Zola's description of a red hole, pink flesh, black specks, and thin streaks of blood (123). Laurent is confident that the wound will heal quickly and untraceably, but this auto-scopic assurance only feeds his desire for more body-viewing, leading him to the Morgue and the reader to some of the most audacious writing of the entire novel (Chapter 13).[6]

Laurent's obsessive visits to the Morgue are motivated by a complex need for bodily evidence: at the most basic level, he longs for the material proof that Camille is dead; he is desperate for the administrative 'closure' that a death certificate would deliver; above all, he has a strong voyeuristic instinct that is legitimated by the avid spectatorship engaged in by regular visitors to the Morgue. Body-gazing nourishes speculative fantasy in the men who treat it as a form of louche theatre, and in the women who derive a vicarious pleasure from the visual consumption of dead male flesh, the ultimate fetish (127).[7] Laurent, in turn, has his scopic desire aggravated by the sight of bloated bodies, blue-skinned cadavers, and dissolving flesh ('[The jet of water] was digging a hole to the left of the nose. All of a sudden the nose collapsed and the lips came away, showing the white teeth below' (75) ['[Le jet d'eau] creusait un trou à gauche du nez. Et, brusquement, le nez s'aplatit, les lèvres se détachèrent, montrant des dents blanches' (125)]).

When Laurent finally confronts the mass of wasting flesh that was Camille, Zola's description of dehumanised horror draws the reader into that same intense process of visualisation. A perspectival inversion of the assumed viewing subject/viewed object relation (whereby the dead Camille is staring up at Laurent) opens the way to the graphic description of decomposition that extends from the language of medicine ('[the head] showing signs of tumefaction', 'the clavicles had torn through the skin of the shoulders' ['[la tête] légèrement tuméfiée', 'les clavicules perçaient la peau des épaules' (129)]) to the nightmare detail of a blackened tongue, falling flesh, and white, protruding eyes.[8] The effect is to depersonalise and objectify the victim ('body', 'corpse'). At the same time, the 'objectivity' of the description constantly veers towards gothic horror ('the lips were twisted . . . in a horrible sneer' (78) ['les lèvres tordues . . . avaient un ricanement atroce' (129)]) as Zola combines competing styles. The Morgue scene becomes the catalyst for the series of hallucinations experienced primarily by Laurent; in these oneiric episodes the writing reaches a new figurative intensity.

Zola's compelling description of Laurent's mental torture begins in Chapter 17, some fifteen months after the murder, at the point where the culprits have determined to marry. Laurent resists returning to his garret for fear of finding someone lurking there, and the use of free indirect style reveals his struggle to quell his anxiety: 'he had never before been subject to such ridiculous imaginings' (91) ['[j]amais il n'avait été sujet à de pareilles poltronneries' (149)]. Gradually, the intensity of those fears heightens, and the close-up view of matches splitting under Laurent's agitated fingers reveals not only Zola's meticulous attention to minor detail, the hallmark of the realist or naturalist novelist, but illustrates his investment of the material world of the narrative with the pressured subjectivity of his protagonists (150).

Zola charts a mind gripped by terror and self-reproach. The disturbing play of shadows on the wall conjures up 'monstrous shapes' in Laurent's mind (92), the narratorial present tense of 'the huge, weirdly-shaped shadows which . . . always flit to and fro' (92) ['les grandes ombres bizarres qui vont et viennent' (150)] drawing the reader further into the mental world of the culprit. The obsessions crowding Laurent's mind give rise to 'spectacles réels' (152), an image founded on oxymoron, one of Zola's preferred structural and stylistic devices. Laurent's fear induces visualisation which produces more acute terror, generating new waves of hallucination. He suffers the repeated nightmare vision of making his way to the Raquin home only to be admitted by the cadaverous Camille. With imaginative force comparable to that of Baudelaire in 'Les Sept Vieillards' (1859), Zola describes Laurent spending hours gazing at the Seine, visualising a flow of drowned men as if the memory of Camille has morphed into a serial hallucination (Chapter 18).

With each chapter, Zola penetrates more deeply the mental agony of his protagonists, unfolding the very *texture* of hallucination. Astonishing descriptions recreate the visual, tactile, even acoustic dimensions of hallucination. Even when they fall silent, the culprits' exchanged gazes seem to hammer words and sentences like nails into their flesh (191); the torturing psychological presence of Camille becomes physical and tangible when his ghost comes to occupy the space between them in bed:

> They were seized by a feverish delusion which made the obstacle seem real: they could touch the body, see it stretched out there like a greenish, half-putrefied lump of meat, and smell the revolting stench given off by this mass of decomposing humanity. (133–4)

> [La fièvre, le délire les prenait, et cet obstacle devenait matériel pour eux; ils touchaient le corps, ils le voyaient étalé, pareil à un lambeau verdâtre et dissous, ils respiraient l'odeur infecte de ce tas de pourriture humaine. (205)]

Terror produces an unbearably vivid imagination and extreme sensory disturbance when sight becomes a form of hearing ('their senses were becoming distorted, their vision turning into a . . . kind of hearing' (122) ['leurs sens se faussaient, la vue devenait une sorte d'ouïe' (191)]). These migrations between the senses (synaesthesia) connect with the other exchanges (human/animal, the living/the dead, materiality/hallucination, physicality/psychology) to amplify the novel's figurative power.

Laurent had envisaged marriage with Thérèse as a means of curing his nightmares: Thérèse's (legitimate) kiss would heal (symbolically) the wound left by Camille's bite (157). By replacing Camille, Laurent assumed that he could destroy the phantom endlessly surfacing in the form of a material sensation or a mental aberration. The culprits' silent commitment to unite in wedlock is driven, not by desire, but by desperation (Chapter 23). Several premonitory clues suggest that this strategy is doomed: on the wedding day, the actual bite of Camille mutates into the 'bite' of the starched collar around Laurent's neck (180). A series of sharp pricking sensations thus acts as a fleshly reminder of his guilt as he sets off to meet his bride. As the scar becomes intermittently more vivid, standing out angrily against the white of his skin, it is as if Camille 'speaks' through the mark on Laurent's neck. The endlessly self-cloning visions (of Camille or his corpse) contrast with the collapse of Thérèse and Laurent, whose mental breakdown ('a sort of nervous crisis' (99) ['une sorte de détraquement nerveux' (159)]) pushes them to the brink of insanity, indifferentiable in the symptoms – physical and psychic – they suffer.

In contrast with Zola's prefatory insistence on physiology and pathology, the actual narrative is thus more equivocal in its evocation of the tantalising interrelation of flesh and fantasy, real and imaginary, and naturalist and gothic elements.

The brutality of reading

In the writing of *Thérèse Raquin* naturalism is integrated, and resisted. This equivocation shapes the reading experience in ways that are more modern, even modernist, than is generally assumed. Zola's drive to collapse the distinctions between reality and illusion, body and mind, and narrator and character (through free indirect style), challenges the premises of literary naturalism by rendering more complex and more equivocal – in textual practice – the defined positions and assumptions of the Preface. (Free indirect style will become a defining feature of Zola's experimentalism in *L'Assommoir* and, more generally, of the modern novel.) The will to dissolve boundaries and subvert readerly expectations are features associated with the modernist experimentalism that shaped Western literature and art from the later nineteenth century to the mid-twentieth century. Modernism is often viewed as an art of impersonality or aesthetics of dehumanisation, and the Preface deploys terms which, as they echo the intellectual currency of mid nineteenth-century scientific naturalism, also anticipate Cubism's art of dissection, and stress the analytical distance between artist and the object of composition.[9] In what precise ways, then, might the narrative reveal a proto-modernist Zola?

In terms of style and the readerly reception of the text, brutality – so central to the thematics of *Thérèse Raquin* – would appear, for Zola, to translate into an assault on normative readerly assumptions. In his 'Notes générales sur la nature de l'œuvre', Zola affirms the need for the dramatic plot 'to take the audience by the throat' ['prend[re] le public à la gorge']: ideally, the reader should be (metaphorically) destabilised or, at least, altered by the reading experience (RM v 1742–5 (p. 1744)). Zola's embrace of brutality in terms of reader reception has crucial *stylistic* implications for a text saturated in themes of menace and madness, desperation and dread. Certainly, Zola's first readers – detractors and defenders alike – experienced *Thérèse Raquin* as raw and shocking, a brutal and brutalising narrative. How does the novel achieve its 'brutal' effects for today's reader? To answer this, we must consider how readerly expectations are formed, and resisted.

Literary history and traditional academic criticism have tended to identify naturalism, an offshoot of realism, with values of explicitness, emphasis, transparency and predictability, promoted by an omniscient, consistent third-person narrator. It is a view Zola himself encourages in univocal theoretical statements like the preface. Those objectives of transparency and completeness tend to promote features perceived to be distinctly un-modern:

descriptive excess, narrative redundancy, recurrent symbolism, conspicuous plot-building.

In typical naturalist fashion, the opening chapter of *Thérèse Raquin* leads us into a world redolent with the values of the plot and the protagonists, and the narrator's vivid, present-tense evocation of the filthy Passage du Pont-Neuf is saturated in signs of sickness, death, crime and violence. The total immersion of the reader in the 'thickened' description is a stylistic analogue to the metaphorical drowning of Thérèse in the cloying Raquin milieu, and anticipates the literal immersion of Camille in the muddy waters of the Seine, just as it prefigures Sartre's vision of viscous anxiety in *La Nausée* (1939).

The portrait of family dysfunction that the reader constructs in the early chapters draws on myriad material details (of atmosphere and setting) and legible indicators of the pressures and urges that shape the protagonists' lives. Readers of Zola quickly recognise the figurative markers (symbols, metaphors, leitmotivs) whose return and development underpin a grand narrative scheme that is at once prospective and recursive, that takes us forward whilst folding in the symbolic material already revealed and transposing or transforming that material with each subsequent inflection of the plot. The metaphoric thickness of the narrative fabric encourages us to read at speed as we begin to catch and connect themes, ideas and allusions, by dint of their repetition and variation. But, if Zola's novels encourage rapid reading, they repay more patient scrutiny, for it is often in the detail that the author subverts the reader's expectations in proto-modernist ways.

Metaphoric distortions, stylistic elisions, and instances of self-reflexivity introduce a measure of productive unevenness into the smooth naturalist narrative. The novel's structuring irony (whereby the murdered man returns to stalk and destroy the perpetrators of the crime) promotes repeated local unevenness in the form of *mise en abyme*, the device that duplicates (in condensed and transposed form) a significant feature of the plot. In *Thérèse Raquin mise en abyme* is located in Laurent's attempts to paint – and subsequently to avoid painting – the portrait of Camille. Paradoxically, the dauber of crude colours produces a prophetically accurate representation of the fate of his rival and of the imminent development of the plot ('Camille's face had the greenish hue of a drowned man', 34 ['le visage de Camille ressemblait à la face verdâtre d'un noyé', 69]). The tortured features envisioned by Zola (perhaps in anticipation of Francis Bacon's visual depiction of agonised subjects) prophesy the eternal return of horror in the form of hallucination. The story of criminal drowning and its hellish aftermath is thus predicted (in the series of pictorial transpositions of the drowned Camille) before it is actualised, a technique known as prolepsis. When, subsequent to the murder, Laurent attempts to paint anything but Camille, the drowned man keeps resurfacing on the canvas, as if on the surface of the water, in a series of regressive reflections of the initial portrait; thus the character and the reader are repeatedly forced to confront the traumatic image of the victim. The proleptic duplication and retrospective reflection (analepsis) provided by the *mise en abyme* works to open up the narrative vertically, allowing us to view the plot as if mirrored in endless self-reflecting pools.

The will to enrich the linear scheme of naturalism produces such self-reflective, interiorising moments (concentrations, miniaturisations) just as, conversely, it produces expansive instances when writing rips free of its naturalist constraints, and achieves a particular figurative intensity. The raw visionary power of Zola's highly imaged writing takes us deep into the inexpressible: the putrefying vacancy of Camille's corpse. As the external world recedes, writing fills up with images of corporeal dissolution, and the body is abstracted in a swirl of colours. These visions of formlessness and dehumanisation take to a new pitch of intensity the pessimism and the nausea evoked so powerfully in the novel's opening chapter. At the same time, they betoken the visions of dystopia and alienation articulated in twentieth-century literature and art.

In the oscillations of Zola's style, the fuller moments in the narrative produced by self-reflexivity or visual (and visionary) expressivity, summon their opposite – ellipses and elisions. Thus, in Chapter 15, the narrator evokes the grief felt by Madame Raquin as she contemplates her son's empty chair. Chided by her Thursday guests, the sobbing mother reluctantly picks up her dominoes. 'The game began' (83) ['On joua' (136)]) brings this poignancy to a brutal end, the narrator's callous closure absorbing something of the cynicism of the old woman's 'friends'. In free indirect style, the feelings of the characters infiltrate the discourse of the narrator, causing the temporary collapse of the differences between the world of the characters and the world of the reader's intermediary – the normally reliable third-person narrator. Such instances of intentional indistinctness and non-differentiation challenge the naturalist claim to transparency and unequivocal iteration. Related to practices of elision and conflation is the weaving of an unresolved narrative enigma in the person of the intermittently present costume-jewellery seller whose gaze is unfathomable and unsettling for characters and reader alike. With her curious combination of banality, bizarreness and silent visual authority, she appears like a surrogate or 'plant' of the author himself, occupying a narrative level superior to that of the protagonists of the story. A Zolian precursor, perhaps, of the intriguing presence of the film-maker in Hitchcock's films?

As the mental hell of the protagonists intensifies, so the narrative structures themselves come under pressure, and the traditional differences between narrative (*histoire*) and narration (*discours*) begin to break down. Free indirect style is one form of narratorial frame-breaking; another is the collapse of distinctions between fact and fantasy, reality and hallucination, that produces the terrifying symbiosis of a material ghost (a living dead man). In Chapter 21, the phantom of Camille sits down between the culprits and the absence of a naturalising phrase like 'as if' ['comme si'] makes the image absolute, unnegotiably real ('the ghost of Camille . . . had come to seat itself between the newly-weds' (120–1) ['le spectre de Camille évoqué venait de s'asseoir entre les nouveaux époux' (188–9)]). Likewise, the evocation of the 'vanishing' frame of Camille's portrait (195), again without the use of a mediating verb like 'to appear' ['sembler'], reproduces (rather like a cinematic dissolve) the hallucinatory effect, thereby expanding the character's experience to include the reader.

Further disruption to readerly expectations comes in the form of humour, a force at once incongruous and productive in the context of the tragic plot. The high seriousness of the novel's founding themes (murder, grief, remorse, hatred, self-loathing, suicide), in the manner of a Shakespeare play, does not preclude instances of sardonic humour, farce and satire that set up local subversions of the plot-line.

The particular focus for humour is the grotesque Thursday evening coterie. In Chapter 4, the narrator debunks the characters' pretensions (and challenges the narrative's tragic intent) by drawing a wilfully ludicrous comparison between the excitement of the weekly get-togethers and a bourgeois orgy: for the Raquin family, that means staying up until 11 pm! The over-inflation of characters' positions produces similar humorously bathetic effects: when the guests resume the Thursday visits which, since the death of Camille 'had put [their visits] in great danger' (139), this view of the curtailment of a mediocre social ritual as little short of a tragedy provides an ironic counterpoint to the real tragedy to which these 'grotesque death's heads' (140) ['têtes mortes et grotesques' (214)] are oblivious.

Through instances of humour or mockery, the narrator enters into a relationship of complicity with the reader as, for example, when Laurent recounts how he took up painting for an easy life and lived off his father's money, a story which, in the words of the narrator, 'portrayed him very precisely' (my translation) ['le peignait en entier' (60)]. Such narratorial winks arrest our attention, subvert naturalism's serious intent and make us reflect on the text's potential for destabilising the values it purports to promote.

These more 'writerly' instances (*mise en abyme*, visual writing, frame-breaking, narrator–reader complicity) import moments of creative unevenness and pleasurable tension. The writerly style of *Thérèse Raquin* emerges, then, as more pliant, more hybrid and more modernist than 'reading for naturalism' traditionally admits.

* * *

This novel of violent desire and destructive remorse was to have a formative importance for the author of the embryonic Rougon-Macquart series, with its insistence on the body as a site of passion and disgust, its imaginative audacity, and its perspectival power. At the heart of *Thérèse Raquin*, the crime of passion born of exasperation and cupidity leads inexorably to the recognition that desire must have an obstacle, if it is to be sustained. The murder of Camille causes the death of desire and generates, in its place, the inextinguishable energy of hatred and self-loathing, in a novel where naturalist pressures produce unexpectedly modernist responses.

Towards the end of *Thérèse Raquin*, a fortuitous meeting leads a former artist-friend to visit Laurent's studio and view 'five studies, two female and three male heads, painted with real energy' (150) ['cinq études, deux têtes de femme et trois têtes d'homme, peintes avec une véritable énergie' (228)]. As the friend (an authorial incarnation?) marvels at the series of disturbing and singularly accomplished paintings produced by a now near-demented Laurent, his rapt contemplation of '"ces machines-là"' (228) catches the impetus of the writerly creativity and vision that will inspire the compelling modern masterpieces of *Les Rougon-Macquart*.

NOTES

1 Louis Ulbach expressed his ferocious disapproval in an article entitled 'La Littérature putride' (23 January 1868), accusing Zola of belonging to the 'the monstrous school of novelists' ['école monstrueuse de romanciers']. The article is reproduced in the Folio edition of Robert Abirached (ed.), *Thérèse Raquin* (Paris: Gallimard, 1979), from which all references to the novel are taken. The quotations which I translate here are to be found on pages 321 and 323 of the Folio edition.

2 Modern translations include Andrew Rothwell, *Thérèse Raquin* (Oxford University Press, 'Oxford World's Classics', reissued 1998). With two exceptions (see note 8), all translated extracts from the novel are sourced in Rothwell and page-referenced accordingly. Recent critical editions include Brian Nelson's for the Bristol Classical Press (1993), with preface and notes in English. Claude Schumacher's comprehensive monograph explores characters, themes, materiality and naturalism, and considers Zola's stage play (Glasgow: Glasgow Introductory Guides to French Literature, reprinted 2001).

3 René Girard, *Mensonge romantique et vérité romanesque* (Paris: Grasset, 1961), is the classic study of triangular desire and its structuring implications for the modern novel.

4 In *Les Apprentissages de Zola* (Paris: Presses Universitaires de France, 1993), pp. 324–65, Colette Becker discusses the novel's origin, its theoretical substratum,

its structure, and explores the gaze and the fantasmatic component. See also Becker, 'Zola et le mélodrame', in Robert Lethbridge and Terry Keefe (eds.), *Zola and the Craft of Fiction* (Leicester, London and New York: Leicester University Press, 1990), pp. 53–66.

5 The metaphorical 'melting' of one species into another is central to a figurative project that stresses phenomenological transformation and migration. Thérèse assumes the qualities of a cat (for her lover) whereas the real cat (François) becomes (for the culprits) ever more human-like in his role as witness and judge. Both the narrator and Thérèse use the language of animality to evoke her resurfacing passions: for example, Chapter 7 ends with her fantasising aloud that the cat might point accusingly at the lovers and denounce their adultery to the Raquins, before calling for a term of imprisonment. This humorous fantasy, naturally, chills Laurent to the bone.

6 Robert Lethbridge, 'Zola, Manet and *Thérèse Raquin*', *French Studies*, 34 (1980), 278–99, explores Zola's translation of key themes and techniques from Manet in the light of his critical appreciation of the painter.

7 This provides a forward link to *Au Bonheur des Dames*, Zola's sex-and-shopping novel of 1883, where eroticised viewing, consumption and death form an irresistible nexus.

8 I have substituted my own more literal translations here to illustrate Zola's use of the lexicon of anatomy.

9 See Guillaume Apollinaire, *Les Peintres cubistes* (1913) (Paris: Hermann, 1980).

RECOMMENDED READING

Bell, David F., '*Thérèse Raquin*: Scientific Realism in Zola's Laboratory', *Nineteenth-Century French Studies*, 24, 1–2 (Fall–Winter 1995–6), 122–32

Bloom, Michelle E., 'The Aesthetics of Guilt: Crime Scenes and Punitive Portraits in Zola's *Thérèse Raquin*', *Dalhousie French Studies*, 58 (Spring 2002), 26–38

Cousins, Russell, *Zola: 'Thérèse Raquin'* (London: Grant & Cutler, 1992)

Duboile, C. and J. Sonntag, 'De Zola à Carné. L'adaptation de *Thérèse Raquin*', *Les Cahiers naturalistes*, 75 (2001), 255–64

Knutson, Elizabeth M., 'The Natural and the Supernatural in Zola's *Thérèse Raquin*', *Symposium*, 55, 3 (Fall 2001), 140–54

Lapp, John C., 'The Novel as Drama: *Thérèse Raquin*', in *Zola before the 'Rougon-Macquart'* (Toronto: University of Toronto Press, 1964), pp. 88–120

Lethbridge, Robert, 'Zola, Manet and *Thérèse Raquin*', *French Studies*, 34 (1980), 278–99

Mitterand, Henri, 'Une anthropologie mythique: le système des personnages dans *Thérèse Raquin* et *Germinal*', in *Le Discours du roman* (Paris: Presses Universitaires de France, 1980), pp. 49–67

Walker, David, 'Writing between *fait divers* and *procès-verbal*', *French Cultural Studies*, 12 (2001), 237–51

8

VALERIE MINOGUE

Nana: the world, the flesh and the devil

When *Nana*,[1] the ninth volume in the Rougon-Macquart cycle, was published in 1880, it provoked a great deal of condemnation for its bold portrayal of sexuality. It also provoked intense interest and fascination, often for the same reason, selling 55,000 copies almost at once, and during Zola's lifetime outselling all his novels except *La Débâcle*. It would later become the subject of a number of films, of varying degrees of fidelity to the novel. Zola's alluring and terrifying heroine shares many characteristics of the man-eating Monster-Woman of decadent nineteenth-century fiction,[2] but she is a far more complex character who, as a symbol of the Second Empire, also embodies a social and political theme.

'Un sacré coup d'aile'

At the same time as he was writing *Nana*, Zola was writing his *Roman expérimental* defending the 'naturalist', quasi-scientific stance, but, carried by what Huysmans admiringly termed 'a tremendous winged thrust' ['un sacré coup d'aile' (1694)], the novel goes far beyond the naturalist 'method'. In his planning notes Zola had described the subject of this novel as 'a whole society chasing after sex. A pack of hounds following a bitch . . . *The poem of male desire*' ['toute une société se ruant sur le cul. Une meute derrière une chienne . . . *Le poème des désirs du mâle*' (1669)] – hardly the objective view of the detached observer as promulgated in naturalist theory! The animal imagery forcibly expresses the author's contempt for the society in question, while the final sentence points to the transforming impulse of Zola's exuberant poetic imagination: 'Nana', as Flaubert percipiently remarked, 'becomes mythic without ceasing to be a woman' ['Nana tourne au mythe sans cesser d'être une femme' (1667)]. Mythic indeed are Nana's exploits and career: the events and coincidences of the novel strain plausibility beyond the cracking point, and yet it works, so powerfully does Zola build his poetic monument to the lust and greed of a departed age, and the vengeful goddess-whore who helped it on its way to destruction.

Carefully researched details contribute to what Roland Barthes calls the 'effet de réel' (the reality effect), but also carry a powerful moral charge, and provide a springboard for Zola's imaginative 'leap into the stars' ['saut dans les étoiles']. Commenting on the notes that accompany Zola's preparatory explorations of the settings of his novels, Henri Mitterand notes that each observation is transformed even in the act of perception: 'Every detail ceases to be gratuitous and becomes a sign within a signifying whole' ['Chaque détail perd son caractère gratuit et devient un signe au sein d'un ensemble'].[3] Details anchor the work in a specific space and time, and from the very first page of Nana, Zola carries us into the solid reality of the Second Empire, an era already ten years in the past at the time of writing, but still painfully present to Zola's mind. It is nine o'clock in the evening in the expectant emptiness of a real theatre ('Les Variétés'). There, in his spectacular first chapter, Zola introduces not only his heroine but most of the principal characters and themes of the novel, making the theatre itself a metaphor of the age he termed 'a strange era of folly and shame' ['une étrange époque de folie et de honte' (RM i 4)], and never ceased to denounce.[4] Heavy red curtains and gilded adornment create an impression of fabulous wealth, while cracks reveal the plaster beneath. The show, La Blonde Vénus, is, in Zola's eyes, an example, like certain immensely popular works of the period, such as La Belle Hélène (put on in that same theatre), of the reckless iconoclasm of an irreverent age.[5]

Anna Coupeau/Nana

The stage is still dark and silent as Zola directs our gaze from the orchestra stalls to the upper gallery, and up to the domed and painted ceiling on which the nude figures of women and cherubs present a gas-stained parody of heaven, prefiguring the display of naked flesh in the 'cardboard Olympus' ['Olympe de carton'] on stage. Nana will make her appearance within this ordered space, to become part of the compelling order of the corrupt Second Empire regime, and part, too, of Zola's own compelling programme. For the first-night audience, she is still an unknown quantity, but she has a pre-history in Zola's fictional world, in which she was born Anna Coupeau (known as Nana) in L'Assommoir – 'a filthy past' ['un sale passé' (1127)], as Mme Lerat remarks, and one that foreshadows her future. Zola had outlined, eleven years before, in 1869, his ideas for a novel on the world of the courtesans, with the daughter of a working-class family as its prostitute heroine. Nana is that heroine, through whom he will dramatically expose the deadly effects of heredity, upbringing and the contemporary social milieu. Nana's role is, in that sense, pre-scripted. Zola's prostitute will be far removed from the sentimentalised 'fallen women' of Romantic literature and even from those presented in the spate of novels on the world of the courtesans that appeared in the 60s and 70s. Indeed, reviewing one by Achille Faure in 1866, Zola had commented: 'This novel does not present the reality of contemporary behaviour. I look forward to the true history of the *demi-monde*, if someone ever dares to write it' ['Ce roman ne présente pas les mœurs de mon temps dans leur réalité. J'attends l'histoire vraie du demi-monde, si jamais quelqu'un ose écrire cette histoire' (1659)]. Thirteen years later, Zola would be that someone.

Nana enters the novel not as a free agent but in her appointed role as the prostitute heroine planned by Zola, and in her role as Venus, a role that carries far beyond the stage, haunting her whole life and even her death. Her various sorties into other roles – as a respectable housewife with Fontan, a devoted mother with Louiset, or a romantic virgin in her idyll with Georges – inevitably fail, but she does succeed in moving up from street-walker prostitute to rich and fashionable courtesan. Nana is caught in a textual web that reflects her entrapment in a determinist net, and Zola does not allow her to write herself out of it. Indeed he does not allow her to write at all. She cannot write to Daguenet without the pen of Mme Maloir and the imagination of Mme Lerat (1130), and Fontan writes her letters to Georges Hugon (1304). The 'programming' of Nana continues throughout the novel, as she is perpetually 'written' and 'read', in a series of what Ross Chambers usefully terms 'textual mirrorings'.[6]

The 'Nana' printed in black letters on yellow on the theatre posters (1097) being read by men 'hooked' as they pass by, echoes the black on yellow cover of the 1880 Charpentier edition of Zola's novel. Nana is introduced as 'une invention de Bordenave' (1096), and oblique intertextual references remind us that she is in fact also 'une invention de Zola'. She dances, in the second act of *La Blonde Vénus*, in a dance-hall just like the one where she danced in *L'Assommoir*, and later in the novel, she and Satin will humiliate her aristocratic lover, Muffat, and his friends with their reminiscences of drunkenness and brutality in the slums, recalling Nana's laundress mother, her drunken father, and the rue de la Goutte-d'Or where she grew up.

Nana will be further 'written' in Fauchery's article, which, in terms that echo those of Zola's planning notes, presents her as 'The Golden Fly' ['La Mouche d'Or'], bred in the swamps of the Paris slums and carrying pestilence into the highest strata of society (1269). Zola mentions various readings of that article – first by Daguenet, who sees its brutal side, then by Nana, who sees it only as an extension of her fame, then by Muffat, in whom it reawakens feelings of self-disgust. In the final pages of the novel, Zola repeats in his own narrative voice (1470) the terms and message of Fauchery's article. Fauchery will 'write' Nana yet again, in his play *La Petite Duchessse*, as Géraldine the tart, though Nana will want, and disastrously try, to play the Duchess. The textual net is highlighted again when Nana reads a novel about a prostitute, indignantly rejecting it as 'filthy books of that sort, claiming to be true to life' ['cette littérature immonde, dont la prétention était de rendre la nature' (1369)] – a splendidly ironic judgment from the lips of the heroine of a novel about a prostitute which does indeed claim to be true to life. Janet Beizer has commented on the way Zola embeds such texts within his own, texts which 'precede – and therefore inevitably shape – our own reading responses', as in this instance, where Nana's reading serves effectively as an 'anti-model' for our own.[7] Nana seems constantly to generate further invention: in the last chapter, when she has left Paris, even her absence provokes rumours and stories of all sorts as she becomes a distant jewel-laden icon (1471).

The theatre

The theatrical world in which Nana makes her début is one Zola knew well. His work as a journalist, particularly as theatre critic for *Le Bien public* from April 1876, as well as his own ventures as a playwright, had taken him behind the scenes into the world of actors and actresses, contracts and managers, courtesans, costumes and sleazy backstage hangers-on. David Baguley describes the theatre of that time as one of 'unadulterated permissiveness, pleasure, and displays, where all distinctions and signs of distinction were effaced . . . to form a parodic society given over to the great leveler: sex'.[8] In Zola's hands, Nana becomes the irresistible instrument of that 'great leveler'. Two worlds meet across the footlights: the shoddy world of the theatre, and the seemingly respectable audience – the latter described, however, as 'a singularly mixed collection . . . spoiled by every kind of vice' ['[un] monde singulièrement mêlé . . . gâté par tous les vices' (1103)]. In its eager response to sexual titillation, its amused acceptance of adultery, its delight in irreverence, the audience reveals the tastes and mood of a hedonistic society, an ideal climate for the triumph of a sex symbol like Nana.

Zola's narrative camera zooms to and fro between stage and audience, offering the shifting and subjectivised perspectives characteristic of Zola's narrative art. It is Fauchery, the sophisticated and cynical Parisian journalist, who first identifies various members of the audience. Their reactions to the performance on stage are at odds with their outward propriety, while the propriety of the theatre itself is severely challenged when Bordenave insists on calling it his 'brothel'. In the audience, we see the highly respected Muffat family – Count Muffat de Beuville, chamberlain to the Empress, his wife the Countess Sabine, and his father-in-law, the Marquis de Chouard, a 'Conseiller d'Etat' [member of the Council of State]. Their respectability soon becomes questionable when, at the end of the show, we see the mottled face of Muffat, flushed and open-mouthed, and the Marquis with eyes gleaming like a cat (1119). Their image is further dented in the second chapter, when they pay a visit to Nana – under cover of collecting for charity! The backstage world is not without its own duplicities: the husband of the actress Rose Mignon, even while pimping for his wife, indignantly deplores the immorality of the theatre (1109) – a blatant hypocrisy that makes Fauchery smile, a smile indicative of the easy acceptance of vice and corruption in this society.

Zola builds up the anticipation of audience and reader alike, delaying the appearance of the new star whose name – a name 'as much a force of contagion as her body will become', as Janet Beizer puts it[9] – is persistently repeated as the audience grows ever more impatient. When Nana finally appears on stage, she provokes sharp intakes of breath, making hairs bristle and muscles tense as a gale of lust sweeps through the audience. Zola offers no access here to Nana's inwardness: she is an object of the (predominantly male) gaze, herself seeming to express – by her body-language – only amused awareness of her artistic shortcomings, along with total assurance in her 'something else' ['autre chose'], the sexuality that drives the audience to a point of frenzy when, in the third act, she appears draped only in a flimsy veil that emphasises her (almost) nakedness.[10]

Nana's body is such that Bordenave has total confidence in her success, despite her lack of talent: 'by God, yes, she'll go far . . . Such skin, oh, such skin! ['sacredié! oui, elle ira loin . . . Une peau, oh! une peau!' (1098)], he exclaims, and he is right. With one swing of the hips she revolutionises the theatre audience. She has an irresistible animal quality, underlined by the 'golden mane' ['toison d'or'] at the nape of her neck, and she dominates the theatre, 'with her marble-smooth flesh, and her sex powerful enough to destroy all these people, without any damage to herself' ['avec sa chair de marbre, son sexe assez fort pour détruire tout ce monde et n'en être pas entamé' (1120)]. She cannot act and cannot sing, but at the end of the show, it is Nana's song, 'When Venus prowls at night' ['Lorsque Vénus rôde le soir'], that is carried out into the streets of Paris, where the prostitute Satin finds an immediate client in the theatre crowd. Nana's sexual power will carry her, along with her provocative waltz, from the theatre into the elegant drawing rooms of the topmost reaches of society in a headlong course of destruction, as her lovers ruin themselves one after another.

Count Vandeuvres, last scion of a noble family, will throw away a vast fortune along with his honour, cheating at the races and finally killing himself and his horses in the same appalling blaze. The banker, Steiner, wastes a fortune on Nana, and Zola points to the dark underside of Steiner's squandered opulence, when he refers to the coal-begrimed workers in Steiner's foundry, who toil and sweat to provide for Nana's pleasures (1455). From the moment the 'cherub' in the audience, who turns out to be Georges Hugon, responds to Nana with a cry of 'Très chic', the collapse of the Hugon family begins, leading to Georges' death, the disgrace and imprisonment of his brother, and the tragic despair of his mother. The Muffat family is swept along in a current of degradation, while the government, with which so many of these people are closely associated, takes them all further along towards destruction in voting for the disastrous war with Prussia.

At the races

That first spectacular scene in the theatre is balanced much later in the novel by another grand 'set piece' at the Longchamp racecourse, where Zola again brings together most of the principal characters, with Nana at the centre of a throng of admirers, and Muffat in the Imperial box alongside the Empress. Zola is again dealing with a scene he knows well. He had previously written on the races at Longchamp in 1872, again in 1876,[11] and he returned to the Grand Prix in June 1879 to renew his impressions for this scene of the novel. His narrative moves like a ciné camera between vast panoramic views and detailed close-ups, as he describes the changing sky, the lavish costumes, the flow of carriages and people, the glitter of harness, the gestures of the bookies, the gleam of grass in the sunshine after a shower. We hear the hubbub of the crowd, the cracking of whips, the thunder of horses' hooves. The scene is not only vividly descriptive, but also, as in the first chapter, forcefully interpretive: the crowd's frantic roar as the horses gallop by becomes 'the ultimate brutality of a colossal game' ['la brutalité dernière d'une colossale partie' (1403)], exemplifying the Second Empire's reckless pursuit of pleasure, while the fraudulent success of 'Nana' the horse, and the social success of Nana the prostitute, together mark the triumph of vice. Nana lords it over the crowds at the racecourse, just as she had dominated the audience in the theatre, and it is Nana, 'la reine Vénus', who responds to the cheers of the crowd, raising her glass in the victorious pose she had struck on stage (1390). And whereas, in the theatre, Nana was the object on whom the opera-glasses were focused, here Nana trains *her* opera-glasses on the crowd, and even on the Imperial box. Deriding the ill-dressed women in the exclusive weighing enclosure and commenting, with intimate details, on the body of the royal prince beside the Empress (1387), the Nana who stripped for the theatre audience now metaphorically strips the audience.[12]

Patterning

The sheer energy of Zola's writing creates an impression of artlessness, but the echoing and part-inversion at Longchamp of the initial scene in the the-atre is typical of the elaborate patterning that marks this densely rich text: public scenes alternate with private, city with country, *demi-monde* with aristocracy. The visit of Muffat and Chouard to Nana's apartment marks the beginning of a progressive intermingling of the two social worlds. If the decorous atmosphere of the Muffat salon is infiltrated by talk of Nana's party, Nana's far from decorous party in the next chapter includes individu-als, and even topics of conversation, from the Muffat world. In the country, the scene shifts to and fro between Nana's establishment at La Mignotte and the respectable Hugon household at Les Fondettes, providing the occasion for some telling, and at times harshly ironic, humour, as Mme Hugon mar-vels at the surprising influx of visitors from Paris (1240). In this world of hypocrisy and illusion, a good deal of ironic humour arises from the gap between appearance and reality: Nana, trying to play the part of a duchess, walks like a fat hen trying not to get her feet dirty (1336), and the aristo-cratic Muffat imitates her imitation, holding a giant egg-cup in his hand (1341). Mignon's pimping for his wife contrasts sharply with his unremit-tingly edifying discourse to his sons, while the severely sententious opinings of Chouard scarcely chime with his degenerate activities. The *demi-monde* and the world of high society, at first seeming quite distinct, become less and less distinguishable as the infection of Nana spreads.

In his *Ebauche* for the novel, Zola described Nana as 'the central flesh' ['la chair centrale' (1670)], but he has made of her much more than flesh. She is the very substance and life-force of the novel, source and centre of every scene. On stage her flesh indeed dominates, but in the warmth of her kitchen with Mme Lerat, Mme Maloir and Zoé, Zola allows some access into Nana's reactions and reflections – reactions sometimes trivial, like her annoyance at the way Mme Maloir has ruined the hat she had given her, or her superstitious vexation at the crossing of two knives on the table, sometimes more telling, like her delight at the prospect of a whole night to herself (1144).

Nana/Venus

Nana's role as Venus becomes a leitmotiv, underlining her quasi-supernatural sexual power. The names 'Nana' and 'Venus' sometimes alternate sugges-tively, as when 'Nana' drops a make-up brush, but it is the hair of 'Venus' that rolls (with considerable effect!) over Muffat's hand when he stoops to help her retrieve it (1214). The men pursuing Nana are seen as 'following the scent of Venus' ['suivant à la trace Vénus' (1241)] in an image that perpetuates the animal quality suggested by her golden mane, and reinforced by her later identification with the filly at Longchamp. The waltz from 'La Blonde Vénus' accompanies Nana like her scent, carrying in an immaterial, invisible form, the irresistible power of her physical presence. When she attends the Muffat ball, she permeates the whole house with her music and her scent: 'Nana, invisible, spread above the dance-floor with her supple limbs, was corrupting this whole society, penetrating it with the ferment of her scent floating in the warm air, and over the provocative rhythm of the music' ['Nana, invisible, épandue au-dessus du bal avec ses membres souples, décomposait ce monde, le pénétrait du ferment de son odeur flottant dans l'air chaud, sur le rythme canaille de la musique' (1430)].

As Woman the Temptress, Nana is contrasted with Woman as Mother. Mme Hugon, representative of a social and biological order that Nana threatens, is the mother of two sons Nana will destroy. Nana is also a mother, but her child Louiset will die, and she miscarries another. She has bouts of maternal concern, but they do not last long. When she learns she is pregnant, her reaction is one of indignation at Nature's exasperating interference in her affairs: 'It seemed to her a ridiculous accident, a thing that diminished her, made her a laughing-stock' ['Cela lui semblait un accident ridicule, quelque chose qui la diminuait et dont on l'aurait plaisantée' (1411)]. Then, in a characteristic slide from the language of narrative to the language of the character, Zola gives us Nana's own thoughts in free indirect speech: 'Eh? Some joke! Such rotten luck, really!' ['Hein? La mauvaise blague! pas de veine, vraiment!']. Again in the mode of free indirect speech, Nana impatiently asks: 'Shouldn't one be able to do as one likes without all this fuss and bother? Anyway, where did it drop from, this brat?' ['Est-ce qu'on aurait pas dû disposer de soi à sa fantaisie, sans tant d'histoires? Ainsi, d'où tombait-il, ce mioche?' (1412)]. Zola's use of such shifts of language and perspective allow him to move, as if by a surge of empathy, right into his character to find, from the inside, the appropriate movements, gestures and language. Such moments of access into the quick of Nana's feelings greatly contribute to the vitality and credibility of a character who might otherwise be totally overshadowed by the sexual force she represents. From the first scene in the theatre, Zola presents that sexual power as capable of destroying a whole society without any damage to itself, and in the early chapters, sex for Nana seems a weapon and a marketable commodity she can use at will to pay her creditors or satisfy her whims. In the course of the novel, however, it is as if she becomes infected with her own virus as her sexuality becomes progressively more demanding and depraved.

Narcissism/lesbianism

Nana's narcissism is made graphically clear in the startling episode where she gazes rapturously at herself in the mirror, swaying erotically, stroking and kissing her body, watched by a Muffat both fascinated and horrified. Even here, Nana in her velvet skin is not quite naked, covered as she is by her animal-like down of red-gold hair, and veiled by male desire, fear and fantasy. Nana revives Muffat's old horror of Woman as 'the monster of the Scriptures' ['[le] monstre de l'Ecriture' (1271)], 'the golden beast, mindless as a force of Nature, its very smell corrupting' ['la bête d'or, inconsciente comme une force, et dont l'odeur seule gâtait le monde' (1271)]. In a frenzy of mingled frustration and lust, Muffat throws her to the floor and brutally makes love to her. This she accepts, calculating that Muffat will now be willing to leave, but he lingers on, and the scene ends with an impatient Nana telling him his wife is deceiving him. When she sees how extremely badly Muffat takes this revelation, she feels 'un regret mortel' (1276), but she goes on to suggest that she and Sabine are now on an equal footing. Muffat reacts with the fury of one for whom the distance between the two women is essential to the social order, but Zola subverts that 'order' when the naked Nana shockingly arouses in Muffat a vision of a naked Sabine (1278).

A new element in Nana's sexuality enters the novel very discreetly in the first chapter in the figure of Satin, with her pure blue eyes and virginal face. Identified at once by Fauchery as 'a trollop' ['une rouleuse'], she seems at first a very minor character, but she is an old acquaintance of Nana's, and during Nana's time with Fontan, the two women grow close, comforting each other and sharing confidences about their experience of 'the filthiness of men' ['la saleté des hommes' (1298)]. Satin takes Nana to the lesbian restaurant, 'Chez Laure' (1300–1), where Nana at first is uncomprehending and rather repelled, though tolerant. Satin will eventually seduce her, and will become her vice and obsession. Nana's lesbianism seems a natural progression from her narcissism, a reaction against the incessant demands of men and, as Brian Nelson suggests, 'a total rejection of the patriarchal structure of power',[13] in a society ruled by and for men, and regulated by the power of the police, so feared by Nana as 'the vengeance of men' ['cette vengeance des hommes' (1315)]. When finally sated with luxury, and bored, Nana becomes indiscriminately promiscuous, picking up both men and girls from the streets, and, aping the transvestism that earlier baffled her in the lesbian restaurant, dressing as a man to visit the most sordidly depraved entertainments (1453).

'Bonne fille'

Despite the damage she does, Zola repeatedly suggests that there is enough of the natural and the child-like in Nana to allow one to wonder whether in another environment, in a different age, her story might have been different. A sudden longing for countryside and fresh air takes her, with 'a childish delight' ['une joie d'enfant'] to the Bois de Boulogne after her party to drink fresh milk (1193–4), and her first taste of real countryside at La Mignotte totally enchants her as she trudges through the mud, admiring the cabbages and picking strawberries in the rain. Through such bursts of enthusiasm Zola offers a glimpse of a Nana that might have been. The combination of the countryside, the moonlight, bird-song and the naive adoration of the young Georges Hugon, carries her away into a world of romance and blushing adolescence, in which she falls into Georges' arms like the virgin she has long ceased to be (1239). The whole episode with Georges has something of the idyll about it, but it is seriously compromised by elements of narcissism, transvestism and even incest. Nana dresses Georges in her own clothes,[14] and calling him 'bébé', seems to confuse her baby and her lover (1245). Even so, when we read: 'Lord! She could have wept, so good, so really nice, it all seemed' and 'Surely she had been meant to live a decent life' ['Mon Dieu! elle aurait pleuré, tant ça lui paraissait bon et gentil!' and 'Bien sûr qu'elle était née pour vivre sage' (1239)], it is difficult not to feel sympathy for one who has had so little opportunity or hope of a decent life. As a man-eater, Nana is powerfully destructive, but if she is a scourge, she is also a victim, condemned by her heredity, her upbringing, and the age she lives in, an age that has offered her nothing but the possibility of exploiting the only resources she has, her body and her sexuality.

Nana's moments of longing for a better life do not, of course, sit well with her incessant greed for money, luxuries and prestige, but they are intimations of the residual 'bonne fille' in Nana that Zola stresses again and again (1335, 1350, 1366, 1368, 1389, 1432), underlining her lack of malice. Even when the bedroom games with Muffat have become increasingly tyrannical and savage, Zola still assures the reader that it was more a shared madness than cruelty on her part, 'for she was still a good-natured girl' ['car elle demeurait bonne fille' (1460)]. There is some contradiction here, for Zola earlier remarks on Nana's increasingly savage demands for money, and her cruelty in insisting to Muffat that she slept with him only for his money (1450). But contradiction is a basic feature of Nana's character, one moment demanding respect for her squalid family background (1366), and the next, dismissing the lower classes as 'a fine load of rubbish' ['une jolie ordure' (1369)]. She is, after all, very young,[15] and she moves with the volatility of a child from pique and petulance to tenderness, generosity, or tantrums of mindless destruction (1436).

Nana herself believes in her good nature and accepts no responsibility for the disasters she provokes. Even when Georges Hugon has tried to kill himself and his brother is in prison for stealing money for her, she complains: 'People come to me and do stupid things, they hurt and upset me, and I get treated like a scoundrel' ['On vient faire des bêtises chez moi, on me cause de la peine, on me traite comme une coquine' (1446)]. Nana will later expostulate again on what she sees as the general injustice of things: 'God Almighty! It's not fair! This world is all upside-down. It's men who demand things, but women get the blame . . . !' ['Nom de Dieu! Ce n'est pas juste! la société est mal faite. On tombe sur les femmes, quand ce sont les hommes qui exigent des choses . . . ! (1469)]. For all Nana's faults, there is some justice in that cry. Even at the end of the novel, after her long trail of destruction, Zola reminds us that 'she still retained the heedlessness of a superb animal, unmindful of what it has done, still the good-natured girl' ['elle gardait son inconscience de bête superbe, ignorante de sa besogne, bonne fille toujours' (1470)], but a girl who has nevertheless 'avenged her own people' ['vengé son monde' (1470)] for the misery of the slums.

Religion, sin, the devil

Through Muffat and his like, Zola indicates the fragility of the traditional social and moral values of the *ancien régime* which tolerated that misery, and suggests the inadequacy, even the culpability, of their religious traditions.[16] Muffat is the product of an upbringing dominated by religion and starved of affection; he still recalls the chill of his mother's goodnight kiss (1213), and lives with the constant fear of sin, hell and eternal damnation. His relations with his wife are characterised by the coldness and propriety fostered by his repressive religious education. Small wonder then that Nana awakens in him 'a greedy adolescent puberty, suddenly aflame in the chill of his Catholic education and the dignity of his maturity' ['une puberté goulue d'adolescent, brûlant tout à coup dans sa froideur de catholique et dans sa dignité d'homme mûr' (1227)]. Although his religion makes him see Nana as the devil, the epitome of Sin, Muffat cannot resist her temptation. She replaces for him the only voluptuous feelings he has ever known – the ecstasy of religious adoration, which the materialist Zola sees as an unrecognised sublimation of sensuality and sexuality.

Nana's 'religion' is a mixture of fear and superstition; she too can be troubled by 'childish fears' of death and Hell – even in Georges' arms (1244, 1247) – and feeling unwell just before her miscarriage, she asks Muffat: 'do you think I'll go to heaven?' ['penses-tu que j'irai au ciel?']. Such questions painfully prick Muffat's Catholic conscience, while Nana sobs: 'I'm afraid of dying, afraid of dying' ['J'ai peur de mourir, j'ai peur de mourir' (1410)]. She hopes her medal of the Virgin may protect her, but she has been taught that women like her will inevitably go to Hell. As her fear grows, she inspects her face in the mirror in a cruel echo of the earlier mirror-scene of self-adoration, and pulling her face into the semblance of a death mask, she provokes in Muffat a terrifying vision of what she might look like when long dead (1411).

In the penultimate chapter, Nana subjects Muffat to the most demeaning humiliations, the final and worst being his discovery of her on her magnificent bed, displaying her royal limbs like a goddess, with, beside her, the decrepit and skeletal figure of Muffat's father-in-law, Chouard, withered by sixty years of debauchery – 'a corner of the charnel-house amid the glories of the woman's radiant flesh' ['un coin de charnier dans la gloire des chairs éclatantes de la femme']. In despair, Muffat returns to his religion, now finding in the fervour of prayer what seems like a continuation of his love affair, 'his former pleasures, the spasms of his muscles, the delightful disturbances of his brain, and the same gratification of obscure desires of his being' ['ses jouissances d'autrefois, les spasmes de ses muscles et les ébranlements délicieux de son intelligence, dans une même satisfaction des obscurs besoins de son être' (1465)].

Thematic patterns

The progressive corruption of the aristocracy, as represented by the Muffat family, is first imaged in the physical resemblance of Nana and Sabine, and the mole on both their faces, but this becomes a moral resemblance as their lifestyles grow more and more similar, with Sabine finally running off with a department-store employee. The Muffat house, with its sombre aspect and closed shutters, is at first quite unlike the sensuality of Nana's surroundings, but in the Muffat salon, Sabine's red armchair strikes one discordant note (1144), a jarring redness that will spread 'until it fills the whole house with a lazy voluptuousness' ['jusqu'à emplir l'hôtel entier d'une voluptueuse paresse' (1420)], and this in turn will lead to a metaphoric 'final blaze' ['flambée dernière' (1429)], in which the house and its last vestiges of honour would be destroyed. The thematic pattern is sustained with another fire in the final chapter, when people with torches are marching in the streets, chanting 'A Berlin! à Berlin! à Berlin!' in the prelude to the Franco-Prussian War. Of these torches Zola makes a conflagration: 'a glow appeared from the direction of the Madeleine, cutting across the mass of people in a trail of fire, spreading over their heads like a sheet of flame' ['une lueur venait de la Madeleine, coupait la cohue d'une traînée de feu, s'étalait au loin sur les têtes comme une nappe d'incendie' (1473)]. From a mole on the face of two women and a discordant note in the furniture of a salon, Zola carries the reader along in a series of images and metaphors to an anticipation of the burning of Paris (later described in *La Débâcle*), and the destruction of a whole society.

Majesty

Underlying Zola's presentation of France in the Second Empire is the pattern of a larger theme that runs throughout the Rougon-Macquart novels: the potential majesty of a humanity everywhere corrupted and degraded.[17] The theme surfaces in *Nana* in the mockery of majesty in *La Blonde Vénus*, and is perpetuated by Nana as 'la reine Vénus' in her life off stage. When the royal prince visits Nana in the theatre, the narrative comments incisively on this heir to a royal throne hobnobbing with actors masquerading as gods and royalty (1210). Vice and degradation are everywhere, in prostitutes and princes alike. Images of royalty are threaded through Nana's life. The once famous prostitute, Irma d'Anglars, glimpsed coming out of church at Chamont, with her queenly majesty (1256) becomes a focal point for Nana, but Zola balances this picture with another, also of a former celebrated prostitute, Queen Pomaré ['la reine Pomaré'], now a down-and-out drunken rag-picker. She too, 'a queen fallen into the gutter' ['une reine tombée dans la crotte' (1374–5)], becomes an emblematic figure for Nana, and the two 'queens' come together in her mind: 'And seeing this hideous drink-sodden old whore, Nana, suddenly remembering, saw far off in the dark, the vision of Chamont, Irma d'Anglars, the former prostitute, laden with years and honours' ['Nana, devant cette vieillesse affreuse de fille noyée dans le vin, eut un brusque souvenir, vit passer au fond des ténèbres la vision de Chamont, cette Irma d'Anglars, cette ancienne roulure comblée d'ans et d'honneurs' (1375)]. The two queen figures are polarities of Nana's imagination, her dream of being raised to majesty and respect, and her terror of ending up in the gutter like Queen Pomaré, whose ravaged face anticipates, indeed, the horror of Nana's face in the final chapter.

Some critics have seen Nana, and in particular the horror of Nana's death, as an expression of patriarchal misogyny on Zola's part, punishing Nana for her seeming revolt against male domination, her narcissism, her lesbianism, and the sexual supremacy by which she remains, to borrow Brian Nelson's useful term, a 'virgin/whore',[18] ultimately and essentially impenetrable, with her 'marble flesh' ['chair de marbre']. Even at the end of the novel, just before Nana leaves Paris, we see her all dressed up, 'clean and strong, looking fresh and new, as if untouched' ['propre, solide, l'air tout neuf, comme si elle n'avait pas servi' (1470)]. The 'punishment' of Nana is severe: what had been 'radiant flesh' becomes 'a charnel-house, a heap of lymph and blood, a shovelful of mouldering flesh' ['un charnier, un tas d'humeur et de sang, une pelletée de chair corrompue' (1485)]. But the punishment is mitigated in various ways.

Zola shows more sympathy with Nana and women in general than is often granted him: if he denounces loose women for their exploitation of men, he also castigates the patriarchal Establishment that fosters them, and the undisciplined 'masculine lusts' ['désirs du mâle'] that make men so readily exploitable. Women play an important part in Nana's life from the beginning, when we meet the three women who make up her household. When Zoé at last decides to leave her, Nana is devastated. Her friendship, then love affair, with Satin no doubt represents a symptom of decadence, a concretisation of Nana's depravity, but it begins as mutual comfort, when both have been cruelly ill-used by men.[19] After all the vicissitudes of their relationship, when Nana learns that Satin is dying, she remembers her love, and rushes to the hospital. There is a good deal of female camaraderie among the women of the theatre; they attend Nana's parties in Paris, and visit her in the country. At the end, it is Rose Mignon who goes to Nana's rescue, and takes her to the Grand Hotel, and it is these same women who, despite their former rivalries and enmities, and despite the danger of infection, gather round Nana's death-bed, while the men, including Muffat, remain in the street below, out of harm's way.

The narrative describes all the horror of Nana's disfigurement as she dies of the smallpox caught from her sadly neglected son but, with what it is tempting to see as a last compassionate gesture, Zola allows her friends to remember her in her role as Mélusine, the legendary fairy, her beautiful body gleaming in the air, in a sparkling crystal grotto. And above Nana's hideous and suppurating face, Zola shows her hair in all its beauty, like a funeral pyre: 'the beautiful hair, still blazing with solar radiance, streamed down like a river of gold' ['les beaux cheveux, gardant leur flambée de soleil, coulaient en un ruissellement d'or' (1485)]. That final solar blaze is the last of the fires that spread from Nana's 'golden mane' and from Sabine's red chair, to destroy the world they both inhabit and corrupt. With Nana/Venus left alone in the empty room at the end, echoing the empty theatre of the beginning, the crowds outside march along, shouting 'A Berlin!', their torches flaming in the night, heralding the coming of war and France's ignominious defeat at Sedan. The end of Nana is also the end of the Second Empire.

NOTES

1 All references (in parenthesis in the text) to *Nana* and Zola's associated notes are to volume II of *Les Rougon-Macquart*, ed. Henri Mitterand, 5 vols. (Paris: Gallimard, 'Bibliothèque de la Pléiade', 1960–7).

2 See Laurence M. Porter, 'Decadence and the *fin-de-siècle* Novel', in Timothy Unwin (ed.), *The Cambridge Companion to the French Novel from 1800 to the Present* (Cambridge: Cambridge University Press, 1997), pp. 93–110.

3 Henri Mitterand, *Le Regard et le signe* (Paris: Presses Universitaires de France, 1987), p. 72.

4 See Henri Mitterand's magisterial essay, 'Zola, "ce rêveur définitif"', *Australian Journal of French Studies*, 38, 3 (2001), 321–35 (p. 333).

5 See David Baguley's comments on the opera bouffe in *Napoleon III and His Regime: An Extravaganza* (Baton Rouge: Louisiana State University Press, 2000), p. 327.

6 Ross Chambers, *Story and Situation: Narrative Seduction and the Power of Fiction* (Manchester: Manchester University Press, 1984), p. 28.

7 Janet Beizer, '*Au* (delà du) *Bonheur des Dames*', *Australian Journal of French Studies*, 38, 3 (2001), 393–406 (p. 399).

8 *Napoleon III*, p. 307.

9 Beizer, 'Uncovering *Nana*: The Courtesan's New Clothes', *L'Esprit créateur*, 25, 2 (Summer 1985), 45–56 (p. 47).

10 Nana's body and her never-total nudity have been much debated and discussed – see especially Chapter 7, 'Decomposing Venus', pp. 200–33, esp. p. 223, in Charles Bernheimer, *Figures of Ill Repute: Representing Prostitution in Nineteenth-Century France* (Cambridge, Mass. and London: Harvard University Press, 1989); 'Uncovering *Nana*'; Peter Brooks, 'Nana at Last Unveil'd? Problems of the Modern Nude', in *Body Work: Objects of Desire in Modern Narrative* (Cambridge, Mass.: Harvard University Press, 1993), pp. 123–61; Brian Nelson, '*Nana*: Uses of the Female Body', *Australian Journal of French Studies*, 38, 3 (2001), 407–29; Hannah Thompson, *Naturalism Redressed: Identity and Clothing in the Novels of Emile Zola* (Oxford: Legenda, 2004).

11 Zola's graphic account of the Grand Prix de Paris for the *Sémaphore de Marseille* in 1876 is reproduced by Henri Mitterand (RM ii 1662–3).

12 See Valerie Minogue, 'Venus Observing – Venus Observed: Zola's *Nana*', in Patrick Pollard (ed.), *The Emile Zola Centenary Colloquium 1893–1993* (London: The Emile Zola Society, 1995), pp. 57–72.

13 '*Nana*: Uses', p. 412.

14 See *Naturalism Redressed*, pp. 111–16, for an analysis of this episode.

15 Inconsistencies surround Nana's date of birth, thanks to the Empire's collapse in 1870. Zola had to fudge some dates in order to fit events within the frame of the Second Empire, but he makes Nana eighteen when she appears on stage (1107).

16 Part of what Mitterand ('Zola, "ce rêveur"', p. 329) terms Zola's 'endless battle with the Church's discourse'.

17 See Michel Butor, 'Zola's Blue Flame', in David Baguley (ed.), *Critical Essays on Emile Zola* (Boston, Mass.: G. K. Hall & Co., 1986), pp. 101–10.
18 'Nana: Uses', 409.
19 Naomi Schor, *Zola's Crowds* (Baltimore and London: Johns Hopkins University Press, 1978), p. 91.

RECOMMENDED READING

Baguley, David, 'Zola, the Novelist(s)', in Robert Lethbridge and Terry Keefe (eds.), *Zola and the Craft of Fiction* (Leicester, London and New York: Leicester University Press, 1990), pp. 15–27 (esp. pp. 22–5)
Beizer, Janet, 'Uncovering *Nana*: The Courtesan's New Clothes', *L'Esprit créateur*, 25, 2 (Summer 1985), 45–56
Bernheimer, Charles, 'Decomposing Venus', in *Figures of Ill Repute: Representing Prostitution in Nineteenth-Century France* (Cambridge, Mass., and London: Harvard University Press, 1989), pp. 200–33
Brooks, Peter, 'Nana at Last Unveil'd? Problems of the Modern Nude', in *Body Work: Objects of Desire in Modern Narrative* (Cambridge, Mass.: Harvard University Press, 1993), pp. 123–61
Chitnis, Bernice, *Reflecting on 'Nana'* (London: Routledge, 1991)
Cousins, Russell, 'Zola's Shifting Narrative Perspectives: The Challenge to the Film-Maker', *Bulletin of the Emile Zola Society*, 23 (April 2001), 24–31
Griffiths, Kate, 'The Haunted Mirrors of Emile Zola and Guy de Maupassant', *Bulletin of the Emile Zola Society*, 26 (October 2002), 3–13
James, Henry, '*Nana*' (1880) and 'Emile Zola' (1903), in Leon Edel (ed.), *The House of Fiction* (London: Hart-Davis, 1957), pp. 274–80 and 220–49
Little, Rebecca, 'Sexual Politics: Towards a Feminist Interpretation of Christian Jaque's *Nana*', *Bulletin of the Emile Zola Society*, 19 (March 1999), 3–14
Minogue, Valerie, 'James's Lady and Zola's Whore: The Inscription of the Heroine in the Text in *The Portrait of a Lady* and *Nana*', in Brian Nelson (ed.), *Naturalism in the European Novel* (Oxford/New York: Berg, 1992), pp. 245–64
'Venus Observing – Venus Observed: Zola's *Nana*', in Patrick Pollard (ed.), *The Emile Zola Centenary Colloquium 1893–1993* (London: The Emile Zola Society, 1995), pp. 57–72
Nelson, Brian, '*Nana*: Uses of the Female Body', *Australian Journal of French Studies*, 38, 3 (2001), 407–29
Schor, Naomi, 'Polarization', in *Zola's Crowds* (Baltimore and London: Johns Hopkins University Press, 1978), pp. 83–131
Thompson, Hannah, *Naturalism Redressed: Identity and Clothing in the Novels of Emile Zola* (Oxford: Legenda, 2004)

9

DAVID BAGULEY

Germinal: the gathering storm

Ever alert to the differences between Balzac and himself as a measure of his own originality, the young Zola wrote in an article in *Le Rappel* (13 May 1870) that there is no place for the people in Balzac's works, but, he added, the reader can hear in the distance 'the great absent voice . . . the muted surge of the people ready to burst forth into political life, into sovereignty' ['la voix du grand absent . . . la sourde poussée du peuple qui va jaillir à la vie politique, à la souveraineté']. To some degree *L'Assommoir* filled the gap, but the novel of Gervaise Macquart's fate contains no hint of the political aspirations and potential of the working classes. By the early 1880s, however, Zola had included in his plan for the Rougon-Macquart series a second novel about the people, which would deal directly with the political activities of Parisian workers and culminate in the Commune. But, in the developing political climate of the early years of the Third Republic and as the Commune faded into history, the workers' movement came to be a more relevant form of social protest than insurrection and the strike a more topical means of revolt than the barricade. By early 1884, as Edmond de Goncourt noted in his *Journal* (16 January), Zola was thinking of writing a novel about a strike in a mining district and with it a 'profound study of the social question'. The Commune would have to wait until *La Débâcle* (1892), where it is presented as a sequel to the depiction of the Battle of Sedan and the fall of the Second Empire.

In a remarkably short period of time, Zola conceived, planned and prepared his new novel, which he began writing on 2 April 1884.[1] He had never had any direct experience of the mining industry, but, as an opposition journalist during the last months of the Second Empire, he had witnessed the industrial unrest that rocked the regime in its so-called 'liberal' phase. Two bloody incidents stand out: on 16 June 1869 at La Ricamarie in the coal basin of Saint-Etienne, troops fired on striking workers, killing thirteen, including a pregnant woman and a child of seventeen months, and wounding nine; on 7 October of the same year, a similar confrontation at Aubin in the Aveyron left fourteen dead and twenty wounded, when troops with their backs to a wall opened fire on workers who were throwing stones at them. As the radical journalist Henri Rochefort wrote with bitter irony (in *Le Rappel*, 16 October 1869), alluding to an early socialist tract by Louis-Napoléon, the future Emperor (*L'Extinction du paupérisme*, 1844): 'The Empire continues making poverty extinct. Twenty-seven dead and forty wounded, that takes care of a few more poor people!' ['L'Empire continue à éteindre le paupérisme. Vingt-sept morts et quarante blessés, voilà encore quelques pauvres de moins!']

Beyond naturalism

In depicting in all their grim reality the life and strife of the miners of Montsou, *Germinal* is consistent with the naturalist's practice of representing cruel and shameful features of the contemporary world and showing human beings shaped by their environment and motivated by instinctual impulses, by what Zola called the 'fatalities of the flesh'. We see how the miners of Montsou have been formed and deformed by decades of grinding toil in inhuman working conditions, barely subsisting on the meagre rations that they can hardly afford. But, for all its naturalist traits, like all major literary works, *Germinal* defies reductive classification and certainly does not conform to the usual patterns of the typical naturalist text. In any case, by 1884 the novelist was revising many of the presuppositions of his art. The 'Médan Group' had largely dispersed and Zola was looking to broaden the range and impact of his works. This tendency is clearly reflected in the very genesis of *Germinal*, where, for instance, one of Gervaise Macquart's sons, Etienne Lantier, originally destined to appear as a physiological case study of homicidal mania caused by the hereditary effects of the drunkenness of his ancestors, evolves into a more complex character, contending with the demands of his role as a political leader and his exalted feelings for Catherine. The character will never be entirely free of his naturalist ancestry, as he occasionally reverts to his original character type in, notably, his confrontations with Chaval, most dramatically in the flooded mine at the end of the novel, where, 'under the impulse of his hereditary flaw' (502) ['sous la pulsion de la lésion héréditaire' (1571)],[2] he seems to purge his system of the desire to kill. But Zola would need to invent another son for Gervaise, Jacques Lantier, to fulfil the role of the homicidal maniac in *La Bête humaine* (1890) and add him to the family tree.

Thus *Germinal* grew much less out of Zola's earlier naturalist preoccupation with the laws of physiology than out of an increasing awareness of the growing significance of industrial action and of socialist doctrines in contemporary life. Though bound to set his Rougon-Macquart novels during the reign of Napoleon III, as the series progressed Zola became less preoccupied with its historical framework and with his characters' past history than with present-day social issues and the challenges of the future, as the opening statement of the *Ebauche* unequivocally reveals:

> The subject of the novel is the revolt of the workers, the jolt given to society, which for a moment cracks: in a word the struggle between capital and labour. There lies the importance of the book, which I want to show predicting the future, putting the question that will be the most important question of the twentieth century.

> [Le roman est le soulèvement des salariés, le coup d'épaule donné à la société, qui craque un instant: en un mot la lutte du capital et du travail. C'est là qu'est l'importance du livre, je le veux prédisant l'avenir, posant la question qui sera la question la plus importante du XXe siècle.]

A 'socialist' novel

Zola was drawn to writing a novel about the mines by the topicality of the subject, primarily as a social problem but also as a literary theme.[3] Since 1878, the mining industry in France was in crisis, blighted by overproduction, foreign competition and uncompetitive extraction costs. There had been important strikes in Anzin in 1878, Denain in 1880, and in Montceau-les-Mines in 1882. Miners' groups and socialist deputies were vigorously lobbying the government to improve the working conditions of miners. During the summer of 1883 on holiday in Brittany, Zola met one such campaigner, Alfred Giard, a professor at the Faculté des Sciences in Lille and an extreme left-wing deputy for Valenciennes. Their conversations may well have determined Zola's choice of setting for what he regularly referred to at this time as his 'socialist novel'. As chance would have it, he had already begun collecting materials for the novel and Giard had invited him to visit the Valenciennes region when a strike broke out on 21 February 1884 in the Anzin area. Zola spent eight busy days, posing as the deputy's secretary, taking notes and drawing sketches on all that he saw and heard, including details of a short strike at Anzin in 1866, involving troops and mob violence. Zola even mastered his claustrophobia to go down the Renard mine near to Denain, stumbling along dark corridors, recording sensations to be passed on to Etienne in the opening scenes in the novel.[4] Zola's notes show not only the amount of detailed information that he garnered from his visit but also the impressions of people, places, machines, customs, that he gleaned from the experience and that would give his novel the thoroughly authentic atmosphere of lived experience and its characters the vividness of real human beings.

Back in Paris, Zola went with Paul Alexis to hear lectures by Jules Guesde, the Marxist journalist and politician, as well by Paul Lafargue and Charles Longuet, Karl Marx's sons-in-law. He needed to do research on strikes and working conditions during the Second Empire, on female and child labour (banned in 1874). He read books on mines, miners and mining at the time, such as Louis-Laurent Simenon's *La Vie souterraine, ou les mines et les mineurs* (1867) and the *Traité pratique des maladies, des accidents et des difformités des houilleurs* (1862) by Dr H. Boëns-Boissau on the accidents and illnesses of the colliers. Though he would draw upon the incidents at La Ricamarie and Aubin in 1869, he chose to set the action of his novel at a slightly earlier date, in the years 1866–7, when economic conditions of crisis and widespread unemployment were not dissimilar to those of the early 1880s. Only Bonnemort's passing allusions in the first chapter to the Emperor's Mexican expedition and to a cholera epidemic indicate the precise date of the beginning of the action (March 1866, ending in April 1867). Such vagueness permitted the novelist to amalgamate elements of distinct historical periods into a single series of events, combining his thoroughly documented representation of the living and working conditions of the miners at the end of the Second Empire with features of the Anzin strike of 1884 and with his evocation of the workers' struggle, which more feasibly belongs to a later date. Zola has frequently been charged with anachronism, but, in this case at least, it could be argued that the novelist was not writing history, but sought to present what André-Marc Vial calls a 'syncretic vision' of the workers' movement.[5] More problematic, perhaps, are certain improbabilities in the novel such as the inordinate length of the strike and, in particular, the accumulation of violent incidents – an accident, a destructive rampage by striking miners, a grocer castrated, a child dying of starvation, a soldier stabbed to death, unarmed strikers shot by soldiers, the sabotage of a mine, an explosion in a mine, a girl strangled by an old miner, a murder down the mine – which do not make for credible history but produce compelling fiction.

The workers' movement in France had been held in check by the repressive regime of Napoleon III. In 1867, 1868 and 1870, the government dissolved the French sections of the International Working Men's Association, the federation of workers' groups that had been founded in London in September 1864 and had elected Marx as the leader of its General Council. Zola depicts the beginnings of organised working-class militancy through the activities of Pluchart, the secretary of the Northern Federation of the International, who, anxious to recruit members to the Association in industrial areas, indoctrinates Etienne, urges him to form a section in Montsou, pays a flying visit during which he manages to beguile the assembled company into enlisting thousands of miners at a meeting (Part IV, Chapter 4). In France, since 1852, only mutual aid societies under state surveillance were authorised and, even after the fall of the Empire, the workers' movement fared little better under the conservative dominance of the early years of the Third Republic. The Commune had been brutally repressed and the International was widely held responsible for the upheaval. Labour unions, though tolerated earlier, were not authorised until 1884 and only after October 1886, when the first of the French workers' congresses took place, did the movement gain impetus. Under the leadership of Jules Guesde, who had returned from exile in 1877 and had been won over to Marxism, a French socialist party had been formed in 1879, but it failed to gain a consensus. In 1882, the socialist movement split into two rival factions. Paul Brousse and the 'possibilists' broke away from Guesde and his Marxist, centralist faction to found the rival Revolutionary Socialist Party, which was more revolutionary in name than in spirit and came to be called, the following year, the Federation of French Socialist Workers. The divisions among Marxists, anarchists and 'possibilists' reflected those, on the broader European scale, at the heart of the International Working Men's Association, which was riven by competing schools of thought and had split in 1872 to be formally disbanded by the Marxists in 1876, with the anarchists, inspired by Bakunin, failing to keep it alive beyond 1881.

Such divisions are depicted on a smaller scale in *Germinal*, in the radically different solutions to the social question proposed by the three activists and political theorists of the novel: Rasseneur, Souvarine and Lantier, who typify the three basic shades of left-wing thought.[6] As Zola wrote in the *Ebauche*, '[Rasseneur] is a possibilist. Etienne, on the other hand, is an authoritarian collectivist. Souvorine [*sic*] is an anarchist' ['(Rasseneur) est un possibiliste. Etienne au contraire est un collectiviste autoritaire. Souvorine est un anarchiste' (fol. 497/94]). Rasseneur is based on Emile Basly, one of the leaders of the 1884 Anzin strike, a former miner, who had become an innkeeper and would go on to be a socialist deputy in 1885, and is labelled a 'collectiviste évolutionniste' or 'possibiliste', being the most moderate of the three, advocating progressive legislative reforms in collaboration with the capitalists. At the other extreme, Souvarine, whose ideas derive in large part from the theories of the Russian anarchists Mikhail Bakunin and Peter Kropotkin, is scornful of the strike, advocating extreme measures and, as his last illusions about humanity fade, evolves towards an uncompromising nihilism. Of the three main dissidents in the novel he is the most faithful to his convictions, totally lacking personal ambition, yet at the same time always alienated from the workers whose cause he espouses, seeking initially the eventual destruction of the present corrupt society to allow a new society to emerge, then resorting to a violent act of sabotage that destroys innocent lives. As for Etienne, whose precise ideas are more difficult to define, he acquires an education in socialist theory during the course of the novel from Pluchart, Rasseneur, Souvarine, and from his somewhat eclectic readings. His viewpoint shifts alarmingly from an advocacy of violent revolution to an indulgence in utopian visions, from a vigorous promotion of the class struggle to an acceptance of the evolutionary forces of history. Only in the most general of terms can he be said to represent the Marxist position, for the narrator insists upon the confusion of his newly acquired ideas, a confusion which some attribute to Zola's own lack of a firm grasp of political theory but which also derives from the novelist's deep-seated mistrust of demagoguery. Both Rasseneur and Etienne are shown in their alternating roles as leaders of the miners' action in a less than favourable light, locked in a power struggle for the satisfaction of their ambitions. Significantly, in Zola's 'socialist' novel, the socialists prove to be largely ineffective, for, as Etienne comes to acknowledge, events had been and would be determined by a force greater than the individual's ideas, an anonymous force, the will of the masses, in whom alone hope for the future could be invested.

The red peril

Unlike the events that Zola witnessed in Anzin, where calm prevailed, the strike in *Germinal* explodes into uncontrollable violence in the memorable scenes in which the raging miners rampage across the landscape. Their violence, as Zola suggests in his *Ebauche*, is in proportion to the sufferings that they have endured, adding: 'The workers on the loose go as far as criminal acts: the bourgeois reader must feel a shudder of terror . . . abominable savagery' ['Les ouvriers lâchés vont jusqu'au crime: il faut que le lecteur bourgeois ait un frisson de terreur . . . sauvagerie abominable' (fol. 421/20)]. To emphasise the point, Zola skilfully presents this famous sequence at its climax (in Part v, Chapter 5) through the eyes and the fearful reactions of a group of bourgeois characters who have taken refuge in a stable. Thus the reader experiences the scene through the surrogate reactions of these witnesses as they hear the thunderous mob approaching and watch aghast as dishevelled women brandish their starving babies like 'banners symbolising mourning and vengeance', young women 'with firm and warlike breasts' wield sticks, old women scream their hatred, and the men form a seething mass, eyes ablaze with fury, singing the *Marseillaise*, with, above their heads, an axe, which, 'like the battle standard of the band, took on the sharp profile of a guillotine blade against the light evening sky' (348) ['comme l'étendard de la bande, avait, dans le ciel clair, le profil aigu d'un couperet de guillotine' (1436)]. This allegorical scene draws upon the familiar historiography and iconography of Revolution ingrained in the French consciousness, mobilising images that respond to middle-class prejudices and contain for them a frightful resonance. The miners have become a 'band', a 'mass', an 'army', transformed into a bestialised mob, a 'herd' of 'galloping beasts', into an irresistible 'torrent', equated with untamed nature or some natural calamity, inciting the worst fears and phantasms in the dominant class. Indeed, the narrator goes on to evoke the myth of 'Le Grand Soir', of the revolutionary day of reckoning of the people against their oppressors, in an apocalyptic evocation of 'the red vision of revolution' ['la vision rouge de la révolution']:

> That was it, one night the people would rise up, cast caution aside, and run riot like this far and wide all over the countryside; and there would be rivers of bourgeois blood, their heads would be waved on pikes, their strong-boxes hacked open, and their gold poured all over the ground. The women would scream, and the men would look gaunt as wolves, their fangs drooling and gnashing . . . And that was the future out there, tearing down the road like some natural disaster, and buffeting their faces with its great hurricane wind.
>
> (349)

> [Oui, un soir, le peuple lâché, débridé, galoperait ainsi sur les chemins; et il ruissellerait du sang des bourgeois, il promènerait des têtes, il sèmerait l'or des coffres éventrés. Les femmes hurleraient, les hommes auraient des mâchoires de loups, ouvertes pour mordre . . . Oui, c'étaient ces choses qui passaient sur la route, comme une force de la nature, et ils en recevaient le vent terrible au visage.
>
> (1436–7)]

This vision of violent upheaval, already present at the beginning of Zola's *Ebauche*, persisted into the final version of the novel both as a portent for the complacent reader and a foil to the more upbeat revolutionary vision of Etienne with which the novel ends. It also provides a gloss on the novel's intriguing (and untranslatable) title.

Zola considered no less than twenty-three alternatives before deciding upon *Germinal*, titles such as 'The Gathering Storm' ['L'Orage qui monte'] or 'The Burning Soil' ['Le Sol qui brûle'], which denote violent change, or others, like 'The Germinating Seed' ['Le Grain qui germe'], that contain the idea of new growth. But, as the novelist himself later explained (in a letter to his Dutch correspondent, J. Van Santen Kolff, on 6 October 1889), the title *Germinal*, despite its somewhat 'mystical', 'symbolic' air, best conveys the essential themes of the novel and the intentions of its author, 'a revolutionary April, the leap of a ruined society into the spring' ['un avril révolutionnaire, une envolée de la société caduque dans le printemps']. 'If it remains obscure for certain readers,' Zola observed, 'it has become for me like a ray of sunlight illuminating the whole work' ['S'il reste obscure pour certains lecteurs, il est devenu pour moi comme un coup de soleil qui éclaire toute l'œuvre' (Cor. vi 423)].

Appropriately, the title refers directly back to the Revolutionary period, an age of violent change and anticipated regeneration, since 'Germinal' was the seventh month of the Revolutionary Calendar, denoting the spring and extending from 21 March to 19 April. Zola may also have had in mind that, on 12 Germinal in year III (1 April 1795), starving Parisian workers, including a majority of women, rose up against the government of the Convention and its reactionary measures to demand bread and a return to the revolutionary constitution of 1793. Appropriately also, the title, which contains within it key semantic elements of the text (*germe* and *mine*), looks forward to a new age, to the burgeoning society of social justice which the novel predicts, a society emerging from the industrial evils of the present that it depicts.

Art of the novel

For all its value as a historical, social and political document, *Germinal* remains essentially a creative work of impressive scope and effect, employing narrative techniques that both draw the reader vicariously into the lived experience of its dramas and prompt an awareness of the broader meanings and the symbolic effects that the novel conveys. The opening sequence is particularly impressive as we discover, through Etienne's eyes, the eerie landscape with its sinister shapes emerging out of the darkness and, through Bonnemort's words, acquire vital information about the place and its history. There is a compelling vividness in such scenes, which anticipate the visual effectiveness of the cinema in their ability to force the spectator's attention and engage his emotions. Yet the novel retains the suggestiveness of verbal art, even, at a trivial level, in the names of several characters and places. Thus, Maigrat combines 'maigre' and 'gras' ['thin' and 'fat'], indicating the character's intermediary status between the starving miners and the invariably sated bourgeoisie and his power over the miners' families, who eat or not according to the satisfaction of his own appetites. There is La Mouquette, ironically 'the little fly', and Chaval, which rhymes with 'brutal', signifying in *rouchi*, the dialect of the Valenciennes region, 'a rotten beast' ['une rosse'], in keeping with his brutish nature and role. Similarly La Levaque derives from 'L'vaque', the 'cow', a common insult in *rouchi*. True to her character, La Maheude's first name is Constance; Rasseneur reasons; La Veuve Désir's name is linked to her profession, whilst La Brûlé is an appropriate denomination for the terrifying 'witch' who incites the women to destructive acts. Montsou, based, no doubt, on Montceau-les-Mines, is ironically for the miners a 'mountain of money', whilst Le Voreux patently connotes the voracious appetite for human flesh of the mythologised mine monster.

In its broader perspectives, the novel is remarkably paced, beginning in an almost leisurely manner, presenting daily life in the mining community with a Balzacian precision. In fact, the events of almost the first third of the novel (Parts I and II) take place in a single day. Thereafter matters are brought to a head and the pace quickens into a series of violent confrontations among the contending 'forces' at play in the work. Indeed, the rhythm of the novel and its temporal and spatial architecture are structured by a series of carefully contrived clashes, for *Germinal* is a text of significant parallels and oppositions blended into the massive design of the work. After the preliminary exposition, when Etienne has begun to assert his influence, the decision to strike occurs dramatically and appropriately at the centre of the novel. Thereafter, scenes of painstaking description of the miners' misery alternate with episodes of violent action, culminating in the brutal deaths and disruptions above and below ground, before the coda of Etienne's departure in the sun. In the triptych of essential phases – before, during and after the strike – the action evolves horizontally on two planes, frequently describing scenes that take place simultaneously above and below ground. Here the grim daylight world of political struggle, of long periods of hardship and brief bouts of pleasure, of family life and family misfortunes, of a community with its loves and hates, and its dreams; there the dark night below, the hell of brutish toil, the primeval world of nightmares, of fear, of catastrophe, destruction, death, in the bowels of the earth, in the belly of the monster.

Literary and mythical resonances

Germinal is a text of such complexity that critics have been able to unearth in its rich textual seams a variety of themes, myths, allusions and cultural references. It is a work of epic stature, recounting the struggle against oppression of a whole people, beasts of burden imprisoned in the pit of their misfortune, searching for the light of day and dreaming of a world in which they might attain dignity and humanity. The novel recounts their past, their present plight, and their emergence as a mighty force for change. It evokes their communal struggle against the overpowering, all-powerful agencies that are oppressing them. This epic clash between Labour and the god-like Capital is narrated at times in a flowing, elevated style and the famous description of the death throes of the evil machine monster, Le Voreux, crashing to its destruction, adds an almost supernatural dimension to the epic tale. But the miners' life is not all heroic striving, for the novel has its lighter, even comic moments, notably the lively gala episode (the 'ducasse' in Part III, Chapter 2), where a carnivalesque mood prevails in the tableau of the festivities of the community, with its uninhibited display of flesh, bodily orifices, sexuality, and indulgence, its scenes of 'grotesque realism' (in Bakhtin's terms), whose spirit of subversion is summed up here and elsewhere by the defiant display of La Mouquette's ample bottom. Then there is the dark side of the carnival spirit, in the terrifying manifestation of the *charivari* of popular tradition that occurs in the ritual castration of Maigrat, the 'matou' ['tom cat', i.e. 'lecher'].

Germinal is also the novel of an individual and his relationship with that community, the story of the rise and fall of a leader whose ambitions are crushed by grim reality as the limits of his powers are cruelly exposed. Yet, despite his failure, Etienne does fulfil a number of 'heroic' roles. He is the naive outsider of a kind of *Bildungsroman*, who completes his harsh apprenticeship and leaves when his 'education' is complete, having sown the seeds of the future harvest of revolt. He is also the lover in a curiously delicate romance, in which he and Catherine, the 'chaste' object of his quest, the 'virgin' bride whom he finally takes in a moving scene of *Liebestod*, consummate a love that is far removed from the easy promiscuity or the brutal possessiveness so common in the mining community. The love story is intrinsically woven into the fabric of the themes of the novel, for the stages of Etienne's political commitment closely parallel the development of his rivalry with Chaval for possession of Catherine such that his romantic quest adumbrates and even motivates his political crusade. It is paradoxically the death of Maheu, marking the failure of the strike, that provokes the onset of puberty in Catherine, as if a primitive taboo has been lifted on the love of Etienne for his daughter and the flow of germination is finally released, but tragically on the threshold of death.

If *Germinal* is widely appreciated as a masterpiece of realistic fiction graphically depicting contemporary life, it has been no less acknowledged as an inventive fable that draws upon timeless mythical formulations and plumbs the deep recesses of the imagination that the psychoanalyst seeks to explore: the world of Jungian quests, of the traumas of birth or rebirth, of the mysterious links between Eros and Thanatos. Indeed, Etienne's initiatory ordeals and Zola's aggrandised, animistic vision of the mine have been shown to evoke echoes of a whole range of mythical motifs from a variety of traditions: Theseus descending into the lower world to rescue Persephone or slaying the Minotaur in the labyrinth, the myth of the Great Flood, the Furies or Erinyes castrating Uranus, whose blood begets a race of Giants, Cronus the capitalist

God lurking in his lair, the Elysian fields of Catherine's dreams, Dionysus leading the Maenads in their wild fury, Le Voreux as the Moloch of the coal-fields – a kind of tyrannical deity to be propitiated by human subservience or sacrifice. Apocalyptic and evangelical prototypes not only function beneath the surface of the text, inciting the reader's imagination, but operate more explicitly through allusions contained in the text. When, in Chapter I of Part VII, we read how the miners throw stones in anger at Lantier, we might recall Saint Etienne [Stephen], the first Christian martyr, who was stoned to death outside the walls of Jerusalem. Le Tartaret, the legendary abandoned mine that has been burning for centuries with its sulphorous deposits, pro-ducing a stretch of perpetually verdant pastures, La Côte-Verte, creates a metaphorical topography, condensing into a single abstract space in stark and symbolic contrast a representation of the longed for Elysium emerging from the living Hades, evoking explicitly the Tartarus of Greek mythology, the deep hell where the Olympian gods confined the Titans.[7] Zola's novel is indeed, like all great literature, a mine of intertextual allusions to the rich deposits of myth, legend, fable, that make up the whole universe of literature itself.

Political message

Unlike later works of social realism with their clear divisions between heroic workers and evil capitalists, *Germinal* is far removed from such propaganda. Zola himself gave few hints as to how in his view the novel should be inter-preted politically, except to state on more than one occasion that it was a 'work of pity' and not a 'work of revolution'. Critics, even those of the same ideological persuasion, have been divided on the question of the political message of the novel, assuming that it does have a single message. Is it a pro-gressive text, depicting, inciting or advocating revolutionary change, despite the author's apparent disclaimer? Or is it a text about revolutionary change that conveys (or betrays), despite its apparent radicalism, a conservative, reactionary message?

Arguments in favour of *Germinal* as a revolutionary work almost always refer to the general effect or impact of the novel, as if, conversely, those who know the text in better detail and reflect upon its implications are more likely to acquire a certain imperviousness to its rhetoric and develop a degree of scepticism about its political significance. There is accordingly the view that the very subject and substance of the novel constitute a subversive political act. The true picture of the plight of the miners, as the Marxist critic Jean Fréville argues, is in itself an indictment against society and forces Zola to condemn capitalism.[8] There is also the general impression left by the novel's ending, not only the resounding rhetoric of the concluding section but the silent promise of La Maheude's handshake with its vow that, next time, 'it would be the real thing' (520) ['ce serait le grand coup' (1588)]. Indeed, far from being a total failure, the strike has led to the awakening of the conscious-ness of the workers to the true nature of their condition and brought about a readiness to renounce their traditional submissiveness. The radicalisation of Maheu, La Maheude, and the paragon of compliance, Bonnemort, is a better measure of the effectiveness of the industrial action than the advancement of the ideas of the radical thinkers. In *Germinal*, the distant rumble of the 'great absent voice' that Zola discerned in Balzac's works, has come to the fore. Whilst the proletarian characters of *L'Assommoir* remain trapped in their cultural and verbal environment, the miners of Montsou come to articulate their history, their grievances, and their aspirations. As Irving Howe puts it: '*Germinal* releases one of the central myths of the modern era: the story of how the dumb acquire speech', though, on the same theme, Claude Duchet points to the tragic lapse of their new found articulateness into inefficacy and into Etienne's verbosity.[9]

Negative views of *Germinal*'s political message tend to point to specific fea-tures of the text and to argue that, despite some high-sounding rhetoric, the novel offers little prospect of change for the workers. Souvarine, for example, provides an apparently rigorous scientific explanation of their plight when he alludes to David Ricardo's 'Iron Law of Wages', which Zola signalled as '*Important*' in his notes. The British economist, strongly influenced by Malthus, held that the workers' wages inevitably stabilise around the subsis-tence level, only rising, as Souvarine explains (1256), until a surplus of labour makes them fall again, whereby they fall to such a low level that workers die of starvation until the ensuing shortage of workers forces them back up. Though the subsequent development of industrial economies would reveal the fallacy of the theory, the action of Zola's novel in no way contradicts this law. More tellingly, it has been argued that the mythological presen-tation of the capitalist system as an all-powerful God-like entity deforms and displaces the true nature of capitalist exploitation, liberating the indi-vidual capitalist from all responsibility, just as the casting of the workers' aspirations in the form of utopian visions and the promise of a mythical golden age deprives them of an objective and reasoned understanding of their situation. Even in the novel's rhetoric and imagery, which seems to convey a message of hope, there is mystification, for, as Henri Mitterand has pointed out, in such passages political and social realities are subsumed by biological and natural connotations that abolish any sense of histori-cal change.[10] One critic even belligerently devotes a whole volume to cen-suring Zola as a petit-bourgeois writer and to denouncing his novel as a betrayal of the working classes, inspired by bourgeois prejudices, revealing disdain for the workers' movement, and a deeply ingrained distrust of the masses.[11]

Despite the ambiguities of *Germinal*, it is clear that Zola wished to communicate with all the vividness of the realist novel his sense of outrage at the plight of the people. As a witness of the Commune and a scion of the Revolution, he conceived his novel as a warning to the dominant classes that, in the struggle between capital and labour, though present circumstances seemed to favour the former, the exploitation of the people could not continue, for, as the apocalyptic tableau of mass violence and retribution presaged, there were irrepressible forces ready to be unleashed against the oppressors. In the awakened aspirations of the wretched miners and in the buoyancy of the novel's ending, Zola conveys the conviction that the people will prevail and that history has shown that, despite the setbacks, 'tomorrow will be right'.[12] Though *Germinal* proffers as many questions as answers to critics and theorists, it remains a memorable work of fiction that continues to engross, thrill, and inspire generations of silent readers who share the afflictions and the aspirations of the miners of Montsou. On some, like the former leader of the British miners' union, Arthur Scargill, who declared it his favourite book, *Germinal* was a spur to action and left a lasting impression.[13] To others, no doubt, the events of the last century and a half, with their industrial reforms and their much greater cataclysms, will have diminished the impact of the novel. Yet others will continue to see its enduring relevance to different contexts. The last coal mine in France may well have closed down in 2004, but in other parts of the world, there are miners still facing the dangers and the torments that Zola depicted more than a century ago. And there is still no shortage of mercilessly exploited labour in the world. The most moving testimony to the impact of Zola's novel remains the tribute paid by a delegation of miners from the Denain coalfield who joined the 50,000 mourners in Zola's funeral procession on 5 October 1902, uttering a rhythmic chant of 'Germinal! Germinal!' A single word, the title of a single text, was in itself an eloquent homage to a writer whose work had given them and their ancestors a voice and a hope.

NOTES

1 Zola finished the novel on 23 January 1885; it appeared in serial form in *Gil Blas* from 26 November 1884 to 25 February 1885 and was published by Charpentier in March 1885.

2 Unless otherwise stated, referenced quotations in English from *Germinal* are taken from Peter Collier's translation (Oxford: Oxford University Press, 1993) in the Oxford World's Classics series (with an introduction by Robert Lethbridge). The

source for quotations in French is volume III of the Pléiade edition of *Les Rougon-Macquart*.

3 In, for example, Maurice Talmeyr's novel, *Le Grisou* (1880), and, most significantly, in a short story by Paul Heuzy, 'La vie d'Antoine Maheu', in the collection *Un coin de la vie de misère* (1878; 2nd edn 1883), which features a strike, a flooded mine, and a love story between the rebellious hero and a female miner called Catherine.

4 See 'Mes Notes sur Anzin', in Colette Becker (ed.), *Emile Zola. La Fabrique de 'Germinal'* (Paris: SEDES, 1986), pp. 375–413. This volume reproduces with annotations the preparatory dossier of the novel. 'Mes Notes sur Anzin' are also published by Henri Mitterand in his collection *Carnets d'enquêtes. Une ethnographie inédite de la France* (Paris: Plon, 1986), pp. 449–97.

5 See André-Marc Vial, *'Germinal' et le 'socialisme' de Zola* (Paris: Editions sociales, 1975), p. 44.

6 For a useful survey of their views, see Colin Smethurst, *Zola: 'Germinal'* (London: Edward Arnold, 1974); reprinted (Glasgow: University of Glasgow French and German Publications, 1996), pp. 36–40.

7 On some of these themes, see Philip Walker, 'Prophetic Myths in Zola', *PMLA*, 74 (1959), 444–52, and Philippe Lejeune, 'La Côte-Verte et le Tartaret', *Poétique*, 40 (1979), 475–86 (475–8).

8 See *Zola, semeur d'orages* (Paris: Editions sociales, 1952).

9 See Irving Howe, 'Zola. The Genius of *Germinal*', *Encounter*, 34 (1970), 53–61 – also in David Baguley (ed.), *Critical Essays on Emile Zola* (Boston, Mass.: G. K. Hall, 1986), pp. 111–24; Claude Duchet, 'Le Trou des bouches noires. Parole, société, révolution dans *Germinal*', *Littérature*, 24 (1976), 11–39.

10 See 'L'Idéologie et le mythe: *Germinal* et les fantasmes de la révolte', in *Le Discours du roman* (Paris: Presses Universitaires de France, 1980), pp. 140–9. This article appears in English translation in Henri Mitterand, *Emile Zola: Fiction and Modernity*, trans. and ed. Monica Lebron and David Baguley (London: The Emile Zola Society, 2000), pp. 95–103.

11 Paule Lejeune, *'Germinal'. Un roman antipeuple* (Paris: Nizet, 1978); republished (Paris: L'Harmattan, 2002).

12 'Quand même, demain aura raison' ['Nevertheless, tomorrow will be right'] (from an article entitled 'La Démocratie' which Zola wrote in *Le Figaro* on 5 September 1881).

13 See *The Socialist Worker*, 21 July 1984, and *The Guardian*, 26 April 1994.

RECOMMENDED READING

A number of books written in English deal specifically with *Germinal*. E. M. Grant's *Zola's 'Germinal': A Critical and Historical Study* (Leicester: Leicester University Press, 1962) and Richard H. Zakarian's *Zola's 'Germinal': A Critical Study of Its Primary Sources* (Geneva: Droz, 1972) are informative traditional scholarly studies. Philip Walker's *'Germinal' and Zola's Philosophical and Religious Thought* (Amsterdam: John Benjamins, 1984) deals perceptively with Zola's ideas as they may be deduced from the novel. Colin Smethurst's *Emile Zola: 'Germinal'* (London: Edward Arnold, 1974); reprinted (Glasgow: University of Glasgow French and German Publications, 1996) is an excellent short introduction to the background and themes of the novel. Six of Henri Mitterand's incisive essays on *Germinal* have been translated into English in *Emile Zola: Fiction and Modernity*, trans. and ed. Monica Lebron and David Baguley (London: The Emile Zola Society, 2000). Colette Becker reproduces the entire preparatory dossier of the novel in *Emile Zola. La Fabrique de 'Germinal'* (Paris: SEDES, 1986). There are several useful introductory studies in French, notably by Colette Becker, *Emile Zola: 'Germinal'* (Paris: Presses Universitaires de France, 1984) and by Pascal Michel, *Etude sur Emile Zola: 'Germinal'* (Paris: Ellipses, 1999). André Vial's *'Germinal' et le 'socialisme' de Zola* (Paris: Editions sociales, 1975) is an excellent study of the politics of the novel. Two special issues of the journal *Les Cahiers naturalistes*, 50 (1976) and 59 (1985), contain a variety of important studies on aspects of the novel, as do the special centennial numbers of the *Revue d'Histoire littéraire de la France* (no. 85) and *Europe* (no. 63) published in 1985.

10

RAE BETH GORDON

La Bête humaine: Zola and the poetics of the unconscious

The title of *La Bête humaine* clearly links it to Darwin's *Origin of Species* and *The Descent of Man*; notions about primitive instinct, passion and aggression are the novel's very basis. Yet evolution theory itself converged with psychiatric notions about hysteria and madness, as the theory of degeneration meshed with Darwinist fantasies of regression to primitive states. The pathologies of degeneration included, among other problems, epilepsy, alcoholism, hysteria and idiocy, which were believed to be hereditary or to have an important hereditary component, and were defined by their constitutionally regressive character. Regression signalled reverse evolution, but it also referred to the predominance of the lower, automatic forms of human activity – automatic reflexes, thoughts and acts – that characterised epilepsy, somnambulism and hysteria. Zola exploits this convergence and moves beyond previous depictions of these nervous disorders as they recur throughout the cycle (hysteria is at the root of the Rougon-Macquart family tree, in the person of Tante Dide). Whereas he had previously ascribed the nervous disorders to heredity, here in the 1890 novel his treatment is considerably subtler, moving between physiology, heredity and the new psychological theories of the mind proposed by Pierre Janet.

Zola wrote that he wanted the violent drama of *La Bête humaine* to possess 'an aura of mystery . . . something that seems to depart from reality (not hypnosis, but an unknown force)' ['un côté de mystère . . . quelque chose qui ait l'air de sortir de la réalité (pas d'hypnotisme, mais une force inconnue)'].[1] This 'hallucinatory', unknown force will be found in the mechanical, involuntary, automatic aspects of human behaviour that lie beyond the control of reason and the will, behaviour that resembles automatic reflex and locomotor problems such as tics and convulsive movement. This behaviour includes instinct, impulsive acts, *idée fixe*, and passion. The fixation on a single idea is an automatism: it forces itself on the consciousness without the person's willing it. In addition, psychiatrists like Pierre Janet and Jean-Martin

Charcot viewed it in the following way: it is introduced into the person's mind and rooted there in the manner of a foreign body. These automatisms belong to a very rudimentary consciousness beneath normal thought. In the late nineteenth century, the notion of a division between the higher faculties (reason, judgment and the will) and the lower faculties (motor response, nervous reflex, sensation and instinct) was a widely accepted medical concept. These lower forms of human activity were studied by the psychiatrist Pierre Janet during the same period that Zola was working out his ideas for *La Bête humaine*. In 1889, Janet had published what is arguably the most important psychiatric work of the nineteenth century, *L'Automatisme psychologique: essai sur les formes inférieures de l'activité humaine*. It was the culmination of over a decade of case studies and experiments that Janet had carried out in Le Havre before coming to work at the La Salpêtrière hospital in 1890,[2] the same year that Zola published *La Bête humaine* (much of which takes place in Le Havre). Janet demonstrated that in all automatic acts, ideas, or images, there is a second consciousness which has its own laws. Not only is Janet's theory the first coherent, detailed description of the unconscious, but he was also the first psychiatrist to 'insist on a new psychological existence, not in alternation with the normal existence of the subject, but absolutely simultaneous with it'.[3] Pierre Janet's name for this 'new psychological existence' was the subconscious.

Janet observed that all of his hysterical and obsessional patients 'use the same language, the words machines, automatons, mechanical constantly recur' (Janet 283). It is striking to see just how many of Zola's characters, whether or not hysterical, are described as exhibiting these traits. *La Bête humaine* offers the most perfect example of the relation of the mechanical and the unconscious mind, for its two main characters are Jacques Lantier, an engine driver, and . . . his locomotive. This chapter will explore the extent to which Zola was able to make use of contemporary psychology in a more than superficial manner. In *La Bête humaine*, detailed and subtle new conceptions of the mind were rewritten by Zola to create a scientifically grounded, yet lyrical and epic, poem of the unconscious. The process of this reworking can be appreciated by looking at the evolution of the text from the planning notes to the finished novel.

Mystery, madness and the *mécanicien*

Let us return to Zola's central idea about the aura of mystery he wanted to convey in the novel. It is on the first page of the *Ebauche* for *La Bête humaine*, a ninety-seven-page manuscript written in 1888–9, that Zola says that he wants to write a novel with, as its subject, 'a violent drama . . . with an aura of mystery, of other-worldliness, something that seems to depart from reality (not hypnosis, but an unknown force, to work out, to uncover)' ['un drame violent . . . avec un côté de mystère, d'au-delà, quelque chose qui ait l'air de sortir de la réalité (pas d'hypnotisme, mais une force inconnue, à arranger, à trouver)' (fol. 338)]. A few pages later, Zola returns to the core of what he wants to portray, the mystery of the unknown force that will be 'something hallucinatory, terrible . . . And that has to be found physiologically in one of my characters' ['quelque chose d'hallucinant, d'effroyable . . . Et cela, il faut le trouver physiologiquement dans un de mes personnages' (fol. 352)]. However, it is not only in the physiology of his *character* that he will discover it: as we will see, the physiology of the railway is precisely that given to a body governed by automatisms and the nerves. Moreover, the milieu in which the characters evolve is of crucial importance in all of Zola's novels, as befitted a writer as indebted to Hippolyte Taine as he was. The milieu, in the case of *La Bête humaine*, is absolutely dominated by the railway: the tracks and the machines that run back and forth on them between the station at Le Havre, the crossing at La Croix-de-Maufras, and the Gare Saint Lazare in Paris. Jacques' behaviour is reinforced by the environment of smoke, heat, speed, and the vibration of the trains that he drives.

Critics such as Gilles Deleuze, Gisèle Séginger and Geoff Woollen have seen that the locomotive in *La Bête humaine* symbolises not only progress but also regression to primitive drives. This is made explicit in Chapter 7 when the train, 'gone mad' ['prise de folie'], gallops along, before it is powerfully figured as a mad beast at the end of the novel. Towards the end of the *Ebauche*, Zola calls it 'a beast gone mad' ['une bête prise de folie' (fol. 427)]. However, it is the *way* that unconscious drives are assimilated with the train that constitutes the more than superficial and extremely modern aspect of the novel, and which allows us to understand why and how the Primitive converges with Progress in the body of the locomotive. The mechanical movement of the train on its rails is the metaphor for what lies in the very depths of humanity: 'this mechanical rolling along of the train . . . the savagery in the depths of man' ['ce roulement mécanique du train . . . la sauvagerie qui est au fond de l'homme' (fol. 400)]. What I want to show here is that the late nineteenth-century theory of an unconscious located in the body and the treatment of that theory in Pierre Janet's *L'Automatisme psychologique* allow us to see the main character of Zola's novel and the poetry of the text in a new light. The mechanical workings of the unconscious in the body therefore have great pertinence for this novel. One of the 133 titles that Zola considered for the novel, along with several others in the same category, was *L'Inconscient* [*The Unconscious*].

Janet's extraordinary contribution was to see that automatic movements and acts – most visible in epilepsy, hysteria, madness and somnambulism – are part of normal functioning, called the lower forms of human activity. There is simply a difference of degree between the normal and the pathological, as Dr Claude Bernard had shown. Normal automatisms also take place without the participation of reason and without the intervention of judgment and the will. (Other titles considered by Zola for the novel were *Sans le vouloir, Sans vouloir, Vouloir et faire, Sans volonté* [*Without Wanting To, Without Willing, Willing and Doing, Without the Will*].) Jacques Lantier's actions are a mechanical response. In a letter to his publisher, Zola precisely stated that the hero was to be a hereditary criminal 'without being mad' ['sans être fou'].[4] In fact, Janet made a sharp distinction between 'the true madman who abandons himself to his delirium and enjoys it, and the victim of impulse who rejects it as something alien to himself. Here we have a remarkable characteristic that gives to this mental disturbance a quite distinct importance' (Janet 397). (Zola also considered *L'Impulsion* and *Le Meurtre impulsif* as possible titles.) In other words, *la folie impulsive* clearly shows the second consciousness at work. It is this mechanical side of the self that allows one to see the *moi* underneath. The insistent repetition of the vocabulary linked to the theme of what lurks underneath, such as the adjectives 'under', 'underneath', 'at the bottom', 'hole', 'abyss', is remarkable in *La Bête humaine*. This vocabulary must be tied to the vocabulary of the unconscious located in the body, in the lower faculties. Even places where the unconscious force of the passions reveals itself are associated with what lies underneath: for example, one would be hard put to find 'a hole more remote' ['un trou plus reculé' (1025)][5] than La Croix-de-Maufras. Trains and the train yard are also associated with the pull from below: 'the station, this trench . . . boring through' ['la gare, cette tranchée . . . trouant'(997)] like Jacques' headaches 'drilling a hole in your skull', 'holes from which the Self would escape' ['trouant le crâne', 'trous où le moi s'échappe' (1034, 1043)]. One of many examples that link the mechanical to what lies underneath is offered in Chapter 2: 'They can go on inventing better machines, but there will still be wild beasts underneath' ['On aura beau inventer des mécaniques meilleures encore, il y aura quand même des bêtes sauvages dessous' (1032)].

La Bête humaine undeniably plunges the reader into the dark, lower depths of human existence. The scene is immediately set in the first chapter by the noise, smoke and constant agitation of the train yard at the Gare Saint Lazare in Paris, and the violent acts in the novel are invariably accompanied by Zola's return to the trains' movements. The narrative begins with violence in the first chapter when the assistant station-master Roubaud discovers that his wife Séverine has had sexual relations from the age of sixteen with her

protector, the rich and politically powerful magistrate Grandmorin. One of
the myriad examples of the superimposition of submerged drives and the
railway occurs here as the tension mounts between Roubaud and Séverine:
'beneath them, little machines . . . continually came and went' ['Sous eux, les
petites machines . . . allaient et venaient sans repos' (1010)], and after the violence erupts, 'Unceasingly, trains hurried off in the growing darkness, amid
the inextricable network of the tracks' ['Sans cesse, des trains filaient dans
l'ombre croissante, parmi l'inextricable lacis des rails' (1020)]. The darkness
penetrates Roubaud's very being. Not only does a brutal beating ensue upon
his discovery, but Roubaud, 'as though invaded by the darkness of this nightfall' ['comme envahie d'ombre par cette nuit qui tombait' (1020)], forces his
young wife to participate in the murder of Grandmorin, which takes place in
the next chapter. The word 'machine' occurs six times in the paragraph from
which I have just quoted. The narrative will return to Grandmorin's house at
La Croix-de-Maufras and, more specifically, to the bedroom that overlooks
the train tracks. It was in that house that Grandmorin gave the sixteen-year-
old a ring – 'a gold serpent with a little ruby head' ['un serpent d'or à petite
tête de rubis' (1012)] – this ring, which she mechanically twists on her fin-
ger, that causes her to reveal 'in a dreamy, automatic voice' ['dans une voix
involontaire de rêve' (1012)] her relationship with Grandmorin. This object
is highly symbolic, the serpent symbolising Eve and sexual knowledge (here,
specifically Séverine's hidden sexual past and Grandmorin's perverse sexual
drives), and the colour red reappearing numerous times in the novel as the
colour of blood, as the colour that Jacques sees before his eyes when his
illness returns, and as the red triangle of lights at the back of the train. The
little golden ring clearly links the mechanism of passion and the railway,
which is described as 'an iron serpent' ['un serpent de fer' (fol. 360)].

   It should be no surprise that the murder takes place in a train. By chance,
Jacques Lantier witnesses the crime in a fleeting, cinematic perception of
the window of the speeding train. But, in fact, chance plays no part in this
novel: it is fate that has brought him to the scene as he was fleeing from his
own desire to kill; the passion aroused in kissing his childhood friend Flore
triggered the automatic impulse to kill the woman he desires. 'Desire had
always driven him mad, he saw red' ['Toujours le désir l'avait rendu fou, il
voyait rouge' (1040)]. Passion is essential to the narrative of this novel. Janet
writes: 'The most curious manifestation of psychological automatism is passion, which resembles suggestion and impulse. Passion . . . that leads one on in
spite of oneself, completely resembling madness, as much in its origins as in its
mechanism. It does not depend upon the will' (Janet 435–6). The central character of every Zola novel possesses an hereditary flaw, and this is Jacques',
one that he has been combating since he was sixteen years old. He tears

Flore's blouse open and sees her white breasts: 'Then, gasping for breath, he stopped, looked at her instead of possessing her. A fury seemed to take hold of him . . . He spotted the scissors . . . threw them away and fled. Jacques fled into the melancholy night. Galloping, he climbed the path' ['Alors lui, haletant, s'arrêta, la regarda au lieu de la posséder. Une fureur semblait le prendre . . . Ses regards rencontrent les ciseaux . . . Il les rejeta, il s'enfuit. Jacques fuyait dans la nuit mélancolique. Il monta au galop' (1041–2)]. Here, as in the next two passages cited, the vocabulary linked to the trains as well as to Pierre Janet's text is striking.

The explanation is given in the famous passage on the following page: 'The family was hardly in good shape, many had a flaw, a fissure' ['La famille n'était guère d'aplomb, beaucoup avaient une fêlure' (1043)]; and Jacques describes his 'hereditary flaw':

> it was in his being, sudden losses of equilibrium, like cracks, holes through which his Self escaped from him in the midst of a sort of thick smoke that deformed everything. He no longer belonged to himself, he obeyed his muscles, the enraged beast.
>
> [c'étaient, dans son être, de subites pertes d'équilibre, comme des cassures, des trous par lesquels son moi lui échappait au milieu d'une sorte de grande fumée qui déformait tout. Il ne s'appartenait plus, il obéissait à ses muscles, à la bête enragée. (1043)]

'So again . . . he galloped . . . to flee from himself, to flee the other, the enraged beast that he felt inside him. But he was carrying it along with him' ['Alors, de nouveau . . . il galopa . . . pour se fuir, pour fuir l'autre, la bête enragée qu'il sentait en lui. Mais il l'emportait' (1046)]. The reader will see Zola continually juxtapose physiological psychology and Darwinism, yet just how close the novelist's prose is to the psychiatrist's text is striking. Pierre Janet describes the psychological automatism of 'impulsive madness' thus:

> The ill person is perfectly conscious of this Other inside him who forces him to act against his will. He feels himself being pulled along by an unknown force. The simplest acts of this sort are nervous movements, like tics. But other cases are more dramatic; the individual who is conscious of his impulse can resist it for a shorter or longer period of time and only succumbs after a desperate battle. These are violent and sudden desires that push him to commit a criminal act contrary to his will. They try to reject the desire to act and try to flee themselves. They are unable to succeed and remain gasping for breath, in a sweat, in this delirious battle against themselves. (Janet 395–6)

The absolute correspondence between Zola's and Janet's texts is clear both in vocabulary and in concept. It is of crucial importance that when Jacques tries to flee from himself, this is expressed as 'to flee from himself, to flee the other . . . he felt inside him' ['pour se fuir, pour fuir l'autre . . . qu'il sentait en lui' (1046)] and as 'the other, that he had so frequently felt moving in the depths of his being, that unknown person who had come from so far away' ['l'autre, celui qu'il avait senti si fréquemment s'agiter au fond de son être, cet inconnu venu de très loin' (1209)]. Cases of 'impulsive madness', such as that of Jacques Lantier, guide the psychiatrist in his study of the co-presence of two consciousnesses. One may be aware of the impulses in the consciousness underneath, but the will is too weak to combat them.

I have left out an important passage between Jacques' attack and its explication: the train's sudden apparition, which symbolises the surging forth of 'psychological automatism': 'Suddenly . . . a train arrived . . . He saw in front of him the round opening, the black maw of the tunnel. The train was disappearing into its depths, screaming and whistling, leaving . . . a long shudder that made the earth tremble. So it had come back, this abominable illness . . . the urge to kill a woman' ['Brusquement . . . un train arrivait . . . Il aperçut devant lui l'ouverture ronde, la gueule noire du tunnel. Un train montant s'y engouffrait, hurlant et sifflant, laissant . . . une longue secousse dont le sol tremblait . . . Il était donc revenu, ce mal abominable . . . tuer une femme' (1042)]. Of course, the less than subtle metaphorising of the sexual act by the train in the tunnel is also an enactment of the body's instinctual force. Two other trains follow on the (w)heels of the first, and it is in the last one that Jacques views the murder. True to his project in the *Ebauche*, Zola tightly interweaves the unknown forces of the unconscious with the train, just as he does in the other scenes of violence and passion in the novel. The chapter ends with a macabre and powerful vision of trains passing: 'The trains sped by in their inexorable mechanical power, hurrying to their far-off destination in the future, oblivious to the half-severed head alongside the tracks' ['Tous se croisaient, dans leur inexorable puissance mécanique, filaient à leur but lointain, à l'avenir, en frôlant, sans y prendre garde, la tête coupée à demi de cet homme' (1053)].

The violence of humans is also punctuated by the catastrophic violence of train derailments (which were in fact quite frequent in the nineteenth century); there are three of them in this novel, and the second one is caused by Flore's jealous passion directed against Séverine. Sex, violent death, and hurtling locomotives are joined in a drama of mythic dimensions. Jacques will become Séverine's lover with the tacit accord of her husband, to keep Jacques from revealing what he had seen. It appears at first as if Jacques' uncontrollable homicidal impulse is not triggered by the mysterious and sensual Séverine. Is it because she has committed the act that he has always wanted to accomplish but feared to do? 'She had killed, was this the dream of his flesh?' ['Celle-ci avait tué, était-ce le rêve de sa chair?' (1146)]. Will the

hero of this fatalistic drama be able to know passion without an accompa-
nying urge to kill? The reader suspects early on that death and sexual desire
are inseparably joined as surely as the railway joins the places where the
two are enacted. It is in fact in Chapter 8, when Jacques insists that Séverine
recount the murder in detail, that his instinctual desire to kill surges up from
the unconscious, pictured here as the unknown, surging up from inside the
body. 'Inside him the unknown was awakening . . . rising from his gut' ['En
lui, l'inconnu se réveillait . . . montait des entrailles' (1204)]. The lovemaking
that follows is a presage of what is to come: 'They took each other, and they
found love in the depths of death' ['Ils se possédèrent, retrouvant l'amour
au fond de la mort' (1205)]. This scene offers a brilliant illustration of the
workings of psychological automatism.

The psychological concept of the association of ideas was essential for
Freud. Several years before Freud developed his theory of psychoanalysis,
Janet had stated that the association of ideas was one of the most important manifestations of psychological automatism, because 'thoughts awaken
each other mechanically' (Janet 56). And this automatic succession of images
brings about the mechanical repetition of gestures and movements. After
Séverine falls asleep, Jacques remains awake, powerless to control the association of ideas surrounding Grandmorin's murder. He experiences 'a prodigious cerebral activity . . . ceaselessly unwinding the same skein of ideas . . .
The same images passed before him, awakening the same sensations with
mechanical regularity' ['une activité cérébrale prodigieuse . . . dévidant sans
cesse le même écheveau d'idées . . . Les mêmes images défilaient, éveillaient les
mêmes sensations avec une régularité mécanique' (1206)]. The association of
ideas is accompanied by 'the doubly intensified labour of the brain, a grinding of the whole machine' ['le labeur décuplé du cerveau, un grondement de
toute la machine' (1206)]. Automatic gestures and movements quickly ensue.

> He was suddenly afraid of his hands . . . imprisoning them beneath his body, as
> if he feared . . . an unwanted act, yet one that he would nevertheless commit . . .
> He could feel them restlessly moving about, in rebellion, stronger than his will.
> Were they going to cease to belong to him? These hands that came to him from
> Another, handed down by some Ancestor . . . in the woods.

> [La peur le prit de ses mains . . . les emprisonnant là, comme s'il eût redouté . . .
> un acte qu'il ne voudrait pas et qu'il commettrait quand même . . . Il les sentait
> bien qui s'agitaient, révoltées, plus fortes que son vouloir. Est-ce qu'elles allaient
> cesser de lui appartenir? Des mains qui lui viendraient d'un autre, des mains
> léguées par quelque ancêtre . . . dans les bois. (1207)]

One again admires how cleverly Zola intertwines Darwinism and psychology. Jacques is 'submerged by the *idée fixe* . . . where . . . one gives in to the

urges of instinct' ['submergé par l'idée fixe . . . où . . . l'on cède aux poussées de l'instinct' (1208)]. *L'Idée fixe* also figured among the possible titles for the novel, and it is worth mentioning that the French theoretician of the *idée fixe* in the nineteenth century was Pierre Janet, whose study *Névroses et idées fixes* dates from 1898. In order to escape from his uncontrollable desire to strangle Séverine, expressed by his hands, Jacques goes out into the Paris night and wanders aimlessly, mechanically, 'like a somnambulist' ['en somnambule' (1209)]. It was thanks to the strange nineteenth-century phenomenon of a double personality in somnambulism that the discovery of the unconscious was made. The unconscious was seen to be the state that a person experienced in somnambulism, outside consciousness, memory and the will.

It is not until Chapter 11 that Jacques kills the woman he loves. It is – as indeed it must be – in the house she has now inherited from Grandmorin at La Croix-de-Maufras. She is – and must be – naked, so that the abyss into which one risks falling becomes 'the black abyss of woman's sex, love unto death' ['le gouffre noir du sexe, l'amour jusque dans la mort' (1297)]. Love and death are united one last time. And the train must speed by at precisely the same moment that Jacques strangles her, causing the mechanical resurgence of the fatal compulsion to coincide with the surging of the machine: Séverine's face expresses the terror of seeing the 'unknown force' – the mystery – as Jacques' hands are strangling her, and the text describes this as 'a railway-effect on her' ['un effet de chemin de fer sur elle' (1297)]. 'Had she cried out? That very second the Paris express was passing with such violence and speed that it shook the floor, and she was dead as if this tempest had destroyed her' ['Avait-elle crié? . . . A cette seconde passait l'express de Paris, si violent, si rapide, que le plancher en tremblait, et elle était morte, comme foudroyée dans cette tempête' (1297)].[6]

Cavemen and criminals

Is Jacques a born criminal, a popular contemporary concept forged by Cesare Lombroso? Certainly, Lombroso was an extremely important medical source for Zola, and Lombroso's *L'Homme criminel* has been vital to interpretations of Jacques Lantier's 'monomania', what Zola calls, in the *Ebauche*, his 'criminal insanity' ['folie du crime'] or 'homicidal madness' ['folie homicide']. The born criminal is a 'moral madman' *and* a savage. Indeed, two of the other titles considered by Zola were *Folie morale* and *Bêtes sauvages*. What is more, Lombroso signalled a criminal tendency in epilepsy. He identified a number of physical anomalies common to criminals and to 'savage peoples'. Although he also possesses non-atavistic characteristics, 'in pathology, nothing better than the epileptic can at the same time reunite morbid and atavistic phenomena. For some time now, alienists have observed that the epileptic in his convulsions often reproduces phenomena specific to savages and to lower animals.'[7] And the adjective *atavistic* should be taken literally: these epileptic criminals are indeed throwbacks with a 'monstrous development of the jaws and teeth' (Lombroso 71). This 'physical degeneration in the skull, face, teeth, and brain [is] a return to the early brutal egotism natural to primitive races, which manifests itself in . . . crime' (Lombroso 73). Jacques in fact possesses a prominent jaw and large, uncontrollable hands. The moral madman supposedly bears a perfect resemblance to the epileptic[8] in the specific form of epilepsy that accentuates the criminal tendency of certain people 'until it reaches the atavistic form' (Lombroso 70). The amalgam of these theories originated with Lombroso and was already largely accepted in psychiatry in the period when Zola was writing. The novelist therefore has no hesitation in combining atavism with unconscious drives emanating from the nervous system: his hero will kill by atavism, the ancient primitive man will manifest himself in Jacques, but it will also be a murder provoked by the nerves, 'a nervous derailment'. 'There is the heredity of the beast . . . I have a brutish, jealous husband blinded by blood and who commits murder; I have the atavistic murder [committed by] Lantier, originating in his nerves, in nervous derailment' ['Voilà l'hérédité de la bête . . . J'ai le mari brutal et jaloux que le sang étourdit et qui tue; j'ai le meurtre par atavisme chez [Lantier], le meurtre des nerfs, du détraquement nerveux' (fols. 400–1)]. It is in fact instinct that serves as the glue joining regression to the lower faculties.

The criminal form of epilepsy does not provoke the terrible motor attacks that are normally associated with the nervous disease, but instead causes 'a constant brain irritation which clouds and disturbs his intellectual and moral nature' (Lombroso 70). Zola describes Jacques' headaches in exactly this manner: 'A great disturbance climbed into his soul with the blood of his veins . . . a huge cloud of smoke' ['Un grand trouble montait à son crâne avec le sang de ses veines . . . une grande fumée' (1040)].

As we have seen, Jacques Lantier is an extraordinarily interesting mixture of two different scientific currents: Darwinism and psychiatry. And since the two are closely linked in French thought, connected by thinkers less flamboyant than Lombroso, the character is layered with both series of ideas. Only because Darwinism is so apparent was the more subtle psychiatric exploration of the unconscious less visible. Zola was therefore not vacillating between two wildly divergent themes when he hesitated between various titles for his 1890 novel. The 'dangerous classes', as we know, were also equated with primitive beings; prehistoric humans and the lower classes supposedly both exhibited instinctual behaviour. This behaviour in turn was composed entirely of automatisms.

Yet, the novel would have far less interest and possess very little mystery if Zola had limited the development of his hero's psychology and physiology to Lombroso's criminal man. This portrait was all too well known by his 1890s public. What Zola achieved was thus far riskier: he took less well-known scientific theories that were nonetheless in the air at the time and magnified them to create a picture of Jacques Lantier's psychology, a picture where the crisscross of normal and pathological phenomena was complex enough to radiate out into a portrait of the whole of society – a society that could be metaphorised as the railway. The mystery is no longer circumscribed by one man's brain, nor by his bestial and atavistic regression to a prehistoric epoch; it is the mystery of the unconscious underneath the behaviour and desires of Second Empire society (of all societies?), whether that particular technologically advanced society appears to be headed towards the future of progress, or whether it looks as though it were returning to a primitive moment in time. The primitive is always within us, and our mechanical acts and thoughts are reminders of that.

Moreover, Jacques Lantier's crime is a perfect example of the psychological automatism in one of its most illuminating manifestations: specifically, 'impulsive madness', as described by Janet. In the *Ebauche*, Zola says that he wants to show Jacques' 'stupor, his anguish at having acted in defiance of his reason, of his will. In short, psychology giving way to physiology' ['stupeur, son angoisse d'avoir agi en dehors de son raisonnement, de sa volonté. En somme, la psychologie cédant à la physiologie' (fols. 344–5)]. In other words, Jacques' reason cedes to his body. Automatisms were seen to emanate from the body, specifically the spinal cord and the nervous system. Before Janet's work, they were already described as being outside consciousness, situated in a corporeal unconscious. Nervous disorders such as hysteria and epilepsy are simply the dominance of 'spinal life over cerebral life' ['la vie spinale sur la vie cérébrale'], as Dr Paul-Max Simon wrote in his 1877 *Hygiène de l'esprit* [*Hygiene of the Mind*]. It is very likely that Zola was familiar with this theory. Janet took this theory, based in physiological psychology, and refined it. He then extended it, bringing it into the larger realm of normal and abnormal psychology.

Runaway trains

Why did Zola link the regressive surging up of unconscious drives to the railway? Let us now try to answer the question more directly with reference once again to the *Ebauche*. We will see that the railway offered itself as the perfect image of the corporeal unconscious, the body as a machine with its instinctual drives always pushing, urging forward and trying to break free from restraints. 'And against this background, against this mechanical rolling along of the trains . . . show the savagery that is in the depths of man . . . my mysterious drama' ['Et sur ce fond, sur ce roulement mécanique des trains . . . montrer la sauvagerie qui est au fond de l'homme . . . mon drame mystérieux' (fol. 400)]. In the depths of humanity, at bottom, is the other 'fond' [underlying ground], the continuous, mechanical movement of the trains: the surroundings – the milieu – is already deep inside the body. The *Ebauche* continues:

> Finally, the railway as the frame. I'd like to keep present throughout the entire novel the great circulation of a railway line as a continuous accompaniment. Make the terrifying and mysterious drama stand out against the great modern transit system . . . The *head* station in Paris, and this being, this iron serpent whose spinal cord is the line, the members, the branchings-off with their nerve-branches; finally, the destination towns that are like the extremities of a body, the hands and feet. *I would like to make this life underneath felt.*

> [Enfin, les chemins de fer comme cadre. Je voudrais garder pendant tout le roman la grande circulation d'une ligne comme accompagnement continu. Détacher tout ce drame mystérieux et effrayant sur le grand transit moderne . . . La gare de *tête* à Paris, et cet être, ce serpent de fer dont la colonne vertébrale est la ligne, les membres, les embranchements avec leurs rameaux nerveux; enfin les villes d'arrivée qui sont comme les extrémités d'un corps, les mains et les pieds. *Je voudrais bien faire sentir cette vie . . . de dessous.*
>
> (fols. 360–1; my emphases)]

As for La Croix-de-Maufras, the place of Grandmorin's murder and also the site of the couple's passion and resulting murder, it too must be a part of this body: 'This town has to be . . . a [nervous] offshoot' ['Il faudrait que cette ville fût . . . un embranchement' (fol. 367)]. The corresponding passage is in Chapter 2 of the novel. What is more, everything that the word 'roulement' has come to signify is linked in the novel to the crowd, a link underlined by sound repetition:

> Que de monde! Encore la *foule*, la *foule* sans fin, au milieu du *roule*ment des wagons, du sifflement des *machines* . . . ! C'était comme un grand *corps*, un être géant *couché* au *travers* de la *terre*, la *tête* à Paris, les *vertèbres* tout *le* long de *la ligne* . . . Et *ça passait, ça passait, mécanique . . . mécanique.* (1035)

> [So many people! The crowd, the endless crowd again, amidst the rolling of the wagons, the whistling of the machines . . . It was like a big body, a giant being lying across the earth, the head in Paris, the vertebrae all along the line . . . And it passed by, it passed by, mechanically.]

Joining the two again a few pages later, Zola makes us feel the rhythmic repetition of the train through assonance, alliteration and word repetition: 'sous ce *roule*ment continu . . . cette *foule* toujours si haletante' ['under this continuous rolling along . . . this crowd still panting for breath'].

In fact, this description of the physiology of the railway is, as I indicated earlier, precisely that given to the corporeal unconscious, a body governed by the spinal cord and the nervous system at the expense of the head. The head is situated in Paris, far from the mysterious drama. 'This is the head that I will show once' ['C'est la tête que je montrerai une fois' (fol. 365)]. Indeed, the head is largely absent from the novel, except for the magistrates representing the higher faculties, the head. Nonetheless, they are so far removed from the drama that they cannot comprehend the mechanical, instinctual forces that brought about the crime, even when one confesses to them. The passion of jealousy causes Flore to lose her head, and her cadaver is found with the head crushed into pudding after she walks into a speeding locomotive. Substituted for the head that reasons is the little ruby red serpent's head of the gold ring, symbol of hidden sexual drives, just as the iron serpent of the railway is a symbol of what is 'hidden and always lively' ['caché et toujours vivace' (1035)]. Jacques' head is literally separated from his body at the end of the novel, as is that of the driver transformed in the heat of passion. 'They'll be found without a head, without feet, two bloody torsos' ['On les retrouva sans tête, sans pieds, deux troncs sanglants' (1330)]. The parallel with the train is evident when it is 'deprived of its driver, like a beast gone mad' ['privé de son mécanicien, comme une bête prise de folie' (fol. 427)]. But, in fact, the driver in this novel is never separate from his machine: they are one. 'This job isolates him, he's only happy on his locomotive' ['Ce métier l'isole, il n'est heureux que sur sa locomotive' (fol. 369)]. Jacques is only happy, tranquil, 'when he is detached from the world, on his locomotive. When it carried him off in the shaking vibrations of its wheels at great speed . . . he didn't think any more' ['détaché du monde . . . sur sa machine. Quand elle l'emportait, dans la trépidation de ses roues, à grande vitesse . . . il ne pensait plus' (1044)]. Happiness depends on a state devoid of thought: becoming part of the machine, one is all body and no consciousness.

Zola makes us feel the life of the second consciousness underneath, always present as an accompaniment in the 'mechanical rolling along of the trains' ['roulement mécanique des trains']. Zola writes: 'I'll have the moving train with the locomotive, for the crime' ['J'aurais le train en marche avec le loco-motive, pour le crime' (fol. 361)]. The physiology of the train and the physiology of the criminal whose drives surge up from below are indissolubly joined in this affirmation. Shortly after this statement (about twenty lines), Zola decides exactly what his hero must be: 'What I need would be to know what Lantier is. I'd really like him to be a mechanic, driving a locomotive. The driver gives me everything; the operation/driving of the train, etc.' ['Ce qu'il me faudrait, ce serait de savoir ce qu'est Lantier. Je l'aimerais bien mécanicien, conduisant une locomotive. Le mécanicien me donne tout; la conduite du train, etc.' (fol. 363)]. The reader has already understood that it is this 'etc.' that we are interested in exploring.

We might ask why Zola abandons the term 'locomotive' in favour of 'machine' when he moves from the planning notes to the writing of the novel.[9] For even if he did not speak Spanish (*loco* is colloquial for 'crazy'), the word locomotive suggests locomotive disorder, the most common form of automatisms in nervous pathology. This disorder affects the extremities, the hands and feet. That would have fit perfectly the *topos* of the corporeal unconscious. But by shifting from the term 'locomotive' to the word 'machine', Zola makes the notion of the automatism immediately comprehensible to his readers, used to seeing the words 'automatic gestures, mechanical movement' used to describe hysterics and somnambulists, as well as the most popular *café-concert* performers of the 1870s and 1880s.

Automatisms can become so powerful that they dominate the head, and when they surge up they 'shake the foundations as high up as the administrative council' ['ébranl[e]nt jusqu'au conseil d'administration' (fol. 598)]. Then we see 'the whole Nation shaken by the crime, because the Empire is traversing a crisis and this business that happened to *a former magistrate* could hasten its *collapse*' ['Tout l'Etat ébranlé par le crime, car l'Empire traverse une crise et cette histoire arrivée à un *ancien magistrat* pourrait hâter *l'écroulement*' (fol. 404)]. Impulses issuing from the lower faculties attack the higher faculties. This causes what Janet called *désagrégation*, but we can settle for *écroulement* here. And we might even find the word more fitting, since it contains the mechanical *roulement* of the trains.

It is just three pages from the end of the *Ebauche* that the vision of how the novel must end comes to Zola.

> Something occurs to me: it's to end with the train deprived of its stoker and its driver moving ahead at full steam, like a beast gone mad . . . Put inside the train raucous soldiers unconscious of the danger and singing patriotic tunes. That way, the train is the image of France.
>
> [Je pense à une chose: ce serait de finir par le train privé de son chauffeur et de son mécanicien passant à toute vapeur, comme une bête prise de folie . . . Mettre le train plein de gais soldats inconscients du danger qui chantent des refrains patriotiques. Le train est l'image alors de la France.   (fols. 427–8)]

In the wake of the Franco-Prussian war, fears of degeneration and the startling rise of cases of hysteria would have been enough to justify the symbolism of disintegration. In addition, the crowd – inseparable from train travel in the novel – carries with it a strong tendency to give in to automatisms, as the sociologist Gustave Le Bon wrote in *Crowd Psychology* (the individual in a crowd is not himself, but rather an automaton). But it is not just the French, it is all of humanity that is in danger of derailment. The mysterious forces in the unconscious are extended in this novel to a vision of humanity, symbolised by the locomotive, the machine without a head, 'this train gone mad' hurtling forward 'like a prodigious and irresistible force that nothing can stop'. The machine with its primitive drives refuses to stay underneath, on the tracks that the higher faculties ignore or are helpless to redirect.

In the corresponding passage in the novel, Zola's vision becomes a clear evocation of the Unconscious.

> And on the engine raced, now out of control, onward and onward. At last this restive, unpredictable beast could let herself go completely . . . having slipped the clutches of her keeper and gone galloping off across the countryside . . . the pressure rose wildly . . . Galloping blindly, head down, the animal raced ahead . . . this lunatic train, this machine without driver or stoker, the cattle wagons full of soldiers singing patriotic songs for all they were worth . . . [The] runaway monster . . . was approaching . . . like some irresistible, prodigious force that nothing now could stop . . . On it raced, onward and onward into the dark night, bound they knew not where, simply onward.
>
> [Et la machine, libre de toute direction, roulait, roulait toujours. Enfin, la rétive, la fantasque pouvait céder à la fougue . . . échappée des mains du gardien, galopant par la campagne rase . . . la pression monta follement . . . C'était le galop tout droit, la bête qui fonçait tête basse . . . ce train fou, cette machine sans mécanicien ni chauffeur, ces wagons à bestiaux emplis de troupiers qui hurlaient des refrains patriotiques . . . [Le] monstre échappé . . . arrivait . . . comme une force prodigieuse et irrésistible que rien ne pouvait plus arrêter . . . Il roulait, il roulait, dans la nuit noire, on ne savait où, là-bas.   (1330–1)]

Here indeed is the 'grandeur' and 'poetic fury underneath' (fol. 396) that Zola said in his *Ebauche* he wanted the trains to possess; and, at the same time, he has found the way to describe the 'mystery' of the 'unknown force' evoked by hypnotism but that went beyond hypnotism. Zola said he wanted to find the mystery physiologically in one of his characters, but as we have seen, Jacques' physiology is inseparable from the physiology of the railway. The mechanics of the one is mirrored by the other. Finally, the description of their physiology is informed by the recent theories of the unconscious developed by the new physiological psychology. In picturing the force of the unconscious, Zola's prose in the novel's climactic scene transcribes the 'poetic fury underneath' reality that he said he was trying to capture. Whether it was in reading the work of Pierre Janet, or whether it was intuitive, Zola extended the physiology of the corporeal unconscious to a psychology that he worked out between the project for the novel and the novel itself. In doing so, he found the place where reality and mystery converge: in the human psyche. A mystery that, at the same time as it exists in the real world, appears to be outside reality.

Even Zola, the conductor of the scientific experiment that he called 'the experimental novel', was subject to the troubling effects of the locomotive in 1889. Here are some of the notes he made on the locomotive trip he took during the preparation of his novel: 'My impression on the locomotive. First, a lot of shaking, fatigue in the legs and finally stupor caused by the jolts. The head seems to empty out' ['Mon impression sur la locomotive. D'abord une grande trépidation, de la fatigue dans les jambes et un ahurissement à la longue produit par les secousses. La tête semble se vider'].[10] And since this is one train we can't get off, the best we can do is to try to understand how it works.

NOTES

1 Folio 338 of the planning notes held at the BNF, NAF, Ms 10274. Subsequent references to these notes are given in the text (as fol. 352, etc.).

2 Janet left in 1902 to occupy the Chair of Experimental and Comparative Psychology at the Collège de France.

3 Pierre Janet, *L'Automatisme psychologique: essai sur les formes inférieures de l'activité humaine* (Paris: Alcan, 1889), p. 309. Subsequent references are given in the text (as Janet 283, etc.).

4 Cited by Jean-Pierre Leduc-Adine in his presentation of the *Ebauche* of *La Bête humaine* (*La Bête humaine*, Paris: Babel, 1992), p. 559.

5 All page references to *La Bête humaine* are taken from volume IV of the Pléiade edition of *Les Rougon-Macquart* (Paris: Gallimard, 1966) and included in brackets in the text.

6 When they make love for the first time, their passion is also metaphorised by the train, 'which . . . passed by, rumbling and whistling, making the ground shake' ['qui . . . passa, grondant et sifflant, ébranlant le sol' (1151)].

7 Cesare Lombroso, *L'Homme criminel*; English translation, *Criminal Man*, edited and with an introduction by Gina Lombroso (New York: Putnam, 1911), p. 71. Subsequent references are included in the text (as Lombroso 71, etc.).

8 In his masterful study, 'Zola: la machine en tous ses effets' (see Recommended Reading), Geoff Woollen bases his interpretation of the character on the resemblance between Jacques' madness and epilepsy. However, as Janet demonstrates, the very same phenomena exist outside epilepsy and madness.

9 Woollen also asks the question, giving it a different answer to mine.

10 Cited by Henri Mitterand in Emile Zola, *Carnets d'enquêtes. Une ethnographie inédite de la France*, ed. Henri Mitterand (Paris: Plon, 1986), p. 553.

RECOMMENDED READING

Deleuze, Gilles, 'Zola et la fêlure', in *Logique du Sens* (Paris: Minuit, 1969), repr. in Emile Zola, *La Bête humaine* (Paris: Gallimard, 'Folio', 1977), pp. 7–24

Duffy, Larry, 'Beyond the Pressure Principle: Bestialisation, Anthropomorphism and the "Thermodynamic" Death Instinct in Naturalist Fiction', in *Le Grand Transit Moderne: Mobility, Modernity and French Naturalist Fiction* (Amsterdam and New York: Rodopi, 2005), pp. 195–234, *passim*

Hamon, Philippe, *'La Bête humaine' d'Emile Zola* (Paris: Gallimard, 'Foliothèque', 1994)

Harrington, Anne, *Medicine, Mind, and the Double Brain: A Study in Nineteenth-Century Thought* (Princeton: Princeton University Press, 1987)

Kanes, Martin, *Zola's 'La Bête humaine': A Study in Literary Creation* (Berkeley and Los Angeles: University of California Press, 1962)

Leduc-Adine, Jean-Pierre, Presentation of the *Ebauche*, *La Bête humaine* (Paris: Babel, 1992), pp. 555–75

Lombroso, Cesare, *L'Homme criminel*; English translation, *Criminal Man*, edited and with an introduction by Gina Lombroso (New York: Putnam, 1911)

Woollen, Geoff (ed.), *Zola: 'La Bête humaine', texte et explications* (Glasgow: University of Glasgow French and German Publications, 1990)

Woollen, Geoff, 'Zola: la machine en tous ses effets', *Romantisme*, 41 (1983), 115–24

II

JULIA PRZYBOS

Zola's utopias

Zola is a pivotal figure in late nineteenth-century French culture. His works both attracted and alienated key figures of the time. He moved from a phase of literary recognition to a late career marked by political and social utopianism. He is best known as the author of *L'Assommoir*, and for his open letter to the President of the Third Republic written in defence of Alfred Dreyfus. To art lovers, he is the journalist whose art criticism called for recognition of Edouard Manet and the Impressionists. To informed readers, he is the father of naturalism and the author of *Les Rougon-Macquart*. To students of literature, he is the writer who wanted to infuse scientific rigour into fiction. The experiments of Claude Bernard influenced Zola's literary theories, and Hippolyte Taine's trinity of *race, milieu* and *moment* determined the lives of his characters. To his biographers, Zola is a multifaceted man drawn to science and politics; concerned with social ills and their potential solutions; a staunch supporter of secularism in education; and an enthusiast of technological innovations like electricity. From Zola's biographies, a psychological portrait emerges of an obdurate believer in progress who 'frequently succumbed to one or another of the various forms of pessimism then circulating in France'.[1]

As a young admirer of Romantic poets, Zola began *La Chaîne des êtres* [*The Chain of Being*], a long poem on the progress of civilisation in the vein of Victor Hugo's *La Légende des siècles*. He soon abandoned poetry for prose and, with the exception of the powerful *Thérèse Raquin* (1867), published such undistinguished volumes as *La Confession de Claude* (1865), a semi-autobiographical novel retracing his unhappy beginnings in Paris; *Le Voeu d'une morte* (1866), a tearjerker depicting a poor orphan's gratitude, fidelity and renunciation; and *Les Mystères de Marseille* (1867), a serial story based on notorious court cases that, with its rambling plot, followed the melodramatic formula perfected by Eugène Sue in *Les Mystères de Paris* (1842–3). But if these works' banality could be explained by young Zola's allegiance to a sentimental brand of Romanticism, critics are less inclined to

169

defend the programmatic post-Rougon-Macquart novels, which relate the saga of the Froment family. How could the creator of masterpieces such as *L'Assommoir* and *Germinal* have penned *Les Trois Villes* (*Lourdes, Rome, Paris*) and, worse still, the mediocre *Evangiles* (*Fécondité, Travail, Vérité*)? Jean Borie sees in the latter works 'Zola's sad failure to give himself a conclusion in his *Gospels*' ['le pathétique échec des efforts de Zola pour se donner à lui-même, dans ses *Evangiles*, une conclusion'].[2] How are we to account for 'the third Zola', to quote Henri Mitterand's expression?[3] Two years before he finished writing *Les Rougon-Macquart*, Zola was asked to reflect upon the evolution of literature. He confided to the journalist that

> The future belongs to the writer or writers who can grasp the soul of modern society, who will liberate themselves from dogmatic theories for a more logical, compassionate approach to life. I believe in the truth of a larger, more complex painting, a wider window on humanity, a classic naturalism of sorts.

> [L'avenir appartiendra à celui ou à ceux qui auront saisi l'âme de la société moderne, qui, se dégageant des théories trop rigoureuses, consentiront à une acceptation plus logique, plus attendrie de la vie. Je crois à une vérité de la peinture plus large, plus complexe, à une ouverture plus grande sur l'humanité, à une sorte de classicisme du naturalisme.][4]

This mild disavowal of naturalism's strictures by an author penning his last volumes of the series was followed by an admission of lassitude with his own artistic credo. After the publication of *Fécondité* in 1899, he wrote to a friend: 'All this is quite utopian, but what do you want? I've been dissecting for forty years; let me dream a little in my old age' ['Tout cela est bien utopique, mais que voulez-vous? Voici quarante ans que je dissèque, il faut bien permettre à mes vieux jours de rêver un peu' (Cor. x 101, letter to Octave Mirbeau dated 29 November 1899)]. Zola as dispassionate observer became a passionate and optimistic prophet.

By all appearances, Zola's words support the opinion of scholars who periodise his literary career. However, his fiction cannot be neatly divided into first, second and third manners. Just as the lurid *Thérèse Raquin* (1867) seems out of place among his early works, *Le Rêve* (1888) – inspired by Bernardin de Saint-Pierre's idyllic *Paul et Virginie* (1787) – seems out of place in the Rougon-Macquart saga of social, economic and political ambition. Several episodes from *Fécondité*, Zola's first Gospel for a new religion of life, evoke the most squalid scenes from *Pot-Bouille* [*Pot Luck*].

Two opposed outlooks mark Zola's literary career. This contradiction embodied the French brands of optimism and pessimism that coexisted in the second half of the nineteenth century. The perception of physical, moral and social decline of a nation defeated in the Franco-Prussian war of 1870, and the political division resulting from the fratricidal Commune of Paris led to a pessimistic national mood. A tradition of faith in spiritual renewal and social progress, which would avert France's ruin, was equally popular. Optimism characterised the new breed of open-minded Catholics galvanised by Charles Péguy's *Cahiers de la Quinzaine*, as well as members of the secular left: liberal, radical and socialist reformers who opposed rampant political and clerical corruption while advocating secular education and improved living conditions for the masses. Pessimism was winning the day. Intellectuals voiced anxiety about the state of affairs, and the *beau monde* embraced pessimism as a sort of mental fashion statement. These currents of pessimism could be traced back to Schopenhauer's philosophy, scientific scepticism, Darwinian notions of the survival of the fittest,[5] and Max Nordau's diagnosis of the French as a degenerate nation.[6] Pessimism, in both its scientific and apocalyptic forms, seemed to have infected the world. The catastrophic science fiction invented by H. G. Wells was continued by the astronomer Camille Flammarion in his *La Fin du monde* (1894), which describes the death of civilisation and organic life due to the cooling down of Earth. Joris-Karl Huysmans, in *Là-bas* (1891), portrayed a millennialist believer who expects that the world's destruction will precede Christ's return to reign on earth, as prophesied in the Book of Revelations. Unscrupulous journalists exploited the fear of imminent Apocalypse in frequent alarmist articles. This backdrop of optimism and pessimism has provided Zola critics with a convenient system of categorisation. The optimistic view of human nature that pervades early works like *Le Voeu d'une morte* turns pessimistic in *Les Rougon-Macquart*, but not without a view towards redemption. Zola's early optimism resurfaces as utopianism at the end of *Paris*, the last volume of *Les Trois Villes*, and develops freely in *Les Quatre Evangiles*. Indeed his late protagonists are men of action who confront social ills and improve the lot of their fellow men and women. Despite the critical tradition, Zola's novels often combine both outlooks regardless of chronology.

If both pessimistic and optimistic currents of thought are found in Zola's works, their dosages vary from one volume to the next. His literary *œuvre* appears to be a battleground between the forces of pessimism and optimism, with the latter ultimately triumphant in the utopian *Evangiles*. A glance at Zola's early and middle fiction reveals the idealist tendencies that would define his later work.

The early and middle idealist

The hero of *La Confession de Claude* counters the misery of his Parisian life, marred by heartbreak and squalor, by leaving for sunny Provence, hoping for a moral and artistic rebirth among his childhood friends. An equally upbeat ending distinguishes *Le Voeu d'une morte*, in which Daniel Raimbault promises his dying benefactress, Madame de Rionne, that he will watch over her daughter's moral education. Several years later, Daniel falls in love with virtuous Jeanne and sends her anonymous love letters. However, Jeanne falls in love with Daniel's best friend Georges, and assumes that he penned the anonymous epistles. The conclusion rewards Daniel's magnanimity on his deathbed. With Jeanne and Georges at his side, Daniel hears Madame de Rionne's voice thanking him for fulfilling her last wish: 'You marry her to a man worthy of her, and your task is accomplished . . . Come to me' ['Vous la mariez à un homme digne d'elle, et votre tâche est accomplie . . . Venez à moi' (OC i 215)].

In *Les Rougon-Macquart*, the strain of idealism appears beyond its more atypical works, *Une page d'amour* (1878) and *Le Rêve* (1888). Victor Brombert has observed that 'the naturalistic novels of Zola are saturated with moral and moralizing undertones which point forward to the revolutionary lyricism of his later period'.[7] The Rougon-Maquart cycle provides uplifting epilogues to its stories of defeat, revolt, destruction and death. *L'Œuvre* records a discussion of a suicidal painter's friends after his burial. Bongrand the painter and Sandoz the prolific writer (Zola's partially idealised self-portrait) accept the motive behind Claude's suicide: he had fallen victim to his desire to capture unattainable beauty on canvas. Meanwhile the older and successful artists exhort each other to persevere. This ending invokes a central tenet of Schopenhauer, who believed that only art could provide solace for the futility of existence.

The major work of this era is *Germinal* (1885), which concludes with the hero, Etienne Lantier, leaving Montsou after a failed strike. The victims of the strike have succumbed to famine, accidents, explosions and gunshots fired by soldiers called in to quell the unrest. For the workers' charismatic leader, Etienne, however, defeat means a new life: he is bound for Paris to join the ranks of activists fomenting revolution. The optimistic ending is a prime example of Zola's symbolic vision of future rebellious generations: 'Men were springing up, a black avenging army was slowly germinating in the furrows, thrusting upwards for the harvests of future ages. And very soon their germination would crack the earth asunder' ['Des hommes poussaient, une armée noire, vengeresse, qui germait lentement dans les sillons, grandissant pour les récoltes du siècle futur, et dont la germination allait faire bientôt éclater la terre' (RM iii 1591)]. This projection into the future is not an ending but a leap of faith, because the story has not prepared the reader for an optimistic outcome. The strike has served to unify capitalists more than ever, while coalminers have been left to their fate. Etienne's demagoguery,

Rasseneur's cowardly egoism and Souvarine's murderous anarchism do not augur well for the victory of the oppressed masses. Zola's 'revolutionaries are seen as inadequate leaders both of their own class and, potentially, of society'.[8]

La Débâcle provides an even starker contrast between pessimism and optimism. The Second Empire has collapsed in the Franco-Prussian war, which led to the bloodbath of the Commune. Jean is the bereaved peasant-soldier who expresses his renewed hope as Paris burns: 'Above this city in flames a new dawn was already breaking . . . It was the inevitable rejuvenation of eternal nature, of eternal humanity, the promised renewal to those who hope and who work' ['Et pourtant, par delà la fournaise, hurlante encore, la vivace espérance renaissait . . . C'était le rajeunissement certain de l'éternelle nature, de l'éternelle humanité, le renouveau promis à qui espère et travaille' (RM v 911–12)].

The quasi-idyllic ending of *Le Docteur Pascal*, the last instalment in the chronicles of a rapacious family (whose members revert to theft, adultery, treason, incest, prostitution and murder to climb the social ladder) may come as a surprise. The protagonist Pascal is dead, yet the conclusion celebrates a new life: his niece and mistress Clotilde is happily nursing their son:

> The child was come, the redeemer perhaps . . . She, the mother . . . was dreaming about the future. If she devoted her whole life to him and made him big and strong, what would he become? A scholar who would pass on eternal truth, a captain who would add to the glory of his country, or a pastor who would still the passions and usher in the reign of justice?
>
> [L'enfant était venu, le rédempteur peut-être . . . Elle, la mère . . . rêvait déjà de l'avenir. Que serait-il, quand elle l'aurait fait grand et fort, en se donnant toute? Un savant qui enseignerait au monde un peu de la vérité éternelle, un capitaine qui apporterait la gloire à son pays, ou mieux encore un de ces pasteurs du peuple qui apaisent les passions et font régner la justice?   (RM v 1218)]

The birth of Pascal's posthumous child 'is seen as a kind of cosmic victory and a guarantee of continuity and renewal. His son is the social messiah whose destiny will be traced in the careers of Pierre, Mathieu and Luc Froment', in the post-Rougon-Macquart novels.[9]

The early utopian

The general critical consensus on the *Rougon-Macquart*'s final pages is that Zola was positing renewed hope for humanity through his symbolism of budding life. This was the foundation for a new cycle of novels, which would address the obstacles to a better future, in the aftermath of Napoleon III's departure and the establishment of a parliamentary regime. Zola shifted his focus from the country's recent past to contemporary concerns, most notably in *Paris*, which reflects the political scandals and anarchist bombings that shook France between 1892 and 1894.

Zola's most pressing concern was the public's waning enthusiasm for science. Intellectuals and journalists alike conceded that while progress in technology and medicine was indisputable, its practical results were relative. This view can been summed up in a paradox: the more men learn about the world the more there is left to learn. The decline of positivism coincided with the renewal of Catholicism. Young writers like Paul Claudel, Francis Jammes, Charles Péguy (the admirer of the socialist Jean Jaurès) and Ernest Psichari (the grandson of the sceptic Ernest Renan) converted to Catholicism.[10] In contrast with his intransigent predecessor, Pope Leo XIII preached reconciliation with the anticlerical French Republic, and in *Rerum Novarum* (1891), the encyclical that earned him the title of the 'workers' Pope', he laid the foundations of social Catholicism. The revival of faith in France owed much to Bernadette Soubirous, the young girl whose visions of the Virgin Mary in a grotto inspired many pilgrimages to Lourdes.

In the light of the widely recognised 'bankruptcy of science', Zola turned his attention to religion, science's emboldened rival for the minds of the people. He novelised three cities – *Lourdes, Rome, Paris* – in an examination of the theological virtues of Christianity: the primitive hope of the masses expecting miraculous cures in *Lourdes*, the renewed faith of the reformed Vatican in *Rome*, and the charity of saintly priests practising among the poor in *Paris*. As always, Zola was a meticulous researcher: he travelled to Lourdes in 1892 and to Rome in 1894 to collect information and to record his impressions. The same protagonist, a young priest named Pierre Froment, provides continuity to the series that could be called novels of re-education. In the first two volumes, Pierre is an alert observer of people and events, poised to engage in discussions with other characters who embody various concepts of faith and institutionalised religion, and their impact on society.

The plot of *Lourdes* is minimal. Pierre Froment accompanies his adolescent love on a pilgrimage that she hopes will cure her mysterious paralysis. Baffled doctors have not been able to alleviate Marie's symptoms, which resemble those of hysterical women in Charcot's ward in the La Salpêtrière hospital in Paris. Even though the miraculous spring water has restored the young woman's ability to walk, Pierre remains sceptical about divine intervention. During his stay, he observes the Church's ways of promoting its own glory while increasing its power over the naive masses. In language reminiscent of the Biblical parable of the sower, typical of Zola when describing Herculean projects, he deplores the fact that Bernadette's simplicity and religious fervour have been exploited by Catholic dignitaries. The hallowed city of Lourdes has nothing saintly about it, with its prostitutes, overcharging innkeepers and rapacious merchants. Jean Borie has noted that in *Lourdes* the Church deploys the same commercial mechanisms as department stores, banks and the stock exchange. Like the other institutions, the Church systematically exploits and thwarts the desires of the masses.[11]

In a leap that seems to underscore Pierre's ambivalence towards faith, *Rome* takes our hero to the Pope's doorstep in defence of his *Rome nouvelle*, a tract reminiscent of Lamennais' *Paroles d'un croyant* (1834). According to Pierre's book, the Pope would be master of the universe if he reunited all Christians and championed democracy. The young priest decries the Church's shrinking influence, especially among the dissatisfied workers. Pierre advocates Catholic socialism, a reconciliation between rich and poor, and collaboration for the general good. He praises Leo XIII's *Rerum Novarum* and its compassion for the workers, yet urges the Pope to relinquish earthly power in order to provide a spiritual beacon for the modern world. Only then, he argues, can the Church return to its original ideals of justice and truth. Vatican dignitaries reject Pierre's ideas. The progressive Pope grants Pierre an audience at the end of the novel's 800 pages; and the climactic dialogue reveals to the priest the hypocrisy of the Holy Father, whose proclaimed compassion is a propaganda tool designed to control the restless masses. The idealistic Pierre leaves Rome in disillusion.

The priest's sojourn in Rome turns him into an avid tourist, and much of *Rome* would have read like a Baedeker if Zola had not seized the opportunity to revisit his discussion of aesthetics, distancing himself from contemporary art. In a conversation in the Sistine Chapel between his mouthpiece Pierre Froment and Narcisse Habert, a *fin de siècle* snob, Zola contrasts two conceptions of art. Pierre is awed by the immensity of Michelangelo's creation and enraptured by its clarity, simplicity and strength. Narcisse rejects Michelangelo's art as devoid of mystery, and exalts Botticelli, who fascinated aesthetes with his enigmatic figures of melancholy grace. Zola's late fiction, however, would feature Michelangelo-like figures, men who undertook colossal enterprises requiring talent, strength, tenacity, and plain hard work: Pierre Froment's older brother Guillaume, the brilliant chemist in *Paris*; Pierre's sons Mathieu, the farmer in *Fécondité*; and Luc, the industrialist in *Travail*.

In *Rome*, Pierre's sightseeing goes beyond tourist sites. He visits an unfinished and decaying neighbourhood inhabited by the desperately poor. He perceives the fading splendour of the Church in symbols large and small. His host Cardinal Boccanera's *palazzo* surprises him with its squalor and decrepitude. The white robes of Leo XIII are encrusted from his use of snuff.

He visits the royal court and judges Victor-Emanuel II unequal to the enormous task ahead for a young country mired in an economic crisis that has impoverished the rich and the Vatican. Ancient patrician families are on the brink of extinction. Like Dario, Boccanera's nephew, male scions are the product of an effete bloodline. However, Zola's female characters are strong-willed, as is often the case in Decadent fiction. Princess Celia defies her family's opposition and marries Attilio, the commoner son of the king's minister Sacco; Boccanera's niece Benedetta has her marriage annulled in order to marry her childhood sweetheart Dario. In a far-fetched subplot, Zola employs the staples of Decadent novels: perfidious conspirators, irrepressible passions, lethal poisons and sexual perversions. The young priest witnesses a tryst between beautiful Benedetta and her dying cousin Dario, a sex scene whose extravagance rivals those of Rachilde's *La Marquise de Sade* (1887) and Jean Lorrain's *Le Vice errant* (1902). In contrast to Decadent writers, Zola presents deathbed lovemaking as a spontaneous and desperate act born of frustrated desire.

At the end of *Rome*, Pierre Froment has a vision of the doom of Mediterranean civilisation. Despite his pessimism, Pierre's vision brightens into a scenario of humanity's longing for primordial community: 'the great movement of the nations was the instinct, the need which impelled them to return to unity. Originating in a single family, afterwards separated and dispersed in tribes, thrown into conflict by fratricidal hatred, their tendency was nonetheless to become a single family again' ['le grand mouvement des nationalités était l'instinct, le besoin même que les peuples avaient de revenir à l'unité. Partis de la famille unique, séparés, dispersés en tribus plus tard, heurtés par des haines fratricides, ils tendaient malgré tout à redevenir l'unique famille' (OC vii 1008)]. According to Zola's planning notes, this dream of human solidarity would have triumphed in a world free of competition, racism and war in the projected novel *Justice*, the unwritten final *Evangile*.

After Pierre's crisis of faith in *Lourdes*, and his lost hope for renewed Catholicism in *Rome*, Zola would test charity – the third and last cardinal virtue – in *Paris*. Pierre's inborn urge to do good would require a harrowing experience to prove the impotence of charity. In the morning, Pierre finds a sick worker and crisscrosses the capital knocking for help on the doors of plutocrats, aristocrats and wealthy foreigners. They all send him away empty-handed. By nightfall, he has cajoled the help of one charity, but finds the worker dead in his freezing garret. The irony is not lost on Pierre: 'What! After so many centuries of Christian charity not a sore had healed. Poverty had only grown and spread, festering badly' ['Après tant de siècles de charité chrétienne, pas une plaie ne s'était fermée, la misère n'avait fait que grandir, que s'envenimer jusqu'à la rage' (OC vii 1245)]. Pierre's re-education has begun. The chemist Bertheroy convinces him of science's omnipotence, since science alone sweeps away dogmas and brings light and happiness. Pierre meets Guillaume Froment's busy and serene atheistic family: three sons, mother-in-law and a young ward, Marie, who impart to him the belief in work as both necessity and moral guide for people liberated from religion. Pierre and Marie fall in love and the priest leaves the Church to get married. He learns that human affection is the source of spiritual strength. At the end of *Paris*, Pierre Froment's re-education is complete: science replaces faith, love and work replace hope, and social justice will accomplish what charity could not.

In accordance with Zola's totalising vision in his late novels, *Paris* departs from *L'Assommoir* and *Le Ventre de Paris*, which compartmentalised the city's social milieus. Zola reworks familiar situations on a larger scale. Janzen, the travelling anarchist, evokes the rootless Souvarine in *Germinal*. The stories of Salvat, a desperate unemployed worker turned bomb-thrower, and Victor Mathis, the anarchist intellectual, add a tragic dimension to the ludicrous conspiracy in *Le Ventre de Paris*, in which shopkeepers, inspired by Florent (a Republican escaped from a penal colony), prepare an insurrection against the Emperor, their secrets spreading like brush fire throughout the neighbourhood. As a *dilettante* infatuated with Schopenhauer, Ibsen, Tolstoy, Nietzsche, and anarchism, Hyacinthe Duvillard is an intellectualised version of the effeminate Maxime, incestuous son of Saccard in *La Curée*. His crippled sister Camille is a malevolent reincarnation of Maxime's sickly wife Louise. The tenement house where the worker dies surpasses in horrific details the building in *L'Assommoir*. In *Paris*, Zola's vision of the city is more extreme than the ones we find in *Les Rougon-Macquart*: the bourgeoisie's selfishness is magnified, ridicule of the *beau monde* emphasised, courtesans' influence increased, parliamentary ineptitude amplified, political scandal deepened, and economic crisis inflamed, leading to anarchic outbursts of violence.

Paris reads like a concentrated version of several Rougon-Macquart novels, and like some of its predecessors, it contains a promise of a better future. Pierre has a prophetic vision reminiscent of Victor Hugo's imagery: 'Paris seemed to him to be a huge vat, in which a world fermented, something of the best and something of the worst, a frightful mixture such as witches might have used; precious powders mingled with filth, from all of which was to come the philter of love and eternal youth' ['Paris, c'était la cuve énorme, où toute une humanité bouillait, la meilleure et la pire, l'effroyable mixture des sorcières, des poudres précieuses mêlées à des excréments, d'où devait sortir le philtre de l'amour et d'éternelle jeunesse' (OC vii 1556)]. In Pierre's vision, Guillaume's explosive designed to blow up the Sacré Coeur has a peaceful application: a powerful engine, noiseless and odourless: 'And what a huge step! What sudden progress! Distance again diminished, all roads thrown open, and men able to fraternise!' ['Et quel nouveau pas de géant, quel progrès brusque, les distances rapprochées encore, toutes les voies ouvertes, les hommes fraternisant enfin!' (OC vii 1564)]. With its final image of the city looking like an immense field of wheat, *Paris* echoes the ending of *Germinal* and announces the *Evangiles*: Marie shows the magnificent view to her firstborn son: 'Look, Jean! Look, little one, it's you who'll reap it all, who'll store the whole crop in the barn!' ['Tiens! Jean, tiens! mon petit, c'est toi qui moissonneras tout ça et qui mettras la récolte en grange!' (OC vii 1567)]. Pierre Froment fathers four sons with Marie, each destined to be the hero of a Gospel for the twentieth century: *Fécondité, Travail, Vérité*, and the unwritten *Justice*. The first two volumes are of most interest to us because *Vérité* is best read as a transposition of the Dreyfus case that Zola situated in the milieu that he abhorred – schools run by priests, one of them guilty of paedophilia and murder, the others of cover-up.

Fécondité and Travail

Zola explained in a letter to his English translator that his *Gospels* fulfil a duty which the terrible state of affairs in France had imposed on him. He was not trying simply to amuse people or give them thrills: 'I am merely placing certain problems before them, and suggesting in some respects certain solutions, showing what I hold to be wrong and what I think would be right.'[12]

Zola wrote his first *Gospel* in response to France's sluggish population growth, which was a matter of national concern in light of the 1870 defeat. If the *fin de siècle* trend were to persist, the most populous country of the eighteenth century would be outnumbered by its victorious enemy, the united German states under the Kaiser of Prussia. Public concern about France's declining birthrate was mitigated by the lasting influence of Malthus' *Essay on Population* (1798), in which the author posited that realisation of a happy society will always be hindered by the miseries resulting from the tendency of populations to grow faster than food supplies. In a later edition, the economist acknowledged people's 'moral restraint' as a potential deterrent to human growth. Malthus' doctrine was popular among the higher ranks of society because it relieved the rich and powerful of responsibility for the condition of the working classes. The poor had chiefly themselves to blame, and not the negligence of their superiors, or the institutions of the country.

Like many contemporary writers, Zola worried about France's depopulation, but rejected Malthus' pessimistic conclusions.[13] He believed in indefinite future progress built on technical innovations and scientific discoveries, both fostered by the spread of education. According to Zola, an expanding population should not face starvation. In *Fécondité*, Mathieu Froment's wife Marianne declares that 'children grow, we must accept them, after all they bring with them joy and wealth' ['des enfants poussent, il faut bien les accepter, c'est quand même de la joie et de la richesse qui viennent' (OC viii 107)]. While Marianne speaks from experience to comfort a woman carrying an unwanted child, Mathieu and Dr Boutan develop arguments to counter the nihilism that reigns in the drawing rooms of Paris. For Mathieu, '[e]ven if the world should become densely populated, even if food supplies, such as we know them, should fall short, chemistry would extract other means of subsistence from inorganic matter' ['Si le monde se peuplait entièrement, et si même les subsistances venaient à manquer, la chimie serait là pour tirer des aliments de toute la matière inorganique' (OC viii 59)]. Yet for Dr Boutan the high birthrate of the working classes is 'the most hateful natality' ['la natalité la plus exécrable], but maintains that 'an endless increase of starvelings and social rebels' ['celle qui multiplie à l'infini les meurt-de-faim et les révoltés' (OC viii 38)] is not the fault of the destitute masses but a law of capitalism that requires a constant supply of cheap labour. In turn Mathieu concludes that, to avert social revolutions, a just apportionment of wealth is necessary.

Zola sides with the prolific Froment couple, and illustrates that in the higher ranks of society fertility is the foundation of happiness and prosperity, whereas sterility or the 'only' child lead to unhappiness, moral dissolution and tragedy. The novel takes place in two contrasting locations: the city, whose citizens avoid pregnancy in their sexual mores, and the country, where the Froments produce twelve healthy children, some forty grandchildren, and a growing number of great-grandchildren in the course of the novel's fifty-year span. *Paris'* prophetic ending notwithstanding, societal renewal will not happen in the city, where the elite first embraces Schopenhauer's stoical pessimism, then an unbridled hedonism influenced by Nietzsche's ideal of the 'superman'. When Charles Santerre, a popular drawing-room novelist, declares the right to pursue pleasure regardless of stifling moral norms, he expresses indifference to the survival of Paris: 'If it wants to die I will not oppose it. As far as I am concerned I am determined to help' ['S'il veut mourir, je ne m'oppose pas à ce qu'il meure. Pour mon compte, je suis résolu fermement à l'y aider' (OC viii 61)].

While Malthus propounded 'moral restraint', Zola demonstrates that the low birthrate among the bourgeoisie is due to greed, selfishness, lust, and anxiety about maintaining social rank. To avoid pregnancy or control the birthrate, wealthy Parisians practise abstinence, adultery, *coitus interruptus*, abortion and hysterectomy. When unwanted children were inevitable, Parisians would send them to the infamous 'baby farms' that sprang up throughout the coutryside, within train distance from Paris. The peasant women who developed this industry understood that they were paid to provide draconian conditions which no abandoned child would survive.

All contraceptive methods bring punishment in *Fécondité*. The industrialist Alexandre Beauchêne has a sole sickly son Maurice, destined to inherit the family fortune. With his wife Constance's tacit approval, he strays outside his marriage for sexual satisfaction. Alexandre-Honoré, a child born from his affair with worker Norine, is sent to a baby farm in Normandy. Some twenty years later, the illegitimate son returns as a seasoned criminal, feared by Norine yet courted by Constance, who is desperate for an heir after Maurice's premature death. When Alexandre-Honoré vanishes in the criminal underground, the rancorous Constance allows a deadly accident to claim the life of Mathieu and Marianne's son Blaise, to prevent the young man from inheriting Beauchêne's factory.

Beauchêne's accountant Morange keeps up bourgeois appearances by skimping on necessities to show off on Sunday outings. Valérie Morange's social ambitions bring worse results than those of *Pot-Bouille*'s Madame Josserand, who catches a rich son-in-law and imprisons her daughter in a disastrous marriage. When Valérie's accidental pregnancy quashes her hopes of climbing the social ladder, she undergoes an abortion and dies, leaving a bereaved husband unable to raise their daughter Reine. The adolescent Reine falls prey to a debauched countess, Sérafine de Lowicz, Beauchêne's widowed sister, who takes her to elegant orgies. When Reine becomes pregnant, Sérafine arranges for a hysterectomy. Reine bleeds to death. The death scenes in *Fécondité* are vintage *Rougon-Macquart* naturalism, with blood seeping through mattresses to form puddles on the floor. The celebrated hysterectomist Dr Gaude is murdered and castrated by an angry patient. His demise evokes the death of Maigrat in *Germinal*, the lecherous shopkeeper who fell off a roof, chased to his death by women whose starvation had transfigured them into castrating furies. Sérafine survives her surgery but meets a tragic end. The hysterectomy that was meant to enhance sexual pleasure ages her prematurely. In pursuit of an elusive orgasm, she stalks the streets of Paris for lovers, and finds fleeting satisfaction with Alexandre-Honoré, her criminal nephew. Zola's modern-day Messalina brings to mind Félicien Rops' engravings of women (*Les Sataniques*, 1883), and rivals the debauchery of decadent heroines like Octave Mirbeau's Clara in *Le Jardin des supplices* (1899).

The interlocked urban plots play out Zola's fundamental idea: nonprocreative sex among the higher classes causes social problems. Its inevitable by-product is a child 'born chance-wise, and then cast upon the pavement, without supervision, without prop or help, rots there and becomes a terrible ferment of social decomposition' ['né au petit bonheur, lâché ensuite sur le troittoir, sans surveillance, sans soutien. Il s'y pourrissait, il y devenait un terrible ferment de décomposition sociale' (OC viii 427)].

The cumulative misery and deaths of *Fécondité*'s subplots contrast with its upbeat central plot: the story of Mathieu and Marianne Froment illustrates Zola's conviction that sexuality must be liberated but tamed in marriage, whose role is reproduction and the production of wealth to sustain it. The Froments retreat to Chantebled in the country to stretch the husband's salary earned at Beauchêne's machine factory. Mathieu leases fallow land and marshes and, with the use of irrigation and technology, transforms wasteland into a bread-basket. His successful return to the land is Zola's response to the potential scarcity of food supply, which so worried Malthus' followers.

The story of Mathieu and Marianne is simple and repetitive. The rhythm of *Fécondité* is dictated by Marianne's gestations and nursing of her twelve children. Each two-year period is framed by inspired lovemaking that leads to conception: 'Desire passed like a gust of flames – desire divine and fruitful, since they possessed the power of love, kindliness, and health. And their energy did the rest – that will of action, that quiet bravery in the presence of the labour that is necessary, the labour that has made and regulates the world' ['Le désir passait en coups de flamme, le divin désir les fécondait, grâce à leur puissance d'aimer, d'être bons, d'être sains; et leur énergie faisait le reste, la volonté de l'action, la tranquille bravoure au travail nécessaire, fabricateur et régulateur du monde' (OC viii 279)]. The Symbolist poet Gustave Kahn admired the repetition of such passages; he read *Fécondité* like a long hymn in praise of human fertility and Earth's fecundity.

But what if fertility were to surpass fecundity, proving Malthus right? Not to worry: beyond France's borders there are vast lands waiting to be ploughed. The story of Mathieu and Marianne's entrepreneurial son Nicolas illustrates the influence on Zola of Prévost-Paradol's *La France nouvelle* (1868). The young man leaves Chantebled for Africa and embarks on a colonising mission with his new wife, fathering eighteen children and bringing prosperity to the region, which will produce a surplus of grain to feed France, with the introduction of machinery from Beauchêne's factory. The twin brother of the murdered Blaise, Denis Froment, is the factory owner. Only adventurous colonists can make Africa bountiful: native Africans are incapable of cultivating the wilderness. Nicolas leaves the settled Niger valley to explore its western frontiers, and becomes a successful landowner. He looks forward to the promise of a trans-Saharan railway that will unite the

French colonies into an empire, a dream inconsistent with Zola's previous treatment of the concept in *Paris*. The idyllic picture of colonial life presents one problem: a hostile indigenous population that must be freed from Islam to embrace French reason and enterprise.

Zola ignored the wretched conditions of French sub-Saharan colonies, documented by the military men who conquered the region. The optimism of *Fécondité* contrasts with early colonial fiction, which negatively portrayed French experience in that part of the world. Africa was a lethal place in novels like Pierre Loti's *Le Roman d'un spahi* (1881). After Zola, the continent became a land of spiritual and material rebirth in propagandistic literature. To the chagrin of humanist Charles Péguy, who welcomed *Paris*' promise of social justice, Zola had embraced imperialism in his first Gospel for the twentieth century.[14]

After showing in *Fécondité* that a growing population need not face starvation, Zola addressed in *Travail* the question that, with the advance of the industrial revolution, had dominated political debate in the Third Republic: the workers' deepening poverty, which led to innumerable strikes that threatened to disrupt the status quo. Political thinkers on the left condemned the pauperisation of the masses and conceived a number of different remedies. The discussions between the characters of *Travail* reflect ideas of Saint-Simon, Auguste Comte, Proudhon, anarchists, and collectivists. 'Beaming with charity, faith and hope', the novel's hero, the young engineer Luc Froment, rejects quick and violent revolution in favour of slow and peaceful evolution, his belief in the ultimate triumph of science having taught him patience and resolve. He has infinite trust in the capacity of human goodness and solidarity to overcome material obstacles and dispel psychological fears. A vehement critic of society, Luc is also a man of action ready to work tirelessly for the betterment of society. A crumbling society must be rebuilt from its foundations up: labour must be reformed first if the world is to avert bloody revolutions. He explains to his friend Jordan, the open-minded capitalist turned scientist: 'Well, it is just that that I want to attempt here. I shall, at least, be able to make my experiment an example; it will be a reorganisation of labour on a small scale, a fraternal factory, a rough draft, as it were, of what society may become in the future' ['Eh bien! C'est cela que je veux tenter ici, c'est du moins un exemple que je veux donner, une réorganisation du travail en petit, une usine fraternelle, l'ébauche de la société de demain' (OC viii 670)]. Luc believes that work is both a necessity and a panacea, provided that it is made easier and its dignity restored.

To make us appreciate Luc's monumental task, Zola describes L'Abîme, a steelworks founded by Quirignon's ancestor. Over the years, harsh working conditions had transformed steel-workers into wretched slaves, while the immense profits generated by their work had turned once entrepreneurial capitalists into incompetent pleasure-seeking egoists. The founder's reckless great-grandsons die young, his kind great-granddaughter Suzanne marries an idle dandy, Boisgelin, who spends the family fortune on the wife of L'Abîme's director, Fernande Delaveau, the novel's *femme fatale*-cum-Messalina.

The young engineer is an enthusiast of Charles Fourier (1772–1837), whose social ideas had been implemented with some success in the first half of the nineteenth century. According to Fourier, a *phalanstère* (phalanstery) composed of 1,600 people cultivating some 5,000 acres of land are at the basis of a future harmonious society in which each individual follows his/her impulses and passions completely. The phalanstery's members act not only in their own interests but also in the interest of the community and society as a whole. Fourier's ideas were popularised by his disciples, who wrote voluminously and attempted to put his ideas into practice. Victor Considérant founded a phalanstery in San Antonio, Texas. In the United States more than thirty phalansteries were founded throughout the Middle West and Middle Atlantic regions. The longest lived were the Wisconsin Phalanx (1844–50) and the North American in New Jersey (1843–56). In France abortive attempts at phalanxes were made at Condé-sur-Vesgres in 1833 and at Citeaux in 1841. Jean-Baptiste Godin's famous profit sharing establishment at Guise, the *Familistère*, had Fourieristic features.

From Fourier Luc takes the notion of capital, talent and labour joining forces for the collective good. He wins over La Crêcherie's owner, the scientist Jordan, who gives him capital and *carte blanche*. Jordan pursues his technical experiments. Luc transforms the foundry into an association of employees, and starts a steelworks whose modern technology returns a better profit than the antiquated L'Abîme. With the introduction of Jordan's revolutionary electric furnace, the new Crêcherie triples its revenue. After many difficulties and a short-lived desertion of workers unhappy with the prohibition of alcohol, Luc Froment's association is a great success, bringing 'the most happiness to the most people'.

Next to the modernised industrial plants is the new city, a community of single family houses standing in lush gardens watered by fresh streams. At the centre of the city, there is the community house with its facilities: an assembly hall, a library, and public baths. Religion and its vestiges are gone, their demise symbolised by an old church fatally crushing the priest. Knowledge is dispensed to all children in co-educational schools, where boys and girls learn the values of partnership. With passing time, inter-class unions flourish, and social hierarchy dissolves.

After years of competition, La Crêcherie takes over the ruined L'Abîme, when the guilt-ridden patriarch Qurignon orders his heirs to surrender all their possessions to the new collective. After his death, they settle down in the idyllic community and become active members. The wife, Suzanne Boisgelin, helps Luc's life-partner Josine and Jordan's sister Soeurette to run social projects for the needy women, children and the elderly. The husband quits his lazy habits, enticed to work by the sight of busy men and women. His supervisor's job cures his boredom and improves his general health.

La Crêcherie's example is imitated by many groups that form associations according to their professions, abolishing competition. Textile workers join forces and share their profits, while local farmers plough their fields together and deliver their produce directly to La Crêcherie, by-passing shopkeepers. Commerce does not die without a fight; merchants gang together, find a pretext, and go to court, seeking financial compensation from La Crêcherie. Naturally, they lose their case, as Zola shared with socialist ideologues and economists a revulsion towards the 'parasitic nature' of commercial activity. On his way home from the tribunal, the victorious Luc faces an angry crowd that hurls insults and a few stones. A nod to Zola's own ordeal during the Dreyfus case, Luc's Golgotha can also be read on a symbolic level: his moral and physical sufferings call to mind the martyrdom of Steven, the first Christian saint stoned to death. As *Travail* is a utopia, Luc will prevail in the end, winning all adversaries to his cause.

Zola does not neglect humanity's ultimate evil, death. A presence even in Nicolas Poussin's painting of idyllic Arcadia (1639), death is neutralised at the novel's conclusion. As a very old man, Luc hears of distant battle whose unprecedented death count has turned humanity against war forever. Before dying, the beloved patriarch and benefactor of mankind looks back with satisfaction at his achievements, and sees the fruits of his titanic labour: 'Then Luc, with one last look, took in the town, the horizon, and the fields, where the reform that he had begun was going on so prosperously. His work was done. He had founded his city. And so he died, passing into the unmeasured flood of universal love and life eternal' ['Alors, Luc, d'un dernier regard, embrassa la ville, l'horizon, la terre entière, où l'évolution commencée par lui, se propageait et s'achevait. L'œuvre était faite, la Cité était fondée. Et Luc expira, entra dans le torrent universel d'amour, d'éternelle vie' (OC viii 969)]. If we compare Daniel Raimbault's peaceful death in *Le Voeu d'une morte* and Luc Froment's serene end in *Travail*, we can gauge how much distance separates the early Zola, and his lonely hero dedicated to the salvation of one person, from the late Zola and his socially conscious protagonist, beloved by women, who devotes his life to improving the lot of humanity.

A future for Zola's utopias?

Over one hundred years after it received a generally positive reception, *Fécondité* has lost its prophetic urgency. As if in mockery of Malthus' predictions, today's French government worries about overproduction and subsidises farmers to leave their fields fallow. Despite immigration from former colonies, the dwindling population remains a concern, and the low birthrate threatens to break down France's retirement system. The legacy of *Travail* has fared better, to judge by its editorial history. In 1979, Verdier published an edition prefaced by workers from LIP, the bankrupt watch plant taken over and rescued by its employees, a 400 strong collective of men and women who worked and lived together between 1973 and 1974.[15] When they came across Zola's *Travail*, they compared their experience with those of the Crêcherie collective founded by Luc Froment. LIP workers debated Luc's pet concept of multi-tasking, which they found to increase rather than relieve stress. They lamented the sense of fraternity once shared by workers, when self-appointed leaders started behaving like the overbearing Luc Froment. Dialogues like those of the LIP workers have fuelled public interest in *Travail*'s utopia. Perhaps the crowning factor of the book's legacy is its perpetually sold-out status within the *Evangiles* series. In our post-communist world, Zola's utopian problematic still resonates within the rising culture of alternative solutions.

Work towards this chapter was facilitated by funds provided by PSC CUNY.

NOTES

1 Philip D. Walker, 'Zola: Poet of an Age of World Destruction and Renewal', in David Baguley (ed.), *Critical Essays on Emile Zola* (Boston, Mass.: G. K. Hall & Co., 1986), p. 178.
2 Jean Borie, *Zola et les mythes, ou de la nausée au salut* (Paris: Seuil, 1971), p. 12.
3 Henri Mitterand, 'Le troisième Zola', in Carlo Menichelli and Valeria de Gregorio Cirillo (eds.), *Il Terzo Zola. Emile Zola dopo I Rougon-Macquart. Atti del Convegno Internationale, Napoli-Salerno, 27–30 maggio 1987* (Naples: Instituto Universitario Orientale, 1990), p. 1.
4 Emile Zola, 'Déclaration à Jules Huret sur l'évolution littéraire', *Echo de Paris* (31 March 1891); repr. in Henri Mitterand (ed.), *Ecrits sur le roman* (Paris: Livre de Poche, 2004), p. 309.
5 Social Darwinism, developed by Herbert Spencer, counted among its proponents the German philosopher Ernest Haeckel and such men of action as General Moltke and the Chancellor Bismarck in Prussia, as well as John D. Rockefeller in America. See Robert J. Niess, 'Zola et le capitalisme: le darwinisme social', *Les Cahiers naturalistes*, 54 (1980), 57–67.
6 Born in Hungary in 1849, Max Simon Nordau studied medicine, travelled widely and settled in Paris in 1880. In *Entartung (Degeneration)*, published in 1892, he

argued that madness, suicide, crime and pathological literature are symptoms of modern times. In a chapter entitled 'Zola and his School' he writes that science can have nothing to do with fiction. Nordau's study was translated into French as *Dégénérescence* in 1894.

7 Victor Brombert, *The Intellectual Hero: Studies in the French Novel 1880–1955* (London: Faber, 1961 [1960]), p. 73.
8 Brian Nelson, 'Zola's Ideology: The Road to Utopia', in David Baguley (ed.), *Critical Essays on Emile Zola* (Boston: G. K. Hall & Co., 1986), pp. 161–72 (p. 164).
9 Brian Nelson, *Zola and the Bourgeoisie: A study of Themes and Techniques in 'Les Rougon-Macquart'* (London: Macmillan/Totowa, New Jersey: Barnes and Noble, 1983), p. 37.
10 For details see Micheline Tison-Braun, *La Crise de l'Humanisme: Le Conflit de l'individu et de la société dans la littérature française moderne* (Paris: Nizet, 1958), vol. I, p. 198.
11 *Zola et les mythes*, p. 221.
12 Ernest Alfred Vizetelly, *Emile Zola, Novelist and Reformer. An Account of his Life and Work* (London and New York: John Lane and The Bodley Head, 1904), p. 498.
13 See David Baguley, *'Fécondité' d'Emile Zola: roman à thèse, évangile, mythe* (Toronto: University of Toronto Press, 1973), pp. 171–2.
14 See Martin Stein, 'L'épisode africain de *Fécondité*', *Les Cahiers naturalistes*, 48 (1974), 164–81.
15 Emile Zola, 'Préface des ouvriers de LIP', *Travail* (Paris: Verdier, 1979), p. 11.

RECOMMENDED READING

Baguley, David, *'Fécondité' d'Emile Zola: roman à thèse, évangile, mythe* (Toronto: University of Toronto Press, 1973)
'*Les Trois Villes*: "Le Voyage de pèlerin" selon Zola', in *Zola et les genres* (Glasgow: University of Glasgow French and German Publications, 1993), pp. 134–46
'Du récit polémique au discours utopique: l'Evangile républicain de Zola', *Les Cahiers naturalistes*, 54 (1980), 106–21; repr. in *Zola et les genres* (Glasgow: University of Glasgow French and German Publications, 1993), pp. 147–60
Becker, Colette, *Les Apprentissages de Zola* (Paris: Presses Universitaires de France, 1993)
Beecher, Jonathan, *Charles Fourier: the Visionary and His World* (Berkeley: University of California Press, 1968)
Borie, Jean, *Zola et les mythes, ou de la nausée au salut* (Paris: Seuil, 1971)
Case, Frederick Ivor, *La Cité idéale dans 'Travail' d'Émile Zola* (Toronto: University of Toronto Press, 1974)
Collin, Pierre, 'L'Eglise catholique dans *Les Trois Villes*', in Michèle Sequin (ed.), *Zola* (Paris: Fayard/Bibliothèque nationale de France, 2002)
Compagnon, Antoine, 'Zola dans la décadence', *Les Cahiers naturalistes*, 67 (1993), 211–22
Cosset, Evelyne, 'L'Espace de l'utopie. Nature et fonction romanesque des utopies dans *Le Ventre de Paris*, *Germinal*, *La Terre* et *L'Argent*', *Les Cahiers naturalistes*, 63 (1989), 137–47

'*Paris*: From Preliminary Sketch to Mythical Vision', *Bulletin of the Emile Zola Society*, 20 (1999), 24–36

Desroche, Henri, *La Société festive: du fouriérisme écrit aux fouriérismes pratiqués* (Paris: Seuil, 1975)

Frye, Northrop, 'Varieties of Literary Utopias', in Frank Edward Manuel (ed.), *Utopias and Utopian Thought* (Boston, Mass.: Houghton Mifflin, 1966), pp. 25–49

Gural-Migdal, Anna, 'Représentation utopique et ironie dans *Le Ventre de Paris*', *Les Cahiers naturalistes*, 74 (2000), 145–61

Mitterand, Henri, 'La Révolte et l'utopie: de *Germinal* à *Travail*', in *Le Discours du roman* (Paris: Presses Universitaires de France, 1980), pp. 150–63

'The Novel and Utopia: *Le Docteur Pascal*', in *Emile Zola: Fiction and Modernity* (London: The Emile Zola Society, 2000), pp. 123–35

Mayer-Robin, Carmen, 'The Formidable Flow of Milk in *Le Docteur Pascal* and *Fécondité*. Two Feminine Allegories for the "République en marche"', *Excavatio*, 13 (2000), 69–80

Mossman, Carol, *Politics and Narratives of Birth: Gynocolonization from Rousseau to Zola* (New York: Cambridge University Press, 1993), pp. 201–27

Nelson, Brian, 'Zola's Ideology: the Road to Utopia', in David Baguley (ed.), *Critical Essays on Emile Zola* (Boston, Mass.: G. K. Hall & Co., 1986), pp. 161–72

Noiray, Jacques, 'De la catastrophe à l'apaisement: l'image du fleuve de lait dans les *Villes* et les *Evangiles*', *Les Cahiers naturalistes*, 67 (1993), 141–54

'L'Imaginaire de la politique dans *Paris*', *Les Cahiers naturalistes*, 74 (2000), 203–21

Ouvrard, Pierre, *Le Fait religieux, notamment le miracle, chez Zola* (Paris: L'Harmattan, 2002)

Pelletier, Jacques, 'Zola évangéliste', *Les Cahiers naturalistes*, 48 (1974), 205–14

Perry, Katrina, '"L'encre et le lait": Writing the Future in Zola's *Fécondité*', *Excavatio*, 13 (2000), 90–9

Ripoll, Roger, *Réalité et mythe chez Zola* (Paris: Honoré Champion, 1981)

Schmid, Marion, 'From Decadence to Health: Zola's *Paris*', *Romance Studies*, 18 (December 2000), 99–111

Steins, Martin, 'L'épisode africain de *Fécondité* et la tradition exotique', *Les Cahiers naturalistes*, 48 (1974), 164–81

Suwala, Halina, 'Regard et parole dans *Lourdes*', in *Autour de Zola et du naturalisme* (Paris: Honoré Champion, 1993), pp. 219–30

Ternois, René, *Zola et son temps* (Paris: Les Belles Lettres, 1961)

Thomson, Clive, 'Une typologie du discours idéologique dans *Les Trois Villes*', *Les Cahiers naturalistes*, 54 (1980), 96–105

Walker, Philip D., *'Germinal' and Zola's Philosophical and Religious Thought* (Amsterdam/Philadelphia: John Benjamins Publishing Company, 1984)

'Poet of an Age of World Destruction and Renewal', in David Baguley (ed.), *Critical Essays on Emile Zola* (Boston, Mass.: G. K. Hall & Co., 1986), pp. 172–85

White, Nicholas, 'Anarchism under the City', in *The Family in Crisis in Late Nineteenth-Century French Fiction* (Cambridge: Cambridge University Press, 1999), pp. 167–75

12

OWEN MORGAN

'J'accuse . . . !': Zola and the Dreyfus Affair

When the Chamber of Deputies approved, in July 1906, the transfer of Zola's ashes to the Panthéon, it sought to honour, first and foremost, not the creator of the fictional Rougon-Macquart and Froment families but the author of 'J'accuse . . . !', the incendiary open letter to the President of the Republic that was the climax of his campaign on behalf of Captain Alfred Dreyfus. For the article published in the newspaper *L'Aurore*, on 13 January 1898, in defence of the Jewish officer who had been wrongly convicted, in December 1894, of betraying military secrets to Germany, the virtual enemy, could be seen in retrospect to have transformed what began as a legal battle over the verdict of a court martial into a much wider conflict opposing, on one side, the advocates of truth, justice and human rights, and on the other the standard-bearers of nationalism, militarism and reasons of State. In the winter of 1898–9, the very survival of the Third Republic seemed threatened, as the extremist anti-Dreyfusards, most of whom were unreconciled to the republican regime and fundamentally opposed to its ideology, fought to gain the upper hand. But in the end, when their opponents emerged victorious, the parliamentary balance shifted from the centre to the left, and a coalition of Radicals and Socialists, augmented by the left wing of the Progressists, as the socially conservative Opportunists were now calling themselves, consolidated the Republic and became the solid foundation for successive governments until the First World War.

In November 1897, when Zola began his campaign, the government was headed by Jules Méline, who was also Minister of Agriculture – he would later urge his compatriots to 'return to the soil' rather than pursue industrial expansion. Méline's ministers were drawn from the ranks of the Progressists, who formed the dominant group in the Chamber: 317 Progressists had been elected in 1893, along with 122 Radicals, 49 Socialists and 88 representatives of the far right, royalists, Bonapartists or former supporters of General Boulanger, the charismatic figurehead of the nationalist and authoritarian movement that had seemed likely to overthrow the Republic at the beginning of 1889. Although the enemies of the republican regime were heavily out-numbered in the Chamber, they were able to agitate public opinion through a number of bitterly polemical newspapers. The redoubtable pamphleteer Henri Rochefort, who had been a strong supporter of the Boulangist move-ment, was still conducting a vituperative campaign against the Republic in *L'Intransigeant*, while his fellow Boulangist Edouard Drumont had increased the circulation of his virulently anti-Semitic *La Libre Parole*, which bore on its masthead the slogan 'France for the French!' ['La France aux Français!'] and claimed to represent the interests of the victims of Jewish capitalism, to 100,000, more than the combined sales of three respected republican newspapers of the centre, *Le Figaro* (40,000), *Le Temps* (35,000) and *Le Journal des Débats* (15,000).[1] The circulation of *La Croix* (170,000) was larger still. This newspaper, published by the Assumptionist Fathers, had suc-ceeded in undermining, in 1892, Pope Leo XIII's policy of conciliation with the Republic and remained vehemently hostile towards Jews, Protestants and Freemasons, castigating them as the true masters of a regime dedicated to the destruction of the Church: its principal editorialist, Father Vincent de Paul Bailly, quickly became a leading supporter of extremist anti-Dreyfusism, while at the same time urging his readers to vote for royalist candidates in the legislative elections of May 1898.

'L'Affaire': September 1894 to November 1897

Before considering the different phases of Zola's campaign on behalf of Dreyfus, it will be useful to recall the sequence of events that led up to it, and in particular the role of the various officers and handwriting experts named in 'J'accuse . . . !' What became known simply as 'l'Affaire' began in September 1894, when an unsigned note in French listing various items of confidential information about military matters was retrieved by a cleaner in the German Embassy from the waste-paper basket of the military attaché, Colonel von Schwartzkoppen. The cleaner was also in the pay of the counter-espionage department of the French War Ministry, a body consisting of five officers and an archivist that operated under the title of the Statistical Section: she delivered the note, which would become known as the *bordereau* (the term normally refers to a form listing the documents contained in a file) to one of the Section's senior officers, Major Henry, who duly passed it on to his chief, Colonel Sandherr. Sandherr was answerable directly to the Deputy Chief of Staff, General Gonse, and through him to the Chief of Staff, General de Boisdeffre; when all three officers had examined the document, it was deliv-ered to the War Minister, General Mercier, who was to play a sinister role from the beginning to the end of the Affair. Other staff officers were then consulted, one of whom expressed the opinion that the *bordereau* must have been written by an artillery officer serving as a probationer on the General Staff. Among this small group was Captain Dreyfus, a graduate of the Ecole Polytechnique and a member of a wealthy textile-manufacturing family of Alsatian Jews: when it was discovered that his handwriting bore some resemblance to that of the *bordereau*, General Mercier became convinced that he had found Schwartzkoppen's informant. Although the only official handwriting expert consulted, Alfred Gobert, reported that the note could well have been written by someone else, Mercier had already decided to place Dreyfus under arrest. The arrest was made, in a highly melodramatic manner, by an officer from the Operations and Training Bureau, Major du Paty de Clam; in the days that followed, he subjected Dreyfus to a series of brutal interrogations, without informing him of the precise nature of the charges. Information about the arrest was leaked to the press, and on 1 November, *La Libre Parole* reported the details under the banner headline: 'High Treason: Jewish Officer A. Dreyfus Arrested' ['Haute trahison: Arrestation de l'officier juif A. Dreyfus'].

It now seems clear that General Mercier was afraid, in the autumn of 1894, of losing his portfolio, as a result of the campaign that *La Libre Parole* and *L'Intransigeant* had been conducting against him since the spring, first for refusing to meet with the inventor of a new explosive, who promptly offered his invention to Germany, then for ordering, in August, the premature release of 60,000 conscripts, without informing either the Army commissions of the Senate and Chamber or the President of the Republic. An unresolved espionage case would have proved disastrous for him, and he needed to identify and convict the author of the *bordereau* as quickly as possible. At the beginning of November, *La Libre Parole* stepped up its campaign: Dreyfus had been arrested on 15 October, but since there was no indication that a trial was imminent, it was obvious, according to Drumont, that Mercier had been slow to act because of Jewish pressure. By the middle of the month, however, Drumont's attacks had ceased, and on 17 November, he congratulated the War Minister on his determination to bring Dreyfus to trial. On 28 November, *Le Figaro* published a statement that Mercier had made in the course of an interview with its military correspondent: Dreyfus' guilt was 'absolutely certain', and he had been communicating with German agents for the previous three years.

In the meantime, the members of the Statistical Section, attempting to find in their files proof of Dreyfus' treason, had discovered an intercepted note from Schwartzkoppen to his Italian counterpart, Colonel Panizzardi: the note referred to 'that scoundrel D.' ['ce [*sic*] canaille de D.'], who had delivered to the German attaché twelve plans of the fortifications of Nice. In

November, Major Bexon d'Ormescheville, guided by du Paty de Clam, began to build the case against Dreyfus. He concluded that the captain should be committed for trial, but the only grounds he offered for the charge of high treason were the resemblance of his handwriting to that of the *bordereau*, his knowledge of German and Italian, and the evidence of his colleagues, which showed him to be of the spy type. The trial began on 19 December and took place in private, at the prosecution's request: the only spectators were the Prefect of Police and a representative of the War Minister, Major Picquart. At the end of the second day, Major Henry declared, under oath, that a 'man of substance' had warned the Statistical Section of the presence of a traitor in the War Ministry. He identified Dreyfus as the traitor. On 22 December, when the seven military judges retired to consider their verdict, they were shown, on Mercier's orders, a secret dossier containing the *canaille de D.* note and two other documents referring vaguely to espionage activities, along with a commentary by du Paty de Clam. Apparently, they were unaware that the production of documents not shown to the defence was illegal in both military and civil courts. Unanimously, they sentenced Dreyfus to deportation for life, to forfeiture of his rank and to military degradation. In April 1894, he was settled on Devil's Island, off the coast of Guiana, in solitary confinement.

A year later, Schwartzkoppen's waste-paper basket produced another alarming document, this time a *petit bleu*, one of the thin blue letter-cards that were used at the time for express delivery within Paris. The card, addressed to a certain Major Esterhazy, was examined by the newly promoted Lieutenant-Colonel Picquart, the officer who had represented General Mercier at Dreyfus' trial and had now replaced Colonel Sandherr at the head of the Statistical Section. Picquart quickly discovered that Esterhazy, the son of a distinguished French general, was a dissolute stock-market gambler, always short of money; in August 1896, he was able to examine letters written by the officer and saw immediately that the handwriting was that of the *bordereau*. At the beginning of September, he reported his findings to Gonse, who was then on leave in the country. He was instructed to 'separate' the Esterhazy case from the Dreyfus case, which was to be considered closed, and an exchange of letters followed, in which Gonse urged extreme caution in dealing with Esterhazy. On 14 September, the newspaper *L'Eclair* published a long article purporting to offer conclusive proof of Dreyfus' guilt. The article revealed that certain secret papers had been shown to his judges and gave a distorted version of the *canaille de D.* note, claiming that it contained Dreyfus' name in full. In the weeks that followed, it became clear to Gonse and de Boisdeffre that Picquart was not going to be dissuaded from his belief that Dreyfus had been wrongly convicted. They decided, with the approval of the new War Minister, General Billot, that he must be removed from the Statistical Section, and on 12 November Billot informed him that he now possessed a document establishing Dreyfus' guilt once and for all. The document, a note from the Italian attaché Panizzardi to Schwartzkoppen referring to their relations with 'that Jew', had been forged by Major Henry: the first, and the most infamous, of the numerous documents he would forge in the months ahead, it would become known as the *faux Henry* [the Henry forgery]. On 14 November, Picquart was ordered to leave on a special mission to organise espionage activities on the German frontier. In January 1897, he was sent to Tunisia, where he soon realised, in spite of the friendly letters he continued to receive from Gonse, that he had lost the trust of his superiors and that Henry was conspiring against him. Consequently, he returned to Paris in June and revealed his situation and what he had learned about the Dreyfus case to his friend, lawyer and fellow Alsatian Louis Leblois, at the same time swearing him to secrecy. In July, however, Leblois, fearing that his friend's life was in danger, divulged what Picquart had told him to Auguste Scheurer-Kestner, the vice-president of the Senate and another Alsatian. Scheurer began his own investigation, continuing it throughout the summer, which he spent in Alsace. He soon had no doubt that Dreyfus was innocent, and on 29 October he met briefly with the President of the Republic, Félix Faure, who was clearly reluctant to talk about the case. On the following day, he had a long conversation with General Billot, the War Minister, who had been his friend for many years. Billot promised to investigate further, but made Scheurer promise to say nothing to the press for two weeks: that evening, Billot revealed what he had been told to a number of journalists, and Scheurer was violently attacked by *La Libre Parole* and *L'Intransigeant*, among other newspapers.

By this time, a small group of men shared the conviction of Dreyfus' family that a miscarriage of justice had occurred. They included Major Forzinetti, the governor of the military prison where Dreyfus had been detained and interrogated following his arrest, and Bernard Lazare, a young journalist and literary critic who had written a short account of the Dreyfus case based on the information provided by Mathieu Dreyfus, the captain's brother and devoted champion: Mathieu's own informants were Forzinetti, his brother's lawyer Edgar Demange, and Dr Joseph Gibert, a close friend of Félix Faure who had learned from the President himself that a secret dossier had been shown to Dreyfus' judges and that the *canaille de D.* note did not contain the full name Dreyfus. Although Lazare had completed his account by the summer of 1895, Mathieu did not authorise its publication until after *L'Eclair*'s revelations of September 1896. It was printed as a pamphlet in Brussels and copies were sent to various influential people in France, among them Zola.

Soon afterwards, Lazare visited Zola to discuss his findings; on 10 November, the newspaper *Le Matin* published a facsimile of the *bordereau*, and a week later an augmented version of Lazare's pamphlet was published in Paris.

'Truth is on the march': November 1897 to January 1898

In October 1894, at the time of Dreyfus' arrest, Zola had been in Rome, doing the preparatory work for his novel about the Italian capital. He had read very little about the case until his return to Paris on 16 December: like most people, he saw no reason to doubt the unanimous verdict of the court martial, although he was, as he wrote later, appalled by the accounts of the harrowing degradation ceremony and thought of using the scene in a novel. On 16 May 1896, he had published an article in *Le Figaro* denouncing anti-Semitism, and in particular the fanaticism of newspapers like *La Libre Parole*, but in November he showed little interest in what Lazare had to say about the Dreyfus case and merely glanced through his pamphlet. A year later, on 6 November 1897, Lazare came to see him a second time, leaving him a copy of his second pamphlet, which included an analysis of the *bordereau* by handwriting experts from six different countries. On 8 November, Louis Leblois paid him a visit: he revealed what he had learned about the Dreyfus case and showed him the letters that Picquart had received from Gonse. That evening, Zola wrote to his wife, who was travelling in Italy: 'The documents I have been shown have left me absolutely convinced that Dreyfus is innocent' ['Les pièces qui m'ont été soumises m'ont absolument convaincu que Dreyfus est innocent' (Cor. ix 96)]. And he added: 'I shall only get involved if I have to, bearing in mind that I am not alone in the world, and that I have children to think about' ['Je ne me mettrai en avant que si je dois le faire, après avoir songé que je ne suis pas seul dans la vie et que j'ai charge d'âmes'].[2] Leblois returned two days later with an invitation to a luncheon meeting at Scheurer-Kestner's home on 13 November, explaining that Scheurer needed the advice of people who were accustomed to addressing the general public, and that another writer, Marcel Prévost, would also be attending the meeting. Zola accepted the invitation and was captivated by Scheurer's account of the Affair: later, Scheurer noted in his diary that he was certain that Zola would 'do something', whereas Prévost would do nothing and regret it later.

The next few days were highly eventful. On 14 November, Emmanuel Arène, a deputy and friend of Scheurer, disclosed in *Le Figaro* the information that Scheurer had gathered since July, adding a few facts about the real author of the *bordereau*, whose name he did not reveal. On the following day, Mathieu Dreyfus, acting on information provided by a stockbroker who had recognised Esterhazy's handwriting on a facsimile of the *bordereau*, accused Esterhazy by name in a letter to General Billot, which the newspapers published on 16 November. The right-wing press stepped up its attacks on Scheurer, who was by now receiving injurious and threatening letters from all over France. Following Mathieu's denunciation, the Military Governor of Paris, General Saussier, ordered a preliminary investigation, which was carried out by General de Pellieux. On 20 November, de Pellieux recommended that no action be taken against Esterhazy, since the only evidence against him was his handwriting and Dreyfus had already been convicted as the author of the *bordereau*. He also concluded that an investigation should be carried out into Picquart, who appeared to have disclosed confidential documents to Leblois. Picquart was summoned back from Tunisia, and on 23 November, on Billot's orders, de Pellieux began an official judicial inquiry into the Esterhazy case.

Two days earlier, Zola had met by chance one of the co-editors of *Le Figaro*, Fernand de Rodays, who had believed for some time that Dreyfus was innocent. On 24 November, he informed his wife that he had written an article for *Le Figaro* on Scheurer-Kestner and the Affair: 'I was haunted, I couldn't sleep at night. I had to relieve my feelings. I was finding it cowardly to remain silent. I don't care about the consequences: I am strong enough, I shall face whatever happens' ['J'étais hanté, je n'en dormais plus, il a fallu que je me soulage. Je trouvais lâche de me taire. Tant pis pour les conséquences, je suis assez fort, je brave tout' (Cor. ix 102)]. His article, entitled 'M. Scheurer-Kestner', appeared on 25 November, and its concluding sentence would become the Dreyfusards' battle-cry: 'Truth is on the march, and nothing will stop it' ['La vérité est en marche, et rien ne l'arrêtera']. A second article, 'Le syndicat', followed on 1 December: it demolished the anti-Dreyfusards' claim that a 'syndicate' of Jewish millionaires was paying huge sums of money to buy support for Dreyfus and to have a Christian convicted in his place. The following day, Zola wrote to his wife: 'I am writing the finest page I have ever written' ['Je suis en train d'écrire la plus belle page de ma vie' (Cor. ix 111)]. On 3 December, de Pellieux submitted his new report, once again concluding that there was no case against Esterhazy and calling for an inquiry into Picquart's conduct. However, Esterhazy's lawyer advised his client to request a court martial: given de Pellieux's recommendation, he was bound to be acquitted, and the proceedings would serve to clear his name. On 4 December, Saussier signed the order to prosecute; the summary of the evidence was entrusted to a retired officer, Major Ravary. On the same day, in the Chamber of Deputies, Méline proclaimed that there was 'no Dreyfus Affair' ['Il n'y a pas d'affaire Dreyfus'], and a motion was passed condemning the leaders of the 'odious campaign' that was 'troubling the public conscience'. Zola had no doubt already completed his third article for *Le Figaro*, 'Procès-verbal' [Assessment], which appeared on 5 December. Two days later, in the Senate, Scheurer-Kestner interpellated Méline and Billot on the motion of 4 December, and both men solemnly declared that Dreyfus was guilty beyond doubt. Once again, Scheurer was the object of vitriolic attacks in the right-wing press, while anti-Dreyfusard students demonstrated against him in the Latin Quarter. Zola was determined to respond in his defence, but by now *Le Figaro*'s more conservative readers were expressing strong disapproval of the newspaper's pro-Dreyfus stance and threatening to cancel their subscriptions. The co-editors took fright, and Zola was obliged to find another means of continuing his campaign. On 14 December, his publisher, Eugène Fasquelle, brought out his pamphlet entitled *Lettre à la jeunesse* [*Letter to the Young Men*], an open letter in the second person upbraiding the student demonstrators. A second pamphlet, *Lettre à la France*, appeared on 7 January 1898.

Zola's writings on the Affair prior to the Esterhazy trial present, over a period of six weeks, a striking transition from comparative restraint to impassioned polemic.[3] The first article is a moving tribute to the venerable senator who has espoused Dreyfus' cause, and Zola's only expressions of anger are reserved for those who have vilified Scheurer-Kestner in a gutter press inflamed by 'imbecilic anti-Semitism' ['l'imbécile antisémitisme']. He refrains from commenting on the Affair itself, since another trial is imminent, except to say how much his novelist's imagination has been captured by the three main characters of the story so far revealed, Dreyfus, Esterhazy and Scheurer, the dispenser of justice: his remarks seem intended to assert his special competence to comment on the Affair, and they anticipate the presentation of the full cast of the drama in 'J'accuse . . . !'. The interests of the Army, he argues, would be better served by redressing a judicial error than by concealing it. In his second article, Zola intensifies his attacks on Drumont and his acolytes by combining telling arguments with an effective use of irony. Exposing the polemical excesses of the anti-Dreyfusards, he justifies the solidarity of other Jews with Dreyfus' family, declaring that it is both their right and their duty to defend an innocent man. There is indeed, he concludes, a growing body of people who have joined forces to fight for truth and justice, but it is not Jewish money that has brought them together: it is rather the vicious propaganda of the anti-Semites in their 'vile press' ['presse immonde']. He has joined the 'syndicate' himself, and he hopes that every decent person in France will do so as well. In 'Procès-verbal', Zola adopts a more passionate tone. Reviewing the escalation of the Affair that has taken place since Mathieu Dreyfus' denunciation of Esterhazy, he uses imagery relating to debauchery and prostitution to attack 'the gutter press in heat' ['la basse presse en rut'], inveighing against the 'poison' of anti-Semitism and its chief purveyors. The public has been led astray, but its true nature will be restored, if only it can hear once again the language of humanity and justice. In the first pamphlet, a new enemy emerges: the student demonstrators, Zola asserts, have been influenced not so much by the press as by those responsible for the motion passed in the Chamber on 4 December, which was a betrayal of the republican ideal embodied by Scheurer-Kestner. He expresses the fear that the Affair could be used to establish a military dictatorship: the prospect would later reveal itself to be a very real one. In his second pamphlet, Zola again rails at anti-Semitism and the 'vile press', and he accuses the nation, personified as a woman always ready to fall in love with a king and sleep with a general, of desiring both military dictatorship and a return to theocracy and religious intolerance: clearly, he has become aware of the campaign conducted by the newspaper *La Croix*.

In the conclusion to his *Lettre à la France*, Zola expresses his concern that the Esterhazy trial will take place in private, so that the War Ministry can keep hidden from the public facts about the Dreyfus case that need to be forced into the light. In reality, he was already convinced, at the beginning of 1898, that the outcome would be an acquittal, which would amount to a second conviction of Dreyfus, and he had devised a strategy, based on a study of the Press Law of 1881, that would, he hoped, rally the Dreyfusard ranks. Until 1881, all actions for defamation came before a police court [*tribunal correctionnel*], where they were heard by a panel of three judges, with no jury. The 1881 law, however, distinguished between libel against private citizens and libel against public servants: cases of the first type continued to be heard by a *tribunal correctionnel* and could take place in private at the prosecution's request, whereas actions of the second type were put to trial by jury at the assizes and heard in public. Articles 30 and 31 of the Press Law, to which Zola would refer explicitly in 'J'accuse . . . !', listed the various categories of public servants, which included members of the armed forces. Zola's aim, therefore, was to force a public trial for libel, and on the day before his second pamphlet came out he revealed his plan to Georges Clemenceau, the former leader of the Radicals in the Chamber of Deputies, who had lost his seat in 1893 and had been, since October 1897, the principal editorialist of Ernest Vaughan's newly founded newspaper *L'Aurore*: Clemenceau had begun to express grave doubts about the legality of Dreyfus' trial, although he was not yet persuaded of his innocence. It was no doubt on 6 January that the decision was taken to publish Zola's planned text in *L'Aurore*. The following evening, Zola read to Eugène Fasquelle what seems to have been a preliminary draft; that morning, *Le Siècle* had published in full d'Ormescheville's report of 1894, making it absolutely clear how flimsy the evidence against Dreyfus was. The Esterhazy court martial opened on 10 January; the military witnesses were heard in private, as were the three handwriting experts, Belhomme, Varinard and Couard, who had examined the *bordereau* in the course of Ravary's investigation and concluded that it had not been written by Esterhazy. On 11 January, shortly after 8 pm, Esterhazy was declared innocent: immediately, Zola informed Ernest Vaughan that his article would be ready by 10 am the following morning. The original title was 'Lettre à M. Félix Faure, Président de la République', but after reading the text, which was long enough to cover the whole front page of *L'Aurore* as well as part of the second, Vaughan followed Clemenceau's advice and placed under the masthead the words that opened, anaphorically, eight paragraphs of Zola's conclusion: 'J'accuse . . . !'

As several critics have pointed out, the structure of 'J'accuse . . . !' corresponds closely to the quadripartite model for forensic discourse prescribed by the ancient rhetors: exordium, *narratio, confirmatio*, epilogue. After a brief appeal, tinged with irony, to Faure's goodwill, Zola announces clearly what will follow: the condemnation of the military judges who have acquitted Esterhazy 'by order' ['par ordre'] and the denunciation of 'the wicked horde of the real guilty men' ['la tourbe malfaisante des vrais coupables'] who conspired to have Dreyfus convicted. The exordium is followed by an account of the courts martial of 1894 and 1898 shaped by Zola's storyteller's imagination into a 'superb drama of life-forces in conflict'.[4] Dreyfus, Zola asserts, is the innocent victim of an evil genius, du Paty de Clam, who is a 'diabolical' figure so powerful that his superiors, Mercier, de Boisdeffre and Gonse, became his 'hypnotised' accomplices. The elevation of du Paty to the status of prime culprit is, of course, a major distortion of the true hierarchy of guilt, although it must have corresponded very closely to Dreyfus' own perception of his principal tormentor. It is clear, however, that Zola has chosen to capture the public's attention through dramatisation rather than argumentation, presenting a highly personal vision of the Affair in which, as Henri Mitterand puts it, 'the implacable accuser' ['l'accusateur implacable'] is at the same time 'the impeccable *narrator*' ['le *narrateur* impeccable'].[5] Casting himself in the role of dispenser of justice, the same part he attributed to Scheurer-Kestner in the first article of his campaign, he is seeking to breathe new life into the Dreyfus story, which the Prime Minister himself had tried to bury by proclaiming that there was no Dreyfus Affair. Having thus presented his main characters, Zola exposes the hollowness of the d'Ormescheville report and dismisses the *canaille de D.* note as a 'ludicrous' document clearly referring to someone other than Dreyfus, before concluding his account of the events of 1894 with a vehement denunciation of anti-Semitism. Turning to the

Esterhazy trial, Zola once again presents a dramatic antithesis, opposing Picquart, 'a man whose life has been without blemish' ['un homme à la vie sans tache'] to the wretched debt-ridden criminal Esterhazy. While Picquart is about to become another victim of the War Ministry – he was indeed placed under arrest on the same day that 'J'accuse . . . !' appeared in *L'Aurore*, put on the retired list on 26 February and arrested again on 13 July – Esterhazy has enjoyed the protection of his superiors, including that of Billot, who had the opportunity to act in the name of truth and justice but has chosen instead to side with the General Staff and become its partner in crime.

In the third part of his article, Zola exposes the sinister factors and the many crimes – the hammer-blow phrase 'c'est un crime' appears six times in a single short paragraph – that lie behind the two courts martial, anti-Semitism, unscrupulous collusion with the 'vile press' to cover Esterhazy and condemn Dreyfus a second time, militarism and clericalism, stressing again the link between the Army and the Church to which he had pointed in his *Lettre à la France* through the image of the nation kissing the hilt of the sabre as though it were a cross. A final antithesis opposes the senior officers, 'a few brass-hats crushing the nation under their boots' ['quelques galonnés mettant leurs bottes sur la nation'], to Scheurer-Kestner and Picquart, 'two decent men, two simple hearts, who left things up to God while the devil was doing his work' ['deux braves gens, deux coeurs simples, qui ont laissé faire Dieu, tandis que le diable agissait']. Abruptly, with a brief apology for the length of his letter, Zola moves into his crowning peroration, the great litany of arraignments in eight short paragraphs 'aligned like stanzas', as Charles Péguy famously wrote, that pillory in turn and by name each of the perpetrators of the 'crime de lèse-humanité et de lèse-justice' committed in 1894 – only Henry, about whose role Zola clearly knew very little in January 1898, is missing from the list – as well as Billot, de Pellieux, Ravary, the handwriting experts Belhomme, Varinard and Couard and, collectively, the judges who convicted Dreyfus and acquitted Esterhazy. A ninth paragraph makes it clear that Zola's accusations are meant to be self-incriminating and indicates the two articles of the Press Law that deal with the type of libel he has knowingly committed. He concludes, calmly, with the briefest of sentences: 'I am waiting' ['J'attends'].

After 'J'accuse . . . !'

The response was carefully prepared. While a quarter of a million copies of *L'Aurore* were being sold in the streets – ten times the newspaper's normal circulation – Billot denounced in the Chamber the 'anti-patriotic attacks' that were weakening the Army's prestige and Méline promised that Zola would be prosecuted. The charge was announced on 18 January. It was confined to the passages of 'J'accuse . . . !' which alleged that Esterhazy's judges had acquitted by order an officer whom they knew to be guilty, a matter on which the defence could presumably produce no evidence; all Zola's other accusations were ignored, so that the Dreyfus case would, in principle, be kept out of the proceedings. In Paris and throughout France, the impact of 'J'accuse . . . !' was enormous. Anti-Semitic demonstrations took place immediately in the Latin Quarter, and the unrest increased in the two days that followed. On 17 January, 3,000 demonstrators marched through the streets of Nantes; in the next few days, the disturbances spread to as many as fifty towns and cities, among them Angers, Bordeaux, Dijon, Marseille, Nancy and Rennes, marking the beginning of what Pierre Birnbaum has called the 'anti-Semitic moment', a 'pogrom without fatalities' that continued, to varying degrees, until the summer of 1899.[6] On 18 January, a serious outbreak of violence took place in Algiers, where the Jewish quarter was sacked and a number of deaths were reported. 'J'accuse . . . !' was also the catalyst that relaunched and strengthened the Dreyfusard movement. The small core of Dreyfus' supporters regained the confidence it had lost with Esterhazy's acquittal, and the first result was the organisation of two petitions in favour of a judicial review of the Dreyfus case (*la révision* in French), which appeared in *L'Aurore* from, respectively, 14 and 16 January onwards. Many distinguished academics from the Sorbonne, the Collège de France and the Faculty of Medicine, as well as younger graduates of the Ecole Normale Supérieure, signed the petition in the first days, as did numerous writers and artists: there were finally 1,482 signatures in 38 lists. Commenting on the petitions in *L'Aurore* on 23 January, Georges Clemenceau wrote: 'Is it not a sign, all these *intellectuals* who have come together from all sides in support of an idea and are unwavering in their belief?' ['N'est-ce pas un signe, tous ces *intellectuels*, venus de tous les coins de l'horizon, qui se groupent sur une idée et s'y tiennent inébranlables?']. His use of the noun *intellectuel*, italicised as a neologism in January 1898, helped to give it the sense that would become familiar in the twentieth century, while the petitions published in *L'Aurore* marked the birth of the modern idea of the intellectual committed, as a member of the group, to the support of a moral or political cause.

When Zola's trial opened on 7 February, in a courtroom full of hostile spectators, the presiding judge, Albert Delegorgue, made it clear that he would restrict the evidence to the single charge laid. Since, under French law, questions put to witnesses during cross-examination are put through the presiding judge, and not by counsel directly, he was able to cut off debate every time the defence strayed from the Esterhazy case, with the words:

'The question will not be put' ['La question ne sera pas posée']. In spite of his vigilance, however, he was unable to prevent Edgar Demange from declaring that he had learned about the use of the secret dossier at Dreyfus' trial, while General de Pellieux rashly confirmed the existence of the *faux Henry*. In response to the prosecution's handwriting experts, Zola's lawyer, Fernand Labori, brought in as expert witnesses a number of distinguished paleographers and historians, all of whom testified that the handwriting of the *bordereau* was Esterhazy's. Another highlight of the trial was the intervention of the Socialist deputy Jean Jaurès. Although he had signed, on 19 January, a manifesto of the parliamentary Socialists presenting the Affair as a 'bourgeois civil war' and calling on the working class to remain neutral, Jaurès agreed to appear as a character witness for the defence, exposing the connivance between Esterhazy and the General Staff and condemning the illegality of Dreyfus' trial. On 21 February, Zola addressed the jury himself, proclaiming passionately his conviction that Dreyfus was innocent. Two days later, he was found guilty and sentenced to the maximum penalty, twelve months in prison and a fine of 3,000 francs.

During the next few months, Fernand Labori used various tactics to keep the case alive, and a crucial development took place in the Affair itself. On 2 April, following an appeal, Zola's conviction was quashed on technical grounds: it was ruled that the action should have been brought by Esterhazy's judges themselves, and not by General Billot acting on their behalf. When the officers duly lodged their complaint, it was decided that the trial would take place at Versailles, on the grounds that the proceedings would be less likely to disturb public order there than in Paris. In the meantime, Zola had been sued for libel by Belhomme, Varinard and Couard, who were seeking damages of 100,000 francs each. Because they were deemed to be private citizens, Labori was unable to have the case put to trial by jury, and a *tribunal correctionnel* awarded them 5,000 francs each on 9 July; another appeal followed. On 23 May, the first day of the Versailles trial, Labori forced a postponement by lodging an appeal against the choice of venue. Following the May legislative elections, which saw a slight movement towards the extremes on both left and right, Méline's government fell on 15 June, and the anti-clerical and anti-Dreyfusard Radical Henri Brisson became Prime Minister. The new War Minister, Godefroy Cavaignac, was determined to put an end to the Affair; after examining the evidence against Dreyfus, he became convinced of his guilt and concluded that Esterhazy had been his accomplice. On 7 July, he announced his conviction to the Chamber, reading, by way of proof, three documents: the *canaille de D.* note, the *faux Henry* and a note from Schwartzkoppen to Panizzardi that Henry had altered so as to incriminate Dreyfus. By a majority of 545 votes to none – Méline and fifteen Socialists abstained – the Chamber approved the placarding of Cavaignac's speech in each one of France's 36,000 communes. Cavaignac also ordered Picquart's prosecution on the almost forgotten charge of showing confidential documents to Leblois. On 18 August, Cavaignac's military aid, Captain Cuignet, would examine the *faux Henry* and discover how the note had been forged.

On 16 July, Zola published in *L'Aurore* a scathing open letter to Henri Brisson in which he ridiculed Cavaignac's three documents, as well as the legend, revived by the War Minister in his speech to the Chamber, that Dreyfus had confessed to his crimes on the day of his degradation. Holding Brisson himself responsible for his minister's action, he declared: 'You have just killed an ideal. That is a crime. You will not get away with it. You will be punished' ['Vous venez de tuer l'idéal. C'est un crime. Et tout se paie, vous serez puni']. Two days later, Zola returned to Versailles for the trial postponed on 23 May. Again Labori sought to have the debate extended to the whole of 'J'accuse . . . !' When his request was refused, he lodged another appeal, but the judges refused to grant another postponement: he promptly left the courtroom, followed by Zola, thus allowing the verdict to go against the defendant by default. He explained to Zola that his case would not be regarded as closed until the judgment had been delivered to him in person by a process server and persuaded him, with the help of Clemenceau, who had assisted in the defence of Zola's co-defendant Alexandre Perrenx, the manager of *L'Aurore*, to leave the country immediately, without returning home. Reluctantly, Zola left for England by the evening boat-train. He would remain there for eleven months, living first in Surrey and then in the suburbs of London, at the Queen's Hotel in Norwood. His leadership of the Dreyfusard cause was, perforce, over.

In Zola's absence, new leaders would emerge. From 10 August to 20 September, Jean Jaurès, who had lost his parliamentary seat in the May elections, published in the socialist newspaper *La Petite République* a series of thirteen articles under the general title 'The Evidence' ['Les Preuves'], in which he demolished the case against Dreyfus; the newspaper was by now totally committed to the Dreyfusards' cause, and it became, along with *L'Aurore*, Zola's main source of information about the Affair during his exile. On 31 August, events took a dramatic turn when Henry, who had been arrested following the discovery of his principal forgery, committed suicide; his arrest had caused de Boisdeffre to resign as Chief of Staff, and his suicide brought about Cavaignac's resignation. Zola believed that the Affair was over, only to discover that the right-wing press would hail Henry as the perpetrator of a 'patriotic forgery' and that Cavaignac's successor, General Zurlinden, would declare himself adamantly opposed to a judicial review of the Dreyfus case. His hopes were raised once again at the end of September, when Brisson's cabinet voted, by a majority of six to four, to refer Madame Dreyfus' request for a review to the Cour de cassation, the Supreme Court of Appeal, but were dashed once more when Zurlinden, who had resigned as War Minister and returned to the post of Military Governor of Paris, signed the order for Picquart's court martial, on the grounds that he had forged the *petit bleu*: a petition launched by the Ligue des Droits de l'Homme [Human Rights League], which had been founded following Zola's trial, on the initiative of the former Justice Minister Ludovic Trarieux and was organising public meetings in support of Dreyfus throughout France, drew between 30,000 and 40,000 signatures. The Criminal Division of the Cour de cassation began its inquiry into the Dreyfus case on 8 December, but in January Zola became convinced that all was lost when the newly founded and anti-Dreyfusard Ligue de la Patrie française [League of the French Fatherland], which would have 400,000 members by the end of 1899, supported an attempt to have the inquiry removed from the Criminal Division and referred to a combined assembly of all three divisions of the Cour de cassation, the other two being deemed less likely to favour Dreyfus. The transfer was approved by the Chamber on 10 February, but another turning-point in the Affair followed six days later, when Félix Faure, by now an intransigent anti-Dreyfusard, suffered a stroke in the arms of his mistress and died without regaining consciousness. The election to the presidency of Emile Loubet, a staunch republican known to be in favour of *la révision*, and the farcical failure of the former Boulangist Paul Déroulède's attempt to stage a *coup d'état*, with the aid of his recently resuscitated Ligue des Patriotes – his intention was apparently to install General de Pellieux in the Elysée Palace and have the Ligue des Patriotes form a provisional and dictatorial government – were grounds for renewed optimism. On 3 March, the Criminal Division of the Cour de cassation ruled that Picquart was no longer subject to military law and transferred his case to a civil court. The combined divisions of the Court began their examination of the Dreyfus case on 21 March; on 3 June, they quashed the 1894 judgment and ordered a new court martial for Dreyfus. Zola left for Paris the following evening; on 5 June, *L'Aurore* announced his return by publishing the article he had completed a few weeks earlier, under the title 'Justice'.

The verdict of the Cour de cassation caused an explosion of rage among the anti-Dreyfusards. On 4 June, at the Auteuil racecourse, a royalist baron struck with his cane the unprotected Emile Loubet. A week later, 100,000 republicans marched in protest to the Longchamp racecourse: the following day, when a Socialist deputy brought to the Chamber evidence of police brutality, the government, now headed by Charles Dupuy, fell. On 13 June, the charge that Picquart had forged the *petit bleu* was dismissed, and on 16 June, Loubet invited the senator René Waldeck-Rousseau to form a government of republican defence. On 26 June, Waldeck's cabinet, which included France's first Socialist minister, Alexandre Millerand, won its vote of confidence by a majority of twenty-five votes. It was enough to ensure that Dreyfus' second trial would take place under a government of the left, with all the anti-Dreyfusards relegated to the opposition. The trial took place at Rennes, lasting more than a month, from 7 August to 9 September. When a second guilty verdict made it clear that no court martial would admit to an error of justice, a presidential pardon was issued: Dreyfus was at last reunited with his family and free, when he had recovered his strength, to fight the last battle for the rehabilitation that would finally come in 1906, four years after Zola's death. Following the pardon, Waldeck's War Minister, General Galliffet, brought the Army to order, while the Prime Minister himself proposed legislation intended to subject the Church to republican discipline by compelling religious organisations, and in particular those engaged in teaching, to apply for state authorisation. Zola was denied his own new day in court by the passage, in December 1900, of Waldeck's general amnesty bill, which covered all crimes and misdemeanours connected to the Dreyfus case. He had the consolation, however, of knowing that 'J'accuse . . . !' and his first trial had inspired the movement that saved Dreyfus' life and re-established the moral principles on which the Republic had been founded. As he put it himself, in a note apparently written during the winter of 1900–1: 'That's where it all came from; since then, not a single development has taken place without making people think back to my trial. It's the Bible. It contained the seeds of everything' ['Tout est parti de là; depuis pas un fait ne s'est produit sans qu'on s'en reporte à mon procès. C'est la Bible. Il a tout contenu en germe' (OC xiv 1548)].

NOTES

1 The circulation figures are those given by Janine Ponty, 'La Presse quotidienne et l'affaire Dreyfus en 1898–1899: Essai de typologie', *Revue d'histoire moderne et contemporaine*, 21 (1974), 193–220.

2 The sentence, which is not included in the fragment published in Cor. ix, is quoted in Brigitte Emile-Zola, 'Extraits des lettres d'Emile Zola à Alexandrine Zola', *Excavatio*, 10 (1997), ix.

3 For an excellent analysis of the rhetoric of these writings, see Richard Griffiths, *The Use of Abuse: The Polemics of the Dreyfus Affair and its Aftermath* (New York and Oxford: Berg, 1991), pp. 123–35. For a translation of the texts themselves,

see Emile Zola, *The Dreyfus Affair: 'J'accuse' and other Writings*, ed. Alain Pagès, trans. Eleanor Levieux (New Haven and London: Yale University Press, 1996).

4 Nelly Wilson, *Bernard-Lazare: Anti-Semitism and the Problem of Jewish Identity in Late Nineteenth-Century France* (Cambridge: Cambridge University Press, 1978), p. 199.

5 Henri Mitterand, 'Politique et littérature: la mesure de *J'accuse . . . !*', in *Le Roman à l'œuvre: Genèse et valeurs* (Paris: Presses Universitaires de France, 1998), p. 300.

6 See Pierre Birnbaum, trans. Jane Marie Todd, *The Anti-Semitic Moment* (New York: Hill and Wang, 2003).

RECOMMENDED READING

Birnbaum, Pierre, trans. Jane Marie Todd, *The Anti-Semitic Moment* (New York: Hill and Wang, 2003)

Bredin, Jean-Denis, trans. Jeffrey Mehlman, *The Affair* (London: Sidgwick and Jackson, 1987)

Burns, Michael, *France and the Dreyfus Affair: A Documentary History* (Boston and New York: Bedford/St Martin's, 1999)

Dreyfus: A Family Affair, 1789–1945 (New York: Harper Collins, 1991)

Cahm, Eric, *The Dreyfus Affair in French Society and Politics* (London and New York: Longman, 1996)

Chapman, Guy, *The Dreyfus Case: A Reassessment* (London: Rupert Hart-Davis, 1955)

Derfler, Leslie, *The Dreyfus Affair* (Westport and London: Greenwood Press, 2002)

Drouin, Michel (ed.), *L'Affaire Dreyfus de A à Z* (Paris: Flammarion, 1994)

Duclert, Vincent, *L'Affaire Dreyfus* (Paris: La Découverte, 1994)

Emile-Zola, Brigitte, 'Extraits des lettres d'Emile Zola à Alexandrine Zola', *Excavatio*, 10 (1997), ix–xiv

Griffiths, Richard, *The Use of Abuse: The Polemics of the Dreyfus Affair and its Aftermath* (New York and Oxford: Berg, 1991)

Johnson, Douglas, *France and the Dreyfus Affair* (London: Blandford Press, 1966)

Mitterand, Henri, 'Politique et littérature: la mesure de *J'accuse . . . !*', in *Le Roman à l'œuvre: Genèse et valeurs* (Paris: Presses Universitaires de France, 1998), pp. 284–305

Zola, tome III: *L'honneur, 1893–1902* (Paris: Fayard, 2002)

Mollier, Jean-Yves and Jocelyne George, *La plus longue des Républiques, 1870–1940* (Paris: Fayard, 1994)

Noiray, Jacques, 'De *La Confession de Claude* à *J'accuse*: formes et significations du sacrifice dans l'œuvre d'Emile Zola', in Leduc-Adine, Jean-Pierre and Henri Mitterand (eds.), *Lire/Dé-lire Zola* (Paris: Nouveau Monde Editions, 2004), pp. 275–93

Pagès, Alain, *Emile Zola, un intellectuel dans l'affaire Dreyfus* (Paris: Séguier, 1991) 'Le discours argumentatif de "J'accuse . . . !"', *Jean Jaurès cahiers trimestriels*, 151 (1999), 23–30

Ponty, Janine, 'La presse quotidienne et l'affaire Dreyfus en 1898–1899: Essai de typologie', *Revue d'histoire moderne et contemporaine*, 21 (1974), 193–220

Rebérioux, Madeleine, *La République radicale? 1898–1914* (Paris: Seuil, 1975)
Reinach, Joseph, *Histoire de l'affaire Dreyfus*, 7 vols. (Paris: Editions de la Revue Blanche et Fasquelle, 1901–11)
Thomas, Marcel, *L'Affaire sans Dreyfus* (Paris: Fayard, 1961)
Wilson, Nelly, *Bernard-Lazare: Anti-Semitism and the Problem of Jewish Identity in Late Nineteenth-Century France* (Cambridge: Cambridge University Press, 1978)
Zola, Emile, *The Dreyfus Affair: 'J'accuse' and Other Writings*, ed. Alain Pagès, trans. Eleanor Levieux (New Haven and London: Yale University Press, 1996)

FURTHER READING AND SPECIALIST RESOURCES

Items listed below are supplementary to the 'Recommended Reading' appended to each essay, the details of which are not repeated here.

Zola's works

Œuvres complètes, ed. Henri Mitterand *et al.* (Paris: Nouveau Monde Editions, 2002–) (14 of the projected 20 volumes plus index had appeared by July 2006)

Œuvres complètes, ed. Henri Mitterand, 15 vols. (Paris: Tchou, 'Cercle du Livre Précieux', 1966–70)

Les Rougon-Macquart, ed. Henri Mitterand, 5 vols. (Paris: Gallimard, 'Bibliothèque de la Pléiade', 1960–7)

Les Rougon-Macquart, ed. Colette Becker, 6 vols. (Paris: Laffont, 'Bouquins', 1991–3)

Les Rougon-Macquart are available on CD-ROM from Chadwyck Healey France (Paris)

Contes et nouvelles, ed. Roger Ripoll (Paris: Gallimard, 'Bibliothèque de la Pléiade', 1976)

Correspondance, ed. Bard H. Bakker *et al.*, 10 vols. (Montreal and Paris: Presses de l'Université de Montréal/Editions du CNRS, 1978–95). A one-volume supplement, edited by Owen Morgan and Dorothy Speirs, is forthcoming.

Les Manuscrits et les dessins de Zola, ed. Olivier Lumbroso and Henri Mitterand, 3 vols. (Paris: Textuel, 2002)

Carnets d'enquêtes. Une ethnographie inédite de la France, ed. Henri Mitterand (Paris: Plon, 1986) (Selections from Zola's planning notes for his novels)

Ecrits sur l'art, ed. Jean-Pierre Leduc-Adine (Paris: Gallimard, 1991)

Useful paperback editions of nearly all of Zola's individual texts exist in popular collections such as Folio, Classiques de Poche and GF Flammarion.

Translations

Nearly all of Zola's novels, including all twenty volumes in the Rougon-Macquart cycle, have been translated into English. Translations of the following are available in Oxford World's Classics (OWC) and/or Penguin Classics (PC): *Thérèse Raquin* (OWC, PC), *La Curée* (OWC), *Le Ventre de Paris* (OWC), *L'Assommoir* (OWC,

PC), *Nana* (OWC, PC), *Pot-Bouille* (OWC), *Au Bonheur des Dames* (OWC, PC), *Germinal* (OWC, PC), *L'Œuvre* (OWC), *La Terre* (PC), *La Bête humaine* (OWC, PC), *La Débâcle* (OWC, PC), *The Attack on the Mill* (OWC).

Bibliographies and 'états présents'

A bibliography (by David Baguley) of Zola studies is published annually in the journal *Les Cahiers naturalistes* (see below)

Baguley, David, *Bibliographie de la critique sur Emile Zola: 1864–1970* (Toronto: University of Toronto Press, 1976)
    Bibliographie de la critique sur Emile Zola: 1971–1980 (Toronto: University of Toronto Press, 1982)
    'An *état présent* of Zola Studies (1986–2000)', *Australian Journal of French Studies*, 38 (2001), 305–20
Brady, Patrick, 'A Decade of Zola Studies, 1976–1985', *L'Esprit créateur*, 25 (1985), 3–16
Hemmings, F. W. J., 'The Present Position in Zola Studies', *French Studies*, 10 (1956), 97–122
Lethbridge, Robert, 'Twenty Years of Zola Studies (1956–1975)', *French Studies*, 31 (1977), 281–93
Nelson, Brian, *Emile Zola. A Selective Analytical Bibliography* (London: Grant & Cutler, 1982)
Pagès, Alain, *Emile Zola. Bilan critique* (Paris: Nathan, 1993)
Schor, Naomi, 'Zola and *la nouvelle critique*', *L'Esprit créateur*, 11 (1971), 11–20
Signori, Dolores (ed.), *Emile Zola dans la presse parisienne (1882–1902)* (Toronto: University of Toronto Press, 1985)
Walker, Philip D., and David Baguley, 'Emile Zola', in David Baguley (ed.), *A Critical Bibliography of French Literature*, vol. v, *The Nineteenth Century* (Syracuse, NY: Syracuse University Press, 1994), pp. 955–1006

A Zola dictionary and an encyclopaedic guide

Becker, Colette, Gina Gourdin-Servenière and Véronique Lavielle, *Dictionnaire d'Emile Zola* (Paris: Robert Laffont, 1993)
Pagès, Alain, and Owen Morgan, *Guide Emile Zola* (Paris: Ellipses, 2002)

Societies, journals and research centres

In France, the Société littéraire des Amis d'Emile Zola promotes commemorative events such as the annual 'pilgrimage' to the Musée Zola at Médan in October, exhibitions and special publications, and also sponsors the specialist annual journal *Les Cahiers naturalistes*, founded in 1955. The current editor of the journal is Alain Pagès (address: B.P. 12 – 77580 Villiers-sur-Morin, France; website: www.cahiers-naturalistes.com)
    The Centre de Recherches sur Zola et le Naturalisme in Paris runs a seminar series during the year, organises occasional conferences, holds a significant Zola archive of manuscript, published and iconographical materials, and, within the framework of ITEM (the Institut des Textes et Manuscrits modernes du CNRS), functions as the

headquarters of Zola research in France, promoting team-based projects, with a particular focus on genetic research. The Centre's address is: 4 rue Lhomond, 75005 Paris. In Canada, the Centre d'Etudes sur le Naturalisme, part of the Joseph Sablé Centre for Nineteenth-Century French Studies at the University of Toronto (website: www.chass.utoronto/french/sable), has a rich collection of research materials and a dynamic programme of research projects. The Centre is directed by Dorothy Speirs and Yannick Portebois.

Also based in Canada is AIZEN (Association Internationale pour l'Etude de Zola et le Naturalisme), which issues the journal *Excavatio* and *The AIZEN Bulletin*. Website: www.ualberta.ca/-aizen

In Britain, The Emile Zola Society organises lectures, occasional conferences and other events at the Institut Français (London), and also publishes the *Bulletin of the Emile Zola Society*. Address: Institut Français, 17 Queensbury Place, London SW7 2DT, UK

Electronic resources

(see also above)

David Baguley's cumulative bibliography of Zola studies from 1981 onwards may be found at www.cahiers-naturalistes.com
The bibliography will be periodically updated.
Carles, Patricia, and Béatrice Desgranges, *Le Musée imaginaire d'Emile Zola*, CD-ROM (Paris: Pages jaunes Editions, 2000)
The Centre de Recherches sur Zola et le Naturalisme (see above) has created an electronic site, the first of its kind, on the server of the Bibliothèque Nationale de France: http://gallica.bnf.fr/Zola
This site is devoted to *Le Rêve*, the sixteenth of the Rougon-Macquart novels. It constitutes an extraordinarily rich collection of resources: the text, with variants, of the novel as it was initially published in serial form; the entirety of the planning notes for the novel; the novel's principal sources; contemporary cartoons concerning the novel and Zola; relevant correspondence; contemporary reviews of the novel; a filmography; translations of the novel; a bibliography (with extracts) of articles, essays and theses devoted to the novel from 1888 to the present day, etc. This site is a superb model for sites on other classic texts.

Biographical studies

Brown, Frederick, *Zola: A Life* (New York: Farrar, Straus, Giroux, 1995; London: Macmillan, 1996)
Hemmings, F. W. J., *The Life and Times of Emile Zola* (London: Elek, 1977)
Schom, Alan, *Emile Zola: A Bourgeois Rebel* (New York: Henry Holt, 1987; London: Queen Ann Press, 1987)

Critical studies

Baguley, David, *Emile Zola: 'L'Assommoir'* (Cambridge: Cambridge University Press, 1992)

Bell, David F., *Models of Power: Politics and Economics in Zola's 'Rougon-Macquart'* (Lincoln, Nebr., and London: University of Nebraska Press, 1988)
Berg, William J., and Laurey K. Martin, *Emile Zola Revisited* (New York: Twayne, 1992)
Bloom, Harold (ed.), *Emile Zola* (Philadelphia: Chelsea House, 2004)
Chevrel, Yves, *Le Naturalisme* (Paris: Presses Universitaires de France, 1982)
Colin, René-Pierre, *Zola, renégats et alliés. La République naturaliste* (Lyon: Presses Universitaires de Lyon, 1988)
Zola et le coup de force naturaliste (Paris: Du Lérot, 1991)
De Lattre, Alain, *Le Réalisme selon Zola. Archéologie d'une intelligence* (Paris: Presses Universitaires de France, 1973)
La Description naturaliste. L'Œuvre d'Emile Zola, in *L'Ecole des Lettres*, 83 (1 March 1992) (A collection of articles)
Dezalay, Auguste, *Lectures de Zola* (Paris: Armand Colin, 1973)
L'Opéra des Rougon-Macquart: essai de rythmologie romanesque (Paris: Klincksieck, 1983)
Dubois, Jacques, *'L'Assommoir' de Zola: société, discours, idéologie* (Paris: Larousse, 'Thèmes et Textes', 1973; Paris: Belin, 1993)
Duffy, Larry, *Le Grand Transit Moderne: Mobility, Modernity and French Naturalist Fiction* (Amsterdam and New York: Rodopi, 2005), *passim*
Frey, John A., *The Aesthetics of the 'Rougon-Macquart'* (Madrid: José Porrúa Turanzas, 1978)
Kaempfer, Jean, *Emile Zola: d'un naturalisme pervers* (Paris: Corti, 1989)
Leduc-Adine, Jean-Pierre (ed.), *Zola: genèse de l'œuvre* (Paris: CNRS Editions, 2002)
Levin, Harry, 'Zola', in *The Gates of Horn: A Study of Five French Realists* (New York: Oxford University Press, 1963), pp. 305–71
Minogue, Valerie, *Zola: 'L'Assommoir'* (London: Grant & Cutler, 1991)
Mitterand, Henri, *Zola journaliste. De l'affaire Manet à l'affaire Dreyfus* (Paris: Armand Colin, 1962)
Le Discours du roman (Paris: Presses Universitaires de France, 1980)
Le Regard et le signe. Poétique du roman réaliste et naturaliste (Paris: Presses Universitaires de France, 1987)
L'Illusion réaliste. De Balzac à Aragon (Paris: Seuil, 1994)
Le Roman à l'œuvre. Genèse et valeurs (Paris: Presses Universitaires de France, 1998)
Zola. La vérité en marche (Paris: Gallimard, 'Découvertes', 2002)
Passion Emile Zola. Les délires de la vérité (Paris: Textuel, 2002)
Mourad, François-Marie, *Zola, critique littéraire* (Paris: Champion, 2003)
Nelson, Brian (ed.), *Naturalism in the European Novel: New Critical Perspectives* (New York and Oxford: Berg, 1992)
Reid, James H., *Narration and Description in the Nineteenth-Century French Novel* (Cambridge: Cambridge University Press, 1993), *passim*
Pagès, Alain, *Le Naturalisme* (Paris: Presses Universitaires de France, 'Que sais-je?', 1989)
La Bataille littéraire (Paris: Séguier, 1989)
Serres, Michel, *Feux et signaux de brume: Zola* (Paris: Grasset, 1975)

Suwala, Halina, *Naissance d'une doctrine. Formation des idées littéraires et esthétiques de Zola (1859–1865)* (Warsaw: University of Warsaw Press, 1976)

Walker, Philip, *Zola* (London: Routledge & Kegan Paul, 1965; New York: Humanities Press, 1968)

Zola et le naturalisme, in *L'Ecole des Lettres*, 81 (15 December 1989) (A collection of articles)

INDEX

anarchism 49, 141, 177
anti-Semitism 15, 189, 193, 195–6,
 199
L'Argent 26, 62, 101
aristocracy 25
 corruption of 132
L'Assommoir 5, 6, 7, 8–12, 14, 16, 22, 26,
 27, 39, 40–1, 68, 86, 87, 89, 90, 92, 93,
 94, 95, 98, 99, 100, 106, 115, 122, 123,
 137, 148, 169, 177
Au Bonheur des Dames 6, 7, 31, 32, 57,
 61–2, 63–4, 99, 101, 120 n.7
Auerbach, Erich 1, 2, 12

Bakunin, Mikhail 141
Balzac, Honoré de 55, 148
 differences to Zola 2, 8, 19, 22, 137
 influence on Zola 1, 3
 La Comédie humaine 2
 precursor to Zola 71, 75, 76
Barthes, Roland 19, 122
Bastien-Lepage, Jules 67, 76, 77
Baudelaire, Charles 67, 77, 113
Bazille, Frédéric 74
Beizer, Janet 124, 125
Bernard, Claude 3, 155, 169
Bête humaine, La 4, 7, 8, 26, 58, 88, 92, 99,
 100, 102, 106, 138, 152–67
Bildungsroman 28, 31, 146
Borie, Jean 170
Bourdieu, Pierre 73
bourgeoisie 48
 attacked by Zola 8–10, 11, 14, 30, 32,
 179
 attitude to sex and marriage 27, 29, 30, 54
 bourgeois ideology 25, 40, 149
 bourgeois mystification 12
 hypocrisy of 60

novel as bourgeois genre 9
 rise of 25
 shocked by Germinal 142–3
 virtues of 16–17
Brousse, Paul 141

capitalism 48, 147, 148, 179, 189
Catholicism 56–7, 174–5
Cézanne, Paul 68–72, 73, 81, 84 n.5
Charcot, Jean-Martin 152
Charles, Michel 23
Chavannes, Puvis de 76
Commune, see Paris Commune
Confession de Claude, La 70, 169, 171
Conquête de Plassans, La 6, 26, 28, 33, 95,
 103 n.19
Corot, Jean-Baptiste-Camille 71, 76
Courbet, Gustave 75, 76, 77
criminality 99, 160–2
Curée, La 6, 7, 8, 26, 33, 34, 42–7, 48, 56,
 59, 61, 64, 92, 95–6, 106, 177

Darwin and Darwinism 3, 7, 95, 152, 157,
 159, 161, 171
Débâcle, La 8, 16, 26, 33, 37, 62, 92, 121,
 133, 137, 173
Decadent movement 17, 176
Degas, Edgar 73, 78
degeneration 152, 161, 165, 171, 185 n.6
Delacroix, Eugène 26, 71, 75
Deleuze, Gilles 23, 154
Docteur Pascal, Le 22, 33–7, 57, 58, 86,
 96–7, 173
Dreyfus affair 2, 34, 178
 Zola's involvement in 14–16, 169, 184,
 188–203
Duchet, Claude 51, 148
Duret, Francisque-Joseph 73, 74

Cambridge Companions to...

AUTHORS

Edward Albee *edited by Stephen J. Bottoms*

Margaret Atwood *edited by Coral Ann Howells*

W. H. Auden *edited by Stan Smith*

Jane Austen *edited by Edward Copeland and Juliet McMaster*

Beckett *edited by John Pilling*

Aphra Behn *edited by Derek Hughes and Janet Todd*

Walter Benjamin *edited by David S. Ferris*

William Blake *edited by Morris Eaves*

Brecht *edited by Peter Thomson and Glendyr Sacks* (second edition)

The Brontës *edited by Heather Glen*

Byron *edited by Drummond Bone*

Albert Camus *edited by Edward J. Hughes*

Willa Cather *edited by Marilee Lindemann*

Cervantes *edited by Anthony J. Cascardi*

Chaucer *edited by Piero Boitani and Jill Mann* (second edition)

Chekhov *edited by Vera Gottlieb and Paul Allain*

Coleridge *edited by Lucy Newlyn*

Wilkie Collins *edited by Jenny Bourne Taylor*

Joseph Conrad *edited by J. H. Stape*

Dante *edited by Rachel Jacoff* (second edition)

Charles Dickens *edited by John O. Jordan*

Emily Dickinson *edited by Wendy Martin*

John Donne *edited by Achsah Guibbory*

Dostoevskii *edited by W. J. Leatherbarrow*

Theodore Dreiser *edited by Leonard Cassuto and Claire Virginia Eby*

John Dryden *edited by Steven N. Zwicker*

George Eliot *edited by George Levine*

T. S. Eliot *edited by A. David Moody*

Ralph Ellison *edited by Ross Posnock*

Ralph Waldo Emerson *edited by Joel Porte and Saundra Morris*

William Faulkner *edited by Philip M. Weinstein*

F. Scott Fitzgerald *edited by Ruth Prigozy*

Flaubert *edited by Timothy Unwin*

E. M. Forster *edited by David Bradshaw*

Brian Friel *edited by Anthony Roche*

Robert Frost *edited by Robert Faggen*

Elizabeth Gaskell *edited by Jill L. Matus*

Goethe *edited by Lesley Sharpe*

Thomas Hardy *edited by Dale Kramer*

Nathaniel Hawthorne *edited by Richard Millington*

Ernest Hemingway *edited by Scott Donaldson*

Homer *edited by Robert Fowler*

Ibsen *edited by James McFarlane*

Henry James *edited by Jonathan Freedman*

Samuel Johnson *edited by Greg Clingham*

Ben Jonson *edited by Richard Harp and Stanley Stewart*

James Joyce *edited by Derek Attridge* (second edition)

Kafka *edited by Julian Preece*

Keats *edited by Susan J. Wolfson*

Lacan *edited by Jean-Michel Rabaté*

D. H. Lawrence *edited by Anne Fernihough*

David Mamet *edited by Christopher Bigsby*

Thomas Mann *edited by Ritchie Robertson*

Herman Melville *edited by Robert S. Levine*

Christopher Marlowe *edited by Patrick Cheney*

Arthur Miller *edited by Christopher Bigsby*

Milton *edited by Dennis Danielson* (second edition)

Molière *edited by David Bradby and Andrew Calder*

Nabokov *edited by Julian W. Connolly*

Eugene O'Neill *edited by Michael Manheim*

George Orwell *edited by John Rodden*

Ovid *edited by Philip Hardie*

Harold Pinter *edited by Peter Raby*

Sylvia Plath *edited by Jo Gill*

Edgar Allan Poe *edited by Kevin J. Hayes*

Ezra Pound *edited by Ira B. Nadel*

Proust *edited by Richard Bales*

Pushkin *edited by Andrew Kahn*

Philip Roth *edited by Timothy Parrish*

Shakespeare *edited by Margareta de Grazia and Stanley Wells*

Shakespeare on Film *edited by Russell Jackson* (second edition)

Shakespearean Comedy *edited by Alexander Leggatt*

Shakespeare on Stage *edited by Stanley Wells and Sarah Stanton*

Shakespeare's History Plays *edited by Michael Hattaway*

Shakespearean Tragedy *edited by Claire McEachern*

Shakespeare's Poetry *edited by Patrick Cheney*

George Bernard Shaw *edited by Christopher Innes*

Shelley *edited by Timothy Morton*

Mary Shelley *edited by Esther Schor*

Sam Shepard *edited by Matthew C. Roudané*

Spenser *edited by Andrew Hadfield*

Wallace Stevens *edited by John N. Serio*

Tom Stoppard *edited by Katherine E. Kelly*

Harriet Beecher Stowe *edited by Cindy Weinstein*

Jonathan Swift *edited by Christopher Fox*

Henry David Thoreau *edited by Joel Myerson*

Tolstoy *edited by Donna Tussing Orwin*

Mark Twain *edited by Forrest G. Robinson*

Virgil *edited by Charles Martindale*

Edith Wharton *edited by Millicent Bell*

Walt Whitman *edited by Ezra Greenspan*

Oscar Wilde *edited by Peter Raby*

Tennessee Williams *edited by Matthew C. Roudané*

Mary Wollstonecraft *edited by Claudia L. Johnson*

Virginia Woolf *edited by Sue Roe and Susan Sellers*

Wordsworth *edited by Stephen Gill*

W. B. Yeats *edited by Marjorie Howes and John Kelly*

Zola *edited by Brian Nelson*

TOPICS

The Actress *edited by Maggie B. Gale and John Stokes*

The African American Novel *edited by Maryemma Graham*

The African American Slave Narrative *edited by Audrey A. Fisch*

American Modernism *edited by Walter Kalaidjian*

American Realism and Naturalism *edited by Donald Pizer*

American Women Playwrights *edited by Brenda Murphy*

Australian Literature *edited by Elizabeth Webby*

British Romanticism *edited by Stuart Curran*

Canadian Literature *edited by Eva-Marie Kröller*

The Classic Russian Novel *edited by Malcolm V. Jones and Robin Feuer Miller*

Contemporary Irish Poetry *edited by Matthew Campbell*

Crime Fiction *edited by Martin Priestman*

The Eighteenth-Century Novel *edited by John Richetti*

Eighteenth-Century Poetry *edited by John Sitter*

English Literature, 1500–1600 *edited by Arthur F. Kinney*

English Literature, 1650–1740 *edited by Steven N. Zwicker*

English Literature, 1740–1830 *edited by Thomas Keymer and Jon Mee*

English Poetry, Donne to Marvell *edited by Thomas N. Corns*

English Renaissance Drama, second edition *edited by A. R. Braunmuller and Michael Hattaway*

English Restoration Theatre *edited by Deborah C. Payne Fisk*

Feminist Literary Theory *edited by Ellen Rooney*

The French Novel: from 1800 to the Present *edited by Timothy Unwin*

Gothic Fiction *edited by Jerrold E. Hogle*

Greek and Roman Theatre *edited by Marianne McDonald and J. Michael Walton*

Greek Tragedy *edited by P. E. Easterling*

The Irish Novel *edited by John Wilson Foster*

The Italian Novel *edited by Peter Bondanella and Andrea Ciccarelli*

Jewish American Literature *edited by Hana Wirth-Nesher and Michael P. Kramer*

The Latin American Novel *edited by Efraín Kristal*

Literature of the First World War *edited by Vincent Sherry*

Medieval English Theatre *edited by Richard Beadle*

Medieval Romance *edited by Roberta L. Krueger*

Medieval Women's Writing *edited by Carolyn Dinshaw and David Wallace*

Lightning Source UK Ltd.
Milton Keynes UK
UKOW05f0300221016

285889UK00007B/347/P

9 780521 543767